THE TRIUMPH OF THE AMATEURS

THE TRIUMPH OF THE AMATEURS

The Rise, Ruin, and Banishment of
Professional Rowing in the Gilded Age

WILLIAM LANOUETTE

LYONS
PRESS

Guilford, Connecticut

To JoAnne

An imprint of The Rowman & Littlefield Publishing Group, Inc.
4501 Forbes Blvd., Ste. 200
Lanham, MD 20706
www.rowman.com

Distributed by NATIONAL BOOK NETWORK

British Library Cataloguing in Publication Information available

Library of Congress Cataloging-in-Publication Data
Names: Lanouette, William, author.
Title: The triumph of the amateurs : the rise, ruin, and banishment of
    professional rowing in the gilded age / William Lanouette.
Description: Guilford, Connecticut : Lyons Press, [2021] | Includes
    bibliographical references and index. | Summary: "The story of the lost
    world of professional rowing in America, a sport that attracted crowds
    of thousands, widespread betting, and ultimately corruption that
    foretold its doom. This book also discusses the rise of amateur rowing
    as America's first collegiate sport, its growth over the twentieth
    century, and current popularity for both men and women competing at all
    levels of the sport"— Provided by publisher.
Identifiers: LCCN 2020044812 (print) | LCCN 2020044813 (ebook) | ISBN
    9781493052769 (hardback) | ISBN 9781493052776 (epub)
Subjects: LCSH: Rowing—United States—History. | Rowers—United
    States—Biography.
Classification: LCC GV791 .L38 2021 (print) | LCC GV791 (ebook) | DDC
    797.12/3—dc23
LC record available at https://lccn.loc.gov/2020044812
LC ebook record available at https://lccn.loc.gov/2020044813

♾™ The paper used in this publication meets the minimum requirements of American National Standard for Information Sciences—Permanence of Paper for Printed Library Materials, ANSI/NISO Z39.48-1992.

CONTENTS

Contents

INTRODUCTION

A SPECTACLE CAUGHT IN TIME

CROWDS STREAMED TO THE BANKS OF THE SCHUYLKILL RIVER IN PHIL-adelphia on a cloudy May afternoon in 1872, eager to see the sports heroes John and Barney Biglin race. At stake was the Championship of North American Waters, and $2,000 (more than $40,000 today). Stalls along the stream sold shares in rich pari-mutuel betting "pools" that multiplied winnings to hundreds of times the rowers' rich prize money.[1]

Gents in dark suits jostled with boys skipping school, young ladies sporting flowered bonnets, and bricklayers let off early from their labors. Families clustered on lawns and rock ledges above the river. Crowds

"The Betting Crowd" at the July 1874 Intercollegiate Regatta, Saratoga.
THE DAILY GRAPHIC, JULY 18, 1874, 1

surged onto the Girard Avenue Bridge that spans Fairmount Park's green river valley—until policemen had to wave and whistle them off, fearing its collapse. Other fans pushed aboard steamboats to follow the race. Easy to spot were the "sporting men" in their black frock coats, fancy hats, ruffled shirts, and gaudy jewels. In town to banter and to bet on the race, this conniving lot had already set three-to-two odds for the Biglins.

"They are both dapper fellows," the *Philadelphia Press* reported about the Biglins, "about medium height, well formed, and with a very determined cast of countenance. . . . They are both in their prime, and have made the art of rowing a study most of their lives." At the time rowing was far more than an "art," or even the admired sport at colleges, schools, clubs, and athletic centers it has become today. Rowing then was big business—and big trouble. Now long forgotten, professional rowing was the most popular and lucrative sport in America's Gilded Age following the Civil War. It thrived until destroyed by betting scandals.[2]

The Biglins' arrival in Philadelphia was historic because they had challenged the world's rowers to North America's first professional race for pair-oared shells. Powerful yet perilous, pairs have two rowers, each swinging one twelve-foot oar. Pairs demand perfect timing and balance. A misplaced stroke could flip the slender cedar shell. To row this quintessential two-man racing craft took grace and guts. The Biglins had plenty of both.[3]

Professional rowing thrived for decades on the fierce ambition of scrappy Irish-American lads who, though oft excluded from more respectable work—yet shying outright criminality—made rowing for money a way to riches and fame. The Biglins personified that ambition, and more than a century after their race on the Schuylkill the *New York Times* declared the brothers "the celebrity athletes and pop stars of the 1870s." The Biglins' era first defined commercial sports in America, during and after the Civil War. Just a year before this pair race, the first professional baseball game was played at Fort Wayne, Indiana. Decades passed before prizefights became legal. Then professional football, basketball, ice hockey, and cycling prospered—with scandals all their own.[4]

The artist Thomas Eakins, himself an avid rower, admired the sport's legendary athletes. He had just begun painting them, and caught the

Biglins in rough sketches, bright oils, and subtle watercolors. Eakins admired the muscular poise needed to power and steer a delicate racing shell for miles of torturous competition. He saw in oarsmen's physiques and prowess a glorious perfection. For Eakins rowing enlivened an American egalitarian spirit—fusing intellect, precision, and stamina for heroic goals. His artworks portraying the Biglins endure as icons of American athleticism.[5]

In a racing shell the Biglins had to perform with intense harmony, but on land their lives were sharp contrasts. Gruff and devious, John Biglin was a ruddy boatman, laborer, and fireman. John's harsh training regime was called "decidedly savage," while brother Barney was more relaxed, both in a shell and ashore. He aspired to easier riches. Glib and genial, Barney was just launching a political career in New York that allied him with Chester A. Arthur and his venal Republican cronies. The Biglins' ambition would lead them to victories, but also to disgrace, in both sports and in politics.

In this book we will discover the messy public and private lives of the Biglins, the artist who painted them, their feisty successors, and the ruin of professional rowing. The motley crew we will meet includes the gloomy American champion sculler Charles Courtney from upstate New York. (Rowers "scull" when using two oars, and "sweep" when pulling just one.) The *New York Times* denounced him as a "clown" and "miserable imposter" for faking injuries, fixing races, and staging mishaps to excuse his losses. We will also meet the exuberant Canadian sculler Edward "Ned" Hanlan from Toronto, who rowed three scandalous races against Courtney. Hanlan won world championships in North America, England, and Australia. Yet he still connived to "lose" easy races at home when betting against himself: one so brazenly performed, a newspaper headlined it an "Aquatic Burlesque." And so shameless a cheat was the cunning professional sculler John Teemer, from Pittsburgh, that he once wrote Hanlan, promising "If you are not in condition, I will do anything you ask me to do to make you win the race."[6]

After printing Teemer's letter, the *New York Times* damned professional rowers as "only so many puppets in the hands of speculators" who seldom waged "honest battles of muscle and skill." And so, increasingly, it was the amateurs who waged those honest battles, redeeming the sport of rowing for pleasure rather than profit. Among them we will meet Benjamin Crowninshield, a Harvard oarsman in the 1850s who fancied himself an amateur although he, too, raced for prize money against professionals. Crowninshield personified tensions between elite college rowers and their rugged Boston-Irish rivals, when races on the River Charles roused ethnic and class discord.

Enthralled by the sport were avid gamblers, from vagrants to Vanderbilts. But with its reckless betting mania, greedy financiers, and easily corrupted athletes, professional rowing spawned America's first—and worst—national sports scandal. Sabotaged boats. Poisoned oarsmen. Bribed officials. Reckless collisions. Secret payoffs. Blackmail. Rigged betting pools. Faked mishaps and illness. Drunken riotous crowds. All this mayhem ruined America's richest sport. As a result, professional rowing was not just sanctioned, or sidelined. It was banned. No other professional sport has been so forsworn.

Soon after the Biglins' acclaimed 1872 pair race, delegates from more than two hundred boat clubs met to found a National Association of Amateur Oarsmen (NAAO)—today's US Rowing—eager to distance themselves from the professionals' greed and guile. Yet distinctions between professional and amateur rowers blurred for decades. In fact, when America's first (and oldest) intercollegiate sports contest, the Harvard-Yale Boat Race, began in 1852, it was financed by a railway corporation. In time, schools and boat clubs deigned to hire the dishonored professional rowers to help train their crews, and some of the most infamous pros became legendary college coaches.

Tension between professionals and amateurs took surprising turns across the centuries as competitive rowing evolved from being at first mainly professional work to now strictly amateur sport. Two best-selling books about Olympic competitors highlight this tension. In *The Amateurs* David Halberstam called the world of amateur sculling "an anomaly" that is "first and foremost a participant's sport." Daniel James Brown's *The Boys in the Boat* celebrated the amateur spirit that drove brawny, working-class students in a University of Washington eight-oared shell to win gold at Hitler's 1936 Olympics. And Daniel Boyne's *The Red Rose Crew* recounts how determined women from diverse backgrounds enlisted legendary Harvard coach Harry Parker to teach and train them for international competition.[7]

Since the turn of the twentieth century, with professional rowing banned, amateur rowing has survived and then thrived. Rowing has evolved to include among today's amateurs not only young men but growing numbers of seniors and women. Indeed, among North America's competitive rowers the women now outnumber the men. Syndicates and gamblers no longer rule the sport, but in some countries amateurs were nationalized. And, in a way, today's most elite amateurs have lifestyles that seem as intense and laborious as they were for the nineteenth century's wily professionals.[8]

As a freshman at Fordham College in New York City I tried out for the crew, my debut in a sport I still enjoy. Often I visited The Metropolitan Museum of Art, and there I first saw two bold rowing pictures by Thomas Eakins: his oil "Max Schmitt in a Single Scull" or "The Champion Single Sculls" and his watercolor "John Biglin in a Single Scull." As an aspiring oarsman I revered both these paintings, but only years later learned a vital difference between them. It wasn't oil versus watercolor. Schmitt, I discovered, was an amateur champion, while Biglin made his living as a professional oarsman. I'm sure most visitors to The Met, or to the eight other American museums with Eakins' rowing works, have no notion there ever *were* professional rowers.

Those races for profit that first created and later destroyed professional rowing set patterns for commercialism in sports that presaged today's avarice and corruption. In this book's personalities and conflicts—in its spectacles and its scams—we will rediscover a sport now long forgotten, yet all too uneasily familiar.

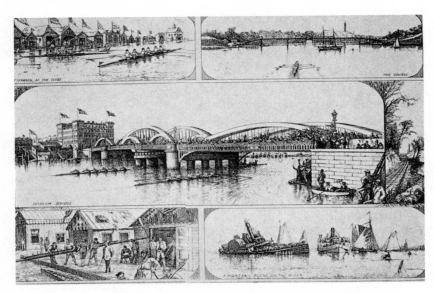

A *Daily Graphic* sketch portrays an 1873 regatta on the Harlem River
THE DAILY GRAPHIC, JUNE 14, 1873

PART ONE

ROWING FOR MONEY AND FAME

CHAPTER I

NO IRISH NEED APPLY—
Except to Row

The brothers Biglin entered the shady world of professional rowing in the 1850s while still in their teens. They had quit school to help support their growing family. John was a laborer and a fireman. Also, as a Battery boatman he rowed passengers and parcels around New York Harbor, hailed by colleagues as a "crack oarsman." John's older brothers worked at a chandelier factory: James as a brass molder, Barney as an apprentice. But as professional rowing gained in popularity and profits, the Biglins were eager for new riches.

"NO IRISH NEED APPLY" signs hung outside factories, specialty shops, and offices—and even became the title of a popular song. Good jobs were scarce, especially for Irish workers with few craft or industrial skills. Back in their homeland, competitive rowing had first developed in the 1830s, but strictly among affluent gents and college boys. This meant that most Irish Americans who immigrated had no native advantage in the sport. What they did bring to professional rowing, though, were ambition, strength, and tenacity.[1]

By 1855, the Irish comprised some 86 percent of New York's unskilled laborers and 74 percent of its domestic servants. Burgeoning Irish families only worsened their own plight by swelling the labor market and suppressing wages. Both for the money—and, no doubt, for some fun—the Biglins rowed their first race in 1856. A crew called the Battery Boys crowed that it could beat anyone afloat. This challenge annoyed John. So he hopped into a two-man boat with brother James. They raced the

braggarts up the East River to Hell Gate and back, a distance of eight miles, and won.[2]

Before the Harlem River became New York's lively Boathouse Row, with more than a dozen amateur clubs, two rowing centers drew racers and crowds to the East River. They were Conrad's Garden around East 110th Street, and Dunlap's Hotel with its busy docks for pleasure boats and ferries at the foot of East 86th Street. In 1856 John and Barney Biglin won $10—then a worker's weekly pay—by racing in a double-scull fishing boat. The start and finish were off Dunlap's pier, and for two-thirds the distance the Biglins struggled along in the widest and heaviest boat, slipping to fourth place. Then, with awesome power they surprised the leader and won with ease. As Charles Peverelly, dean of rowing journalists, recalled: "It was the first time, we believe, their names appeared in print in connection with the 'paddles,' and we have always remembered them with distinctness and pleasure." (Peverelly was editor of *The Aquatic Monthly and Nautical Review* 1872–1881.)[3]

With each race the Biglins improved their style, and broadened their friendships with oarsmen who became both teammates and rivals. John formed a lasting bond with a fellow fireman, the talented professional rower Dennis Leary. For their first pull together, in August 1859, the two rowed double sculls in a race off Nautilus Hall, a popular inn and pub near Staten Island's ferry terminal. They finished second to win $20 in the *Lewis C. Meeks*, a shell named for a patron on the Board of Fire Wardens.[4]

Later that month, John and James Biglin each raced in fishing boats at the Empire City Regatta Club on the Harlem, a meet for both professionals and amateurs. In a hard-fought row James placed second to New

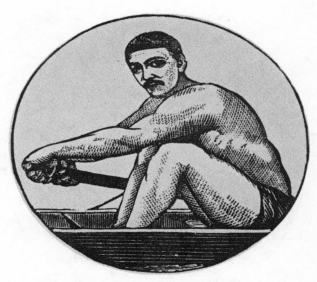

John Biglin woodcut from a photograph by William Notman, Montreal *THE MODERN OARSMAN* BY ED. JAMES, 1878

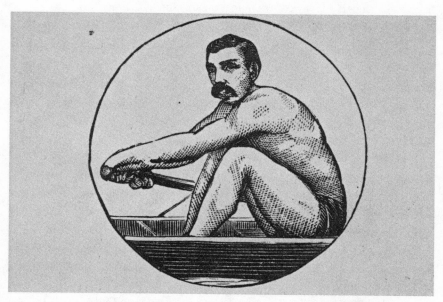

Barney Biglin woodcut from a photograph by William Notman, Montreal *THE MODERN OARSMAN* BY ED. JAMES, 1878

Dennis Leary woodcut from a photograph by Jordan, New York THE MODERN OARSMAN BY ED. JAMES, 1878

York professional James Sheridan, while John failed to finish. Rowing at that regatta, Dennis Leary stroked (set the pace) to victory in the *George J. Brown*, a four-oared shell that he and the Biglins would come to race triumphantly. Over the next quarter-century the Biglins would row more than one hundred races for money, typifying professional athleticism—mostly at its best, but also at its worst.[5]

ENGLAND V. IRELAND

Along America's Eastern Seaboard professional rowing became a spectacular sport—and more. Often it was a proxy conflict between the English and the Irish, especially in New York and Boston. The job of being a "professional" rower in North America began during the 1830s. As in England, it was at first the single scullers who captured public acclaim, and who made rowing a lucrative business.

In New York in 1837 Stephen Roberts and Sydney Dolan rowed high-stakes races that drew huge crowds and stoked national passions. Roberts

6

had emigrated from Jersey in England's Channel Islands. He took up rowing on the East River, and built boats for a living. A frequent winner of pick-up races, he was later active in the Empire City Regatta Club and became a city councilman. Dolan was from Ireland, and their first race embodied the city's latent English-Irish frictions. Roberts had challenged any man to row him for a purse of $200. Dolan accepted. But when he won, Roberts was irate and demanded a rematch. They pulled three more races. All were won by Roberts, and all were well attended, the last for a $400 purse.[6]

The Biglins launched their professional rowing careers when another family of brothers was also joining the sport: the Wards, from up the Hudson. Wards and Biglins would compete for decades, and even try to combine their crews. However, unlike the Biglins and most other professional rowers, the Wards weren't Irish or Catholic. They were WASPs who traced their ancestry to Sir Gilbert Warde, an English nobleman and leader of the Second Crusade in 1145.[7]

The clan's patriarch, Isaac Ward, was born in the hamlet of Middle Hope, near Newburgh, New York. From there he moved his family—in all, nine sons and five daughters—to Cornwall-on-Hudson, between Newburgh and West Point. Despite his noble heritage Isaac Ward was a fisherman. And he taught his sons basic boating skills: to knit fishnets, seine for sturgeon, and angle for shad. He also taught them how to row and sail. Most found work as skippers aboard sloops or schooners. And some became champion professional rowers.

Of the four Wards who gained fame with an oar, William Henry (known as "Hank," born in 1827) was their leader, and later became known as "Old Leatherstocking" or "The Old American Eagle." Other brothers in Hank's many winning crews were Joshua "Josh" (born in 1838), Gilbert (1841), and Ellis (1846). Hank Ward rowed his first race in Newburgh's 1856 July Fourth Regatta, finishing third in a double scull. The next year at Newburgh, Hank and Josh won a close race in the double by "a dip or two." And in 1859, off Staten Island, Josh raced two New York Irishmen, Andrew Fay and Thomas Daw, to win the American Sculling Championship and a solid-silver Tiffany belt.[8]

The Wards' early rivals came from Poughkeepsie, an emerging center for competitive rowing, and then from New York City, where Biglin crews in the *George J. Brown* gave them trouble for years. This four-oared shell was named for a real estate man who became a leading member of the New York Athletic Club. In 1860 Dennis Leary first stroked the *Brown* with John, James, and Barney Biglin—setting a five-mile record that stood for years. From then on, the Biglins and the *Brown* were famous, and fearsome. Although Barney rowed in both the *Brown* and a six-oared shell at Boston in the early 1860s, he mostly left singles and doubles to his brothers: John and James sculling as professionals, their younger brother Philip as an amateur.[9]

By settling in New York, the Biglins had joined an Irish minority then unwelcome to the founding Dutch and English families who owned and ruled the compact island city. Each day brought shiploads of new arrivals—until the steady migration from Ireland surged after a national catastrophe, called "The Great Famine." A potato blight destroyed the country's main food source. Crop failures that began in 1844 had by 1850 killed more than a million people, and forced as many or more to America.[10]

"Immigrants accounted for a higher proportion of the U.S. population in the 1840s and 1850s than ever before or since," observed historian Kevin Kenny, "and the Irish made up between one-third and one-half the total flow. Because they settled in towns and cities the American Irish—and not the slightly more numerous but rural Germans—came to symbolize immigration and its attendant problems. They, and not the Germans, became the primary target of nativist, or anti-immigrant, sentiment."[11]

HARVARD V. HIBERNIA

New York wasn't the only American city drawing immigrants from Ireland, and sparking fresh hatred against them. Philadelphia was an English bastion thanks to Quakers finding comfort and community in what became (at least in name) a city of "brotherly love"—although not always friendly to the Irish. Boston also spawned legendary ethnic tensions. Founded as a theocracy by English Puritans, the port only gradually integrated the eager and needy Irish. These newcomers were welcomed as laborers, although shunned for both their Catholic faith and their rustic ways. Over time, segregation by race and religion and wealth shaped rich and poor neighborhoods throughout Boston and Cambridge. And, as these divisions strengthened and the city swelled with more and more inhabitants, the River Charles became a popular venue for both recreation and rising class conflicts. True, Boston's rowing men nurtured rivalries with other cities: Crews from Worcester, Portland, Saint John, and Halifax were frequent foes. But acrimony was fiercest within the growing metropolis, most ardently among Boston's Irish and the entrenched Anglo-Saxons, then personified by the elite students at Harvard.

Boston's Irish had become skilled watermen by working in and around the thriving port, and like the Thames Watermen in London and the Battery boatmen in New York, they enjoyed racing one another informally whenever a challenge and a bet arose. They also socialized by forming Irish boat clubs that prompted ardent rivalries: the Maid of Erin, Young Men's Catholic Lyceum, St. Mary's Temperance Society, and St. James Young Men's Catholic Total Abstinence.[12]

Boston was America's first city to sponsor an annual July Fourth Regatta, in 1854, and that year the eight-oared shell *T. F. Meagher* won a six-mile race by more than four minutes, establishing its Irish crew as local champs. Often shells were named for a patron, or to honor ethnic heroes, and Thomas Frances Meagher was an Irish nationalist leader. In July 1855, the eight-oared *Maid of Erin* won $1,000 and the championship in the City Regatta, and later that month it bested the *Meagher* in an arduous nine-mile race up and down the Charles. Neighborhoods, too, staged races, and for years each June a Beacon Regatta in Boston's Harbor preceded the city-run July Fourth races on the Charles.[13]

Competition heated up at Boston's 1856 City Regatta when the six-oared *Robert Emmett*—named for an Irish patriot and martyr—bested a Harvard eight. (At the time, boats with different numbers of rowers sometimes competed in the same races by using a time allowance per oar to set handicaps.) "The annual encounter between the Maid of Erin [Club] and Harvard crews on the Charles River reflected a fundamental cleavage between Boston's Irish Catholic neighborhoods and New England's Puritan families," noted sports historian Larry McCarthy.[14]

This rivalry intensified with a three-mile race in June 1858 for six-oared shells when Harvard easily beat *Fort Hill Boy*, *Robert Emmett*, and

Shamrock—all rowed by Irish Americans. Harvard's crew was as tony as could be, including as it did Alex Agassiz, son of the school's noted paleontologist Louis Agassiz; Charles W. Eliot, who in eleven years would become college president; and from a distinguished Massachusetts seafaring family, Benjamin and Caspar Crowninshield.[15]

As an undergraduate Eliot learned to row in a wide-bodied lapstrake boat used to carry classmates into Boston for drinking bouts, the floor boards being ideal to ferry home, he recalled, those "members of the crew who did not propose to return sober" to campus. (A boat's hull planks overlap when lapstrake- or clinker-built, and join smoothly when carvel-built.) Benjamin seems from his breezy private journal to have been a carefree gadabout. Bustling around Cambridge as a member of Harvard's exclusive Porcellian and Hasty Pudding clubs, he savored a self-proclaimed *otium cum dignitate* (leisure with dignity) in the company of the future writer/historian Henry Adams. He also read Dante in a class taught by poet James Russell Lowell, played cello with passion, and enjoyed singing classical and liturgical music.[16]

His journal entry the day of the race captures Benjamin's busy life:

Saturday June 19th 1858—*Loafed round in my room—Post office*

Talked music on the University steps—In Nick's room Gymnasium—Boathouse—Room—Felt nervous generally on account of the race, and tried to do all sorts of things to feel better—dined at 2½ on roast mutton—Eliot and I aled at Lyons'—Got the immense blue flannel pantaloons at Wales' room (we wore the Juniata trowsers) [first worn when rowing a boat by that name] & came round to the room and dressed for the race—We were a hard looking crowd—Went over to the grocery & weighed [for the race] . . .

We went in town at ¼ before 5 o'clk—Loafed round Braman's [public baths] till about 6 when we came out from the "Union" [Boat Club] house—Everybody clapped & cheered us, and my heart came right up in my mouth—We rowed round a little and started at 6—My out-rigger bent the first stroke—but I made out to row—We had hard work till after we turned the stake (No 1)—We came in in 19m. 22s *the quickest time ever made—the Fort Hill Boy 2d boat made 21.18 beaten by us 1m. 58 seconds—I never heard anything like the cheering—We won the "Beacon Cup" a prize this year of $75 in gold—We took in our coats &c and rowed to Cambridge—Took a dress and tea and made for Boston—Went to Parker's [House Hotel] where I found everybody drunk . . .*

Before this race, Benjamin and Charles Eliot set out to buy their teammates new headscarves, to distinguish them from the fourteen other crews on the river. They picked "a very handsome red of certain Chinese silk handkerchiefs," and this choice first established the school color of Harvard crimson.[17]

Distinctions were vague between amateur and professional oarsmen at the time of this race in 1858. Many of the Irish rowers were professional watermen. Two of the six in Harvard's shell weren't even students: Eliot had graduated in 1853 and worked there as a proctor with the title assistant professor; Agassiz had graduated in 1855. And the university crew itself could be considered professional just by racing for the $75 prize.

Indeed, the revered Harvard-Yale Boat Race, America's first and oldest intercollegiate contest, was begun as a way to publicize a New England railroad, making it the earliest example of corporate patronage for college sports. This came about in 1852 thanks to James Elkins, an enterprising agent for the Boston, Concord & Montreal Railroad Co. He saw a chance to attract press and passengers with a rowing regatta on BC&M's new line at the resort town of Center Harbor, at the north end of Lake Winnipesaukee in New Hampshire. Elkins printed posters. He scheduled extra trains. He also paid all travel, lodging, meal, and sundry expenses for the student rowers. And he gave them free passes on the line. One Yale oarsman remembered the event as "an eight days' junket at the expense of a railroad corporation. . . ." Another called it "a jolly lark."[18]

Today's competitive rowers obey strict diet and exercise regimens, shunning alcohol and tobacco. But back then, the college boys partied as much as they practiced—although Yale's crew did try to abstain from pastries. One Harvard rower admitted they "had only rowed a few times for fear of blistering their hands." Elkins scheduled two contests for Tuesday, August 3, with a practice pull in the morning and the two-mile race that afternoon. When Harvard won the morning row, a crewmember recalled how his eager classmates "immediately seized us and took us to their rooms, where we were regaled with ale, mineral water, and brandy." At midday they ate a hearty meal, and, "after a little rest and a cigar," appeared at four o'clock for the race.

While both crews pulled hard, trading the lead through the first mile, it was clear Harvard had stronger rowers. Swinging "better together and steadier," they won by two boat-lengths. On hand to present silver-tipped walnut oars to the winners was General Franklin Pierce, that year's Democratic presidential candidate. Harvard won its next race with Yale, on the Connecticut at Springfield in 1855, although their rivalry failed to become an annual fixture until after the Civil War.[19]

Instead, Harvard kept racing Boston's Irish crews, taking special pride when beating what the college boys considered to be hardy professional opponents. Thus, in 1858 the Harvard students relished their win over Irish watermen who rowed the *Fort Hill Boy*, and a month later an account of the race in *The Harvard Monthly* included churlish song lyrics by junior William Reed Huntington (later a distinguished Episcopal clergyman and rector of Grace Church in New York City).

"Mocking all that is Irish, the accent, the dialect and open self-confidence, the author questions the trustworthiness of the losing crew whose payment of bets was dependent upon victory, an indication of their poverty and professional status," wrote sports historian Ralph Wilcox. "Reversing Irish ridicule of the Harvard 'lady pets,' 'fops,' and 'Beacon Street swells,' Huntington asserts the superiority of the university shell over the Irish crew's flat-bottomed ferry scow. Yet, perhaps, such contests served a cathartic effect, replacing outright conflict with these regularly scheduled and socially sanctioned clashes."[20]

In Huntington's first song, Michael sings to Patrick before the race in a thick Irish brogue:

> Arrah, me Patsy! jist look at the College boat:
> Niver afore did ye see so much knowledge float.

Shure it's a shame that their arms isn't bigger now,
For it is muscle, not brains, that will figure now.

(*Chorus*)
O ye b'ys, ye fops, ye lady pets,
Twinty to wan, and our word that we pay the bets. Etc.

After the race a second song has Patrick serenading Michael.

Look! look! will ye, Mike?
Ye ne'er saw the like:
These childher have waxed us through and through.
The studints is here,
But, bad 'cess! It is clear
We'll wait awhile now for the Irish crew.

(*Chorus*)
Har-r-vard! Har-r-vard! O ye spalpeens [rascals]! Haven't ye scattered
my wages like smoke?
I can't pay a quarter
The bets that I oughter.*
Divil fly off wid yer wondherful stroke. . . .

Let's scuttle our boats:
Nary one of thim floats
But look kond o' shamed about the bows;
And oh! may the crews
In future refuse
To meddle with race-boats, and stick to their scows.

The footnote after "oughter" extended Huntington's insult about Irish rowers not paying their bets: *"The Editor . . . informs us in a foot-note, that he has opened a subscription-book for the benefit of Irish families rendered destitute by similar calamity. Cannot Harvard, he hints, do a little towards it?"[21]

And Harvard's rowers *did* give their competitors some kind and welcome relief a few weeks later. In Crowninshield's journal entry about the next City Regatta on the Charles, he jotted, "As the 'Fort Hill Boy's' crew seemed to think it hard of us to enter and take the prize from them, we agreed that if we took 1st and they second prize we would give them $25. And make the two prizes even each of $75." Harvard finished first, *Fort Hill Boy* second, and the crews did split the difference. As we will see, despite enduring such condescension—or, perhaps fired by it—Irish Americans from Boston, New York, Philadelphia, and other cities became the best rowers, both amateur and professional.[22]

The Irishmen's fans gained a reputation for drunken brawls at regattas, although the college boys were hardly genteel. For years, rowdy crowds disgraced the Harvard-Yale Regatta, especially in the 1860s when rowed on Lake Quinsigamond at Worcester. A newspaper called the students' behavior a "grand bacchanalian carnival," fouled by yelling and obscene songs. One year "china was lobbed from hotel windows shattering on the pavement below, carpets were ripped, furniture smashed, and doors ripped from their hinges," noted sports historian Ronald A. Smith. Faculty members condemned these "gross immoralities" and threatened to ban the regattas, but their efforts failed. In time, the students learned to cheer their crews with a bit more decorum.[23]

CHAPTER 2

From the Nile to New York

THE SPORT THE BIGLINS ASPIRED TO IN THE 1850S HAD EVOLVED AMONG professional watermen for millennia, although rowing gained the structure and style we know today just two centuries ago—at first in England, then in North America. There are many fine histories of the sport, so here are just a few highlights of the changes from professional to amateur competition.

ROWING THROUGH THE AGES
Rowing and racing for a living dates to antiquity and continued as grueling work into the nineteenth century. Wall paintings and bas-reliefs from ancient Egypt depict rowers pulling six-oared boats with gracefully upswept bows and sterns. Races were common in a kingdom defined by its dominant waterway, the Nile. Cornell University classicist (and amateur sculler) Barry Strauss wrote that an inscribed stone found near the Sphinx at Giza "praises the rowing prowess of Pharaoh Amenhotep II" and added how

> Egyptians liked rowing so much that they even paid it the compliment of using it in a tasteful erotic fantasy, a tale of twenty pretty girls rowing back and forth across a lake at the palace, wielding gold-plated, ebony oars and wearing only nets made of pearls instead of clothes.[1]

We remember ancient Greece and Rome from their poetry and artwork, and (thanks to Hollywood epics like *Ben-Hur*) for tumultuous sea battles by mighty triremes: swift warships powered from three decks of oars. Consider the eight-oared shell, today's standard craft for crew races. These eights are about sixty feet long and two feet at their broadest, tapered to points at bow and stern, and propelled by twelve-foot oars. With a modern eight in mind, now imagine a Greek trireme's scale and power. Only about twice as long, but five times wider than an eight, a trireme was driven by twenty times more oars. Typically 170 rowers swung slender thirteen-foot oars in drum-timed unison to propel these sleek wooden hulls across the Aegean and the Mediterranean.[2]

Competitive rowers today perch on seats with four wheels that roll back and forth in metal grooves. This lets them exert on each stroke not only the power and arc of their arms and backs, but also the stronger muscles and length of their legs. Moving seats were first tried in England and North America in the 1870s, although ancient Athenian rowers achieved a similar full-body stroke by sliding on greased sheepskin cushions: their arms, backs, and legs all driving the oar.[3]

Proud citizens of their city-states' navies rowed the Greek triremes. But in Rome slaves powered their warships, giving us a galley-slave image of rowing still common today.

A prosperous city-state built on water, Venice had the first recorded reference to a *regata*, in 1274. Along the Thames at London, professional "watermen" rowed passengers and cargo in small boats. When idle they dared one another to "wager" races. Admiralty official Samuel Pepys viewed one in the spring of 1661, and penned in his diary (best read for court intrigues and lascivious encounters) how one day he

> *found the Thames full of boats and gallys [sic], and upon inquiry found that there was a wager to be run this morning. . . . But upon the start, the wager boats fell foul one of another, till at last one of them gives over, pretending foul play, and so the other row away alone, and all our sport is lost.*[4]

London's professional rowers joined what became the world's oldest race continuing today. In 1715 Thomas Doggett, a famed Irish actor and theater manager, sponsored an annual race for the fastest apprentice waterman on the Thames. Called "Doggett's Coat and Badge," its winners receive a cash prize and a bright red coat adorned with an oval silver badge on its sleeve.[5]

Amateurs in England first rowed what they called a "regatta" at Chester in 1733 and at Walton-on-Thames in 1768. Yet professional-amateur distinctions stayed murky for a century to come. In 1817, for example, the prestigious preparatory school Eton College won money in a four-oared race against professional Thames watermen. And until 1828 Eton crews hired professionals to coach and to stroke their boats. Notably, it was at Eton, and later at Oxford and Cambridge Universities, that the hardscrabble sport of professional rowing began to be gentrified. Amateurs followed the professionals by racing eight-oared cutters when Oxford bested Cambridge in their first regatta in 1829 at Henley-on-Thames, a site where the meander-

James Liddy, winner of Doggett's Coat and Badge in 1842 *ILLUSTRATED LONDON NEWS*, AUGUST 6, 1842, 205

ing river runs a surprising straight course for more than a mile. The first Oxford-Cambridge race drew some twenty thousand spectators, and many more once the venue shifted downriver to London.[6]

Rowing technology advanced in England's industrial north at Newcastle upon Tyne when, in 1828, boat-builder Anthony Brown fashioned a metal "outrigger" that moved the oarlock—in which the oar rotates—from between wooden pins on the gunwales atop the hull to project out over the water. This let rowers pull longer oars for extended strokes, gaining extra leverage and speed. Professional oarsmen went from working

"Henley Regatta—Eight-Oar'd Match" *ILLUSTRATED LONDON NEWS*, JUNE 29, 1844, 416. THOMAS E. WEIL JR. COLLECTION.

boats to sleeker racing shells by 1831 when competing for prize money on the Thames at London.[7]

The piecemeal shift from professional to amateur rowing jumbled along when in 1818 England's oldest surviving boat club was founded: named Leander, for a hero of Greek mythology. With its mock-Tudor clubhouse by the Henley finish line, Leander remains the model for mixing athletic and social delights.

Despite fighting against Britain, Americans still held cultural ties that persist to this day: not only in language and in law, but also with the fuzzy ideal of amateur sports. The Knickerbocker Club in New York City was the first amateur boat club in the United States, established even before Leander in 1811. Two leading boat-builders were Jean Baptiste (later John Baptist) in Manhattan and John Chambers in Brooklyn. Baptist was a French-born cabinetmaker who turned to crafting more delicate boats for racing, whereas John Chambers and his brother William made boats of all kinds, for rowing and for sailing. In what is probably the country's first major rowing race, a Baptist boat beat one built by Chambers in 1807: from a pier at Whitehall Street by the Battery, up the East

River, around Blackwell's (now Roosevelt) Island, and back. It was also in 1811 that Canada's first rowing race was held in Halifax Harbor, between soldiers from The Garrison and sailors from the Royal Navy.[8]

In 1811 Baptist built the four-oared *Knickerbocker* for the Knickerbocker Club, which raced it against the Chambers' *Invincible* to win on a course from Harsimus, New Jersey, to the Battery. In 1818 the Chambers' four-oared *American Star* defeated Baptist's *New York* when racing from Williamsburg in Brooklyn to Governors Island and back. And New Yorkers in *American Star* beat a crew of London watermen from the British frigate *Hussar* in 1824, racing from the Battery to Hoboken and back and winning $1,000.[9]

Britain's rowing gained followers across its empire, with the first race in Australia in 1805. Canada's first recorded regatta was in St. John's Harbor in Newfoundland in 1826. The English also set world standards for boat building, and it wasn't until 1856 that James McKay launched the first American-made racing shell on the East River at Williamsburg.[10]

Whitehall Street, by the harbor in Lower Manhattan, was the center for competitive rowing among the professional watermen, whose

Whitehall racing boat that defeated a Staten Island crew on May 20, 1825 THOMAS E. WEIL JR. COLLECTION

"Whitehall" boats were built for both speed and stability. These workboats delivered goods and sailors to shore from ships at anchor, and ferried passengers about the rivers and bay.

By contrast, rowing and racing by amateurs was spotty during the 1820s and 1830s and, as in England, mostly a pastime for the elite. The best known New York clubs were Wave and Gull—both with members from the richest families and described by one historian as "the first gentlemen in the city." Wave, Gull, and a few other clubs rowed from boathouses

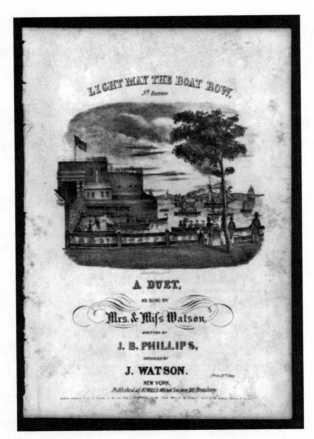

"Light May the Boat Row" sheet music depicting rowers by Castle Garden at the Battery (1836) THOMAS E. WEIL JR. COLLECTION

around the Battery, by Castle Garden: a sandstone fortress converted to a resort with a theater and restaurants that attracted a wealthy clientele. Castle Garden was also where immigrants landed for most of the nineteenth century, until Ellis Island opened in 1892. Besides the Battery another convenient locale for rowers was Elysian Fields, a riverfront park in Hoboken, New Jersey.[11]

And yet, for rowing to attract more athletes and fans it first had to rival and then displace America's most popular ballgame—not yet baseball, but cricket. Into the mid-1850s, New York newspapers ran more column inches on cricket than on either rowing or baseball. As in England, competitive rowing in North America first involved mostly professionals in match races for big-money purses. Often races were for, say, "$500 a side," each rower or his syndicate staking that amount, winner-take-all. This way, rowers and their financial backers might double their money with each race. Only later were more amateurs attracted to the sport, for exercise and competition.[12]

In the South, plantation owners arranged slave races around Mobile, Charleston, Jackson, Savannah, and Atlanta. Betting lavishly, they sometimes rode as coxswains. White men also formed amateur boat clubs in southern cities. Once competitive rowing by professional watermen spread to other ports, New York's Whitehallers in 1826 proposed races for $10,000 against crews from Savannah and Charleston. Nothing came of this, as was revealed later by a "Southern Coxswain" who wrote the weekly sporting paper *Spirit of the Times* inviting rowers to visit "for a trial with our Georgia clipper for a thousand or two? We cannot carry our oarsmen to New York as they are our slaves, else we might be tempted to visit your city with our boats for a trial on the fair Hudson." New York State outlawed slavery in 1827, and there is no record the New Yorkers replied.[13]

Amateurs formed a New York Amateur Boat Club Association at Castle Garden in 1834, arranged only two regattas, and then disbanded. Their few surviving records reveal that the members spent most of their dues on newspaper ads for their regattas, pricey silver urns and goblets as trophies, and plenty of Champagne, Port, Sherry, and Madeira.[14]

Considered semi-professionals because they were working men, the Whitehallers were unbeatable in the few races for money they could muster. When they met a Fulton Meat Market Crew in 1837 one paper reported, "It appeared as if the city had poured forth all its inhabitants to witness some great contest on which their existence depended." Betting was rampant. In 1839, the Whitehallers were odds-on favorites in a four-oared race for $2,000. Improbably, the Fish Market Crew shocked fans and gamblers to finish a boat-length ahead. This upset was widely considered America's first "fix" of a major professional rowing race.[15]

CIVIC PRIDE AND PROFIT

While support by American cities for sports franchises and contests is common today, it was professional rowing that created this practice. Boston was first when its officials funded a July Fourth City Regatta in 1854. It quickly became the country's leading event for both professional and amateur rowers.[16]

Amateur boat clubs gained popularity, in New York City at first, then throughout the country. Upper-crust gents from Providence founded the Narragansett Boat Club in 1838. The Detroit Boat Club was founded a year later. Clubs were launched across the Midwest, and into the South, where freemen replaced slaves at the oars.[17]

Regrettably, it wasn't just southern slave owners who pressed their charges to row. The governors of four public institutions on Blackwell's Island, in the East River, staged an elegant regatta for the amusement of New York socialites in July 1858. They enlisted vagrants from the almshouse, paupers from the workhouse, thieves from the penitentiary, and inmates from the lunatic asylum. The rowers had to pull six-oared barges in a four-mile race around the island. And after the workhouse crew won, the *New York Times* noted pointedly that invited guests "sat down to a jolly dinner, furnished by order of the Governors, at the Lunatic Asylum." The "tables were supplied with every delicacy of the season, and there was a good time generally. Our Reporter noticed that neither paupers,' vagrants' nor lunatics' boats' crew were represented at the table."[18]

Among those free to choose their pastimes, rowing also appealed to the populations moving west. Beyond the East Coast, races for prize money were first staged at San Francisco as early as 1852 and included cash awards for both amateur and professional rowers, with betting a featured attraction. In America's heartland, races began at Chicago, Pittsburgh, and Sandusky, Ohio, in 1855—and at many other places. In 1858 Chicago's Metropolitan Club rowed a four-oared race with Toronto's Shakespeare Club, over five miles for $5,000, and lost badly.[19]

Disputes continued about amateur and professional status and rowing for money. New London, Connecticut, staged its first city regatta in 1858, on the Thames River (there ardently pronounced "Thaymz" not "Temz"), and in 1878 Harvard and Yale moved their boat race there. After Yale won a city regatta on the Connecticut River at Middletown in July 1859, it raced at New London—and lost to crews packed with professional whalers and fishermen. As the *New Haven Palladium* reported:

> *For an explanation of the defeat of the Yale crew, we have only to state that they were beaten, not by clubs, but by professional oarsmen hired for the occasion and trained together. These were, almost without exception, hardy, weather-beaten, middle-aged men, and were picked up in New-London and all along the shore by the New-London clubs, and hired to pull their boats. This was admitted by the captains of the several New-London boats. . . .*[20]

Competitive rowing evolved from being first professional, then social, and finally recreational as amateur clubs by the score formed and dissolved. One explanation for Boston's eventual dominance as a rowing mecca is that it was better sized for the sport with the River Charles at its heart. Likewise, rowing thrived in Philadelphia because its Schuylkill River flowed through the city's magnificent Fairmount Park. By contrast, New York's rivers and harbor were only randomly visible from shore, and not always accessible. Besides, the city's waters churned with the wakes of seagoing ships, ferries, tugs, and scows. Boat clubs had to cluster where waters were calmest: along Newtown Creek on the Brooklyn/Queens boundary, and on the Harlem River between Manhattan and the Bronx.

When Boston drew New York's professional oarsmen to its second City Regatta, editorial writers at the *New York Times* were alarmed. In

June 1855, the paper implored city officials and citizens to hold their own July Fourth regatta. The paper's appeal was stirring, and ripe with civic gumption. The *Times* editorial "Better than Fireworks" chided the Bostonians' "Yankee cunning" for having staged the country's first city-run regatta, and then for making it a popular annual affair. The *Times* praised "the stalwart lungs and broad chests of sturdy oarsmen," and proffered some reasons for supporting a local competition.

> *So we may economize the thousands annually sacrificed to Vulcan in the infernal shapes devised by the pyrotechnist. So we may preserve our military cool and comfortable, instead of fricasseeing them between the sweat and sunshine, about the streets. So we may attain the chief end of all popular amusement, novelty; which surely cannot be predicted of martial displays, wherewith, on the slightest provocation, the ways of the City are harassed from one years' end to the other; or of fireworks, of which we shall haply hear, see and smell quite as much as is consistent with personal safety and comfort, whether the City treasury deal in them or not. We crave a change; a change from exhausting and perilous pageants, to sports athletic and invigorating.*

The paper even carped that the esteemed New York Yacht Club's annual regatta "has nothing of the athletic about it" because "Its heroes go forth in kid gloves. . . . Our need is different."

> *We want something to beguile young men from the sedentary relaxation of the gaming, or the semi-effeminate skill of the billiard table, and lead them out into God's open air, where health, strength, manhood may be earned—where jolly young watermen may, to the eternal benefit of the national marine, come in time to be bold and skillful mariners.*

Grumbling how "most of what boat-clubs we have are entered for the Boston plate," the *Times* urged New Yorkers to host their own regatta the next year, envisioning "what a glorious spectacle our broad Bay will present when its waters shall be thick besprent with gallantly-decorated steamers, sail-boats and row-boats; and the shores, and shipping, and house-tops in every direction alive with masses, enthusiastically alert to witness the stirring novelty of a boat-race." Despite this grandiloquent plea nothing followed in 1856. New York's rowers left town to race on the Charles in three regattas that year, and competed up the Hudson when Newburgh held its own July Fourth Regatta.[21]

The Empire City Regatta Club had for a few years sponsored summer races on the Harlem with prize money (the club's president was champion professional sculler and boat-builder Stephen Roberts). Finally, in 1859, the Empire City Club convinced City Hall to arrange New York's first July Fourth Regatta—at the Battery, funded by the Common Council. The *Times* wrote buoyantly about the races, but on the same page also ran results from the day's Boston City Regatta. The best the paper could do was note proudly which winners at Boston had rowed "New-York built boats."

Then, in 1860, New York's second July Fourth Regatta drew a sprawling crowd to the Battery. And joining the festivities, as rowers, were three brothers named Biglin.[22]

CHAPTER 3

The Biglins Take to the Boats

HOW THE BIGLIN BOYS CAME TO COMPETE IN NEW YORK CITY'S 1860 July Fourth Regatta is a story that personifies America's Irish immigration—both its harsh realities and its comforting myths. Struggle led the Biglins and their compatriots to succeed, often by luck and pluck.

THE BIGLIN FAMILY

When John Biglin and Ellen (also called Eleanor) Hart married at St. James Church on Jay Street in downtown Brooklyn that Saturday, August 4, 1837, they faced a life together that must have seemed daunting—and a bit dangerous. Both had braved crossings from Ireland to New York and secured menial work. Both were then just twenty-one years old.[1]

In Manhattan Eleanor Biglin bore Mary in 1838 and James in 1839, the first two of their fifteen children (the five marked * died as infants or youngsters). Then the couple moved to the mountains of western Pennsylvania near Altoona, where John found work as a laborer. There Bernard (Barney) was born in 1840, Edwin* in 1841, John in 1842, Joseph in 1843, Julia* in 1845, Ellen in 1847, Philip in 1849, Elias* in 1850, and Ann in 1851. The children attended local schools, sharing a life of work and play in the countryside.

The Biglins returned to Manhattan, where Martha* was born in 1853, Amanda in 1854, George* in 1857, and William in 1859. Their apartments, on Third Avenue near 28th Street, were in the Kips Bay neighborhood, then mostly Irish and sharply divided between Democrats and Republicans.[2]

For Irish Americans at the time, financial opportunities were meager but improving, and the Biglins needed their children's help to support the family. A year after returning to New York the two oldest sons, James and Barney, then aged sixteen and fifteen, had both found work as laborers. Construction boomed for residential, commercial, and public buildings, giving some Irishmen both physical and semi-skilled work: as hod carriers and bricklayers most often, but also as masons, plasterers, stonecutters, and blacksmiths. For their part, Irish women boosted family incomes by working as laundresses, nurses, and domestics.[3]

When they couldn't aspire to higher-paid and more prestigious professions, the Irish and their children still found two other ways to survive. One option was to become an apprentice for the skilled building and commercial crafts then dominated by the Dutch, English, Scots, and Germans. But as access was often barred by nepotism and prejudice, the Irish gained more accessible work in certain municipal jobs, as a street-sweeper, jailer, policeman, or fireman. Eldest son James became a molder of molten brass at Mitchell, Vance & Company in Chelsea, where brother Joseph was later a brass finisher and Barney an apprentice. Samuel B. H. Vance ran what was then the nation's largest chandelier and fancy lamp factory. He was active in Republican politics, and Barney's celebrated (later disgraced) intrigues with the party likely began while working for Vance.

Since Republican patronage then ruled federal and state hiring in New York's thriving port, the connection to Vance also explains how Barney was appointed an inspector for the US Customs Service, and later an inspector at the Internal Revenue Department. Elective politics offered another path to prosperity for the Irish, and the Biglins enjoyed several public sinecures arranged by Barney even before he ran for office.[4]

The Biglin family's neighborhood was in the notorious Eighteenth Assembly District, and none in the city had "a political history more stirring and bloody," said the *New York Herald*. "The annals of the XVIIIth are filled with deeds of violence, of 'horrible beatings and murders most brutal,'" according to Dr. Edward McGlynn, a Catholic priest and social worker who lived in the area, studied its residents, and also heard their confessions. "Election day never passed without bloodshed," the *Herald* noted, "and it was an exception when no lives were taken. Not only on election day, but in the early days during the [Civil] war, particularly, it was almost a continuous round of strife."[5]

Both before and during the Civil War, the district's majority Democrats sympathized with the South, further charging the neighborhood's partisan rancor. The Irish feared emancipated slaves would compete for their low-wage jobs. "Republican inspectors had to be taken to and from the polls by a strong escort of Republican fighters, armed, as a rule, with hickory sticks or pistols," reported the *Herald*. "To go out at night alone and unarmed was regarded as the height of rashness." Discord was known, and feared, block-by-block. "Second-ave. was Republican territory, while third-ave. was looked upon as belonging exclusively to the Democrats," explained the *Herald*. "The appearance of a Republican on Third-ave. or of a Democrat in Second-ave. was considered sufficient ground for a fight." The Eighteenth would become Barney's political base, with both he and brother John embroiled in its political violence.[6]

"The Regatta," July 4, 1860. The Biglins were contestants. THOMAS E. WEIL JR. COLLECTION

While Barney would be able to use his connections to enter politics and enjoy its patronage, John seemed content to work on his own: briefly as a dyer, then as a laborer, Battery boatman, and, in 1859, a fireman.

New York's Common Council sponsored a second City Regatta for July Fourth in 1860, when Dennis Leary joined John, Barney, and James Biglin for a memorable race at the Battery. Once the Biglins realized that they could win far more money from an afternoon's row than they earned in a month or a year, they bent their energies to the oar with zeal and tenacity.

These four lads were already colleagues at Knickerbocker Engine Company No. 12, on East 33rd Street, near Third Avenue, where they had helped reorganize that firehouse. At the time, fire companies were manned and run by volunteers who enlisted for the fraternal and social opportunities, as well as the pay for their work and the esteem gained from public service. All volunteer companies were notably casual: forming, disbanding, re-forming, and renaming themselves as if by whim. John Biglin and Leary were volunteers years before their names appeared on the rolls of Knickerbocker Engine Company No. 12 in 1863, and they joined the Fire Department of New York (FDNY) when it formed officially in 1865. That fall, John helped organize Engine Company No. 21, at 142 East 40th Street, between Lexington and Third Avenues. Firemen in the FDNY earned about $700 a year, forcing them to seek other income. At Knickerbocker No. 12, Foreman Bartley Donohue was also a butcher, Assistant Foreman Leary a dock-builder, Assistant Foreman John Biglin a laborer, and James Biglin a brass finisher. Leary was later a policeman, thus holding the two city jobs most common among Irish Americans.[7]

New York's Independence Day celebration in 1860 began as chimes at Trinity Church on Broadway played a medley of favorites, including "Hail Columbia," "Home, Sweet Home," "Last Rose of Summer," airs from Bellini's popular opera *Norma*, and, of course, "Yankee Doodle." Bells pealed as well at churches and at firehouses in Brooklyn, and officials in both cities stood to review military parades. That afternoon, crowds jammed the waterfront along the Battery for the regatta. Pulling in double-scull workboats were John and Barney in the *Jack McDonald* (or *McDonnell*, spelling was erratic among rowing journalists), ready to race four miles against their brother James and Leary in the *H.W. Genet*, the *G.W. Winship*, and five other boats. They started at the Battery, rounded a stake boat anchored near Ellis Island, then returned. The *New York Times* reported a close and exciting race with the *McDonnell* leading the *Winship* most of the way. John and Barney won $75 for first place; James and Dennis Leary took home $20 for third.[8]

CIVIL WAR

America's brutal and calamitous Civil War began on April 12, 1861, when cannons from Charleston, South Carolina, bombarded the federal Fort Sumter in the harbor. Barney, aged twenty, and John Biglin, who was nineteen, each year were winning hundreds more dollars a race, and once a draft was imposed, in 1863, they easily paid the $300 "commutation fee" that hired others to serve in their stead—an opportunity scarcely available to their poorer Irish brethren.

Avidly seeking to join the federal cause was brother Philip S. Biglin, who made a life of his volunteer service. He joined New York's Seventh Regiment (called the "Silk Stocking Regiment" for its many members from the city's social elite), and even composed the popular song "I Want to Be a Soldier."[9]

John and Barney's aspirations were not on the battlefield but on the water, and about the time the war began the Biglins' fire department connections led to a chance and fateful meeting with Charles B. Elliott. He was then with Americus Engine Company No. 6, called "The Big Six" for its huge steam-powered pump engine as well as its outsize political sway. Tammany Hall's "Boss" Tweed and General Daniel Sickles were Big Six members. Both were Democratic political power brokers who would run afoul of the law in nasty ways: Tweed for stupendous public graft, and Sickles for being the first man in an American court to plead "temporary insanity" after shooting his young and flirtatious wife's paramour, a son of Francis Scott Key.

Days after the war's outbreak Elliott organized for the Union cause the Fire Zouaves—a volunteer corps that dressed like the French army units in North Africa by wearing short open-fronted jackets, baggy trousers, and oriental caps and sashes. Huge crowds cheered as they departed

New York City, and their exploits at the First Battle of Bull Run drew constant press attention in July.

By shipping out to war Elliott had to interrupt his new business—building racing shells at a small shop in the Greenpoint section of Brooklyn. (One of Elliott's first shells, *Unexpected*, had won the four-oared race at New York's 1860 City Regatta.) He located his shop at the corner of Franklin and Quay Streets for its easy access to Bushwick Inlet, where a stream afforded an easy place to launch his light and slender shells. However, within sight (and acrid smell) of Elliott's cedar-scented shop stood the Continental Iron Works, a foundry that would soon hammer out the Union ironclad *Monitor* and a fleet of modern warships.[10]

By contrast to the military precision of the Greenpoint ship builders, Elliott, the Biglin Four, and John Biglin were all then just launching their aquatic careers much more tentatively. John joined with two brothers and Leary to take the *George J. Brown* to Boston in July 1861. There they finished a close second to a powerful crew from Poughkeepsie. And that fall John rowed second in a matched race with the more seasoned Poughkeepsie sculler William Stevens. Steadily John was making his way as a professional sculler.[11]

Given their arduous lives raising fifteen children (five died prematurely), it is sad yet no surprise to see that the Biglins' parents went to early graves. They must have been proud of their sons' early victories on the water, and grateful for the riches they earned by rowing. But the glories they could share were brief. Eleanor Biglin died on February 20, 1862, and her husband John died on August 3, 1863—both aged forty-six. They were buried in Calvary Cemetery in Queens.

Still, the next Biglin generation grew and prospered. In April 1862, Barney was the first of the sons to marry, taking as his bride Mary Ann "Polly" Grundy. Barney and Polly had seven daughters and a son. John Biglin wed an Irish woman, Catherine "Kate" Nutley, in 1865, and they had five daughters (two died as infants) and a son, John Jr. The Biglin children gained more and more cousins after James raised a daughter and three sons, and Philip two daughters.

At Boston's 1862 City Regatta, John finished fifth in a two-mile race won by powerful Pittsburgh sculler James Hamill in single-scull wherries (wider and heavier than racing shells). Yet later that day, John, James, and Barney—with Dennis Leary as stroke—won a three-mile race in the *George J. Brown*.

The Biglins rowed the *Brown* to a close second at the 1863 Boston City Regatta, where they won first prize in a six-oared shell. For John Biglin July 1863 may have begun with triumphs in Boston, but back in New York he quickly faced sorrow and violence. His father was ailing, and life in his Kips Bay neighborhood was in turmoil. Congress had recently passed a federal draft that angered Irish Americans and sparked them to riot. Irish mobs terrorized the city for three days and nights. They set afire the Colored Orphan Asylum, and dozens of other buildings. They stoned and looted stores and banks. And they attacked the homes of abolitionists and blacks. John's engine company on East 40th Street was near the worst riots and fires and worked to control the infernos. President Lincoln ordered in federal troops, many battle-weary from their conflict at Gettysburg. But only after New York's esteemed Archbishop John Hughes appealed for calm did the Irish slacken their rampages. More than one hundred people were killed, some two thousand injured, and at least a dozen blacks lynched, making it the bloodiest urban disturbance in American history.[12]

Since he could buy his way out of the draft, John Biglin's only involvement with this tragic outburst came as a firefighter. Adding to that income, he made $550 racing in 1861, only a few hundred dollars in 1862 and 1863 when rowing declined, $1,850 in 1864, and $6,450 in 1865. John also enjoyed extra pay from Republican sinecures brother Barney had contrived at the Custom House.

John Biglin THOMAS E. WEIL JR. COLLECTION (1872)

WINNING WAYS

In September 1863 John Biglin had his first of many encounters with the Ward brothers. At Cornwall-on-Hudson he was third behind the more experienced Gilbert Ward and William Stevens, in a three-mile race, but finished ahead of veteran sculler John Hancon. Biglin bested Hancon again in October, when finishing second to the champion sculler Josh Ward in a regatta at Troy, New York. On the Harlem in October, John won a five-mile race in the single *Elly Biglin*, named for his mom. After snatching what Peverelly called "a fine start," he "went immediately to the front, where he remained during the entire race, winning it with ease. . . ."[13]

At Boston that year, the three Biglins and fellow New Yorker John J. Eckerson rowed the *Brown* to a decisive first at the Beacon Regatta in June. But two weeks later—with no practice in between—they finished a dispiriting second in the July Fourth City Regatta, trailing a shell stroked by the famed Boston-Irish oarsman George Faulkner. Then, as if for revenge, the three Biglins and Dennis Leary joined a six-oared race, which Peverelly wrote "was very soon decided; the Brown's crew, feeling very much chagrined at losing the four-oared race, determined to win this. After the start they soon took the lead, which they kept to the end of the race, winning easily in twenty minutes eight seconds . . . the 'Sixty-Six' [from Harvard's class of 1866] coming in second. . . ." For this race the *Brown* won $175, Harvard won $75.[14]

When Charles Elliott returned from the war in 1864 he became the Biglins' favored boat-builder, and soon their patron. Elliott prospered by his quick mechanical mind and eagerness to innovate. He was among the first to use "Spanish cedar" (*Cedrela*) for his shells—so called because it was used to make boxes for cigars featuring Spanish names, to line humidors, and to craft flamenco and classical guitars. It had the strength of mahogany but weighed less.[15]

The Biglins also used Elliott's Greenpoint shop as their boathouse, practicing on the East River, and often pulling into the calmer Newtown Creek where traffic was lighter. But the creek posed nasty problems. It was fetid from the abattoirs, rendering plants, varnish and glue factories, and kerosene works along its banks. On the Queens shore the Laurel Hill

Chemical Works was then the country's largest sulfuric acid producer. Today the creek is an EPA Superfund site.

Elliott enjoyed tinkering with hull designs and hardware. He rejected the traditional contours of English four-oared shells, instead crafting ones that were notably longer and narrower. Elliott's ingenuity also let the Biglins benefit from the latest technology—especially sliding seats that maximized power from the legs and a rudder controlled by cables moved when the bow rower pivoted his foot.[16]

Year by year the Biglin crews prospered. John, Barney, and James Biglin joined Dennis Leary to win a four-oared race at the popular Citizens' Regatta at Worcester in July 1864, the same day they also won in a six-oared shell. At Poughkeepsie in August, the Biglin four with Leary won $2,000 by besting a strong Pittsburgh crew. In New York that August, John defeated D. O'Brien, racing from Jackson Street (near today's Williamsburg Bridge) up the East River, around Blackwell's Island, then back. And, off Staten Island that November, John won $1,000 when beating sculler William H. Hays from Brooklyn. For perspective, in 1870 a non-farm laborer working six days a week earned about $485 a year, a skilled carpenter about $925 a year.[17]

The year 1865 was momentous for the Biglins, and for the United States. On New Year's Day John Biglin married Catherine E. Nutley, and they moved into an apartment off Lexington Avenue in Kips Bay. In April the Union won the Civil War. But within a fortnight the North sank into mourning when an assassin felled its heroic wartime president, Abraham Lincoln. The country faced daunting challenges as it recovered from the war's devastation and struggled to reconcile the former Confederate States of America to the Union. Yet with the peace came also surging prosperity, affording elites and entrepreneurs a Gilded Age of greed and opulence.

On the water in 1865 the Biglins enjoyed more and more success. They renamed their favorite four-oared shell the *Samuel Collyer* after a generous new patron: a champion bare-knuckle boxer who invested in their races. (Among the Irish Americans especially, boxers and rowers supported and sometimes competed in each other's sports. Boxers who raced, or rowed when training, included John Morrissey, Jake Kilrain, and

The Biglin Four wins at Poughkeepsie, July 19, 1865 *HARPER'S WEEKLY*, AUGUST 5, 1865, 1

John L. Sullivan.) With Dennis Leary as stroke, this four won at Boston's City Regatta, easily defeating a local crew led by George Faulkner. Two weeks later, an "immense crowd" greeted the same *Collyer* crew on the Hudson at Poughkeepsie as "the docks, piers and rocky eminences on either side of the river were filled with thousands of human beings" awaiting the starter's pistol. William Stevens, John Biglin's frequent sculling rival, was stroke in a Poughkeepsie four named the *Floyd T. F. Field*.

At stake was the nation's largest rowing prize: $6,000 and the grandly titled "Championship of American Waters." This race "excited more interest throughout the United States than any other affair of the kind ever gotten up in this country or Europe," declared the *New York Times*. Betting exceeded $200,000, and *Harper's Weekly* depicted the event on its cover. "The sporting celebrities were out in full force, and the light fingered gentry numerously represented." The popular Josh and Gilbert Ward strode around town, and bet on the Poughkeepsie crew. But wagering against them was John Morrissey, the former prizefighter who was also a famous gambler, race promoter, and politician. Gladly he placed hundreds of his dollars on the New Yorkers.[18]

With quicker strokes the *Collyer* at first grabbed the lead, then by easing a bit still stayed ahead. Nearing the stake boat at the mid-course turn, the *Field* pulled a hard sprint, yet failed to sustain it. Still leading after the turn, the *Collyer* pushed steadfastly toward home. "The excitement was now deeper than ever—the New-York boat getting the odds freely, with but few takers." The Biglins won by two lengths, to a din of huzzahs, steamer bells, and boat whistles. Poughkeepsie's crew claimed it had been blocked and fouled when trying to pass. This protest the referee dismissed.[19]

The *Times* reported "the usual amount of thieving going on that is noticeable at all boat-races, and in a miniature riot on the Main-street dock some of the Poughkeepsie police got pretty roughly handled" by thugs from Gotham. But worse trouble was to come. Roused with complaints by the *Poughkeepsie Eagle,* townsfolk screaming "foul," and, with tensions flaring, the referee and four judges agreed to reconsider the *Field* crew's plea. When they sat down that night at Rutzer's Hotel to decide, they faced what the *Eagle* called "scoundrels and thieves" who "filled up the windows of the room, burst in the doors, and flourished pistols, knives and clubs, called out in threatening tones to the referee, Mr. Charles Gausman[n], to decide the question in [their] favor or they would take his life."

"I want to decide fair," Gausmann vowed, prompting cries of "throw him out of the window. Our time is short. Kill him." When he ruled once again for the New Yorkers, the *Eagle* reported that "the thugs congregated about the depot and, while there awaiting the departure of the train, committed the most diabolical outrages"—stealing a watch and chain from an elderly gent, accosting a priest, and picking countless fights and pockets. Aboard the train "the robbers seated themselves, yelling and shouting and using profane and abusive language in an awful manner." On reflection, said the *Eagle,* "The entire track of these devils throughout the day was marked with scenes of violence and bloodshed. These scenes are not entirely new to our citizens. They always happen on the occasion of every boat race opposite this city. How long we are to suffer thus we do not know. . . ."

Then a graver complaint rang through Poughkeepsie's streets: The whole race had been "sold"! Days before, rumors had spread that William Stevens agreed to throw their race as part of a statewide betting scheme. He and his crew denied this, again and again. Still they heard death threats. According to both the *Eagle* and the *New York Herald*, Stevens was standing with friends near Dobbs' Saloon, at Main and Water Streets, when up strode Thomas DeMott. A recently returned soldier, DeMott had bet heavily on the *Field*, and accused Stevens of selling out his friends and his town. Both men had been drinking, friends later vouched. After Stevens boldly dismissed the charge, he bet DeMott he couldn't prove it. "DeMott denounced Stevens in strong terms, which exasperated Stevens to such a degree that he struck DeMott a powerful blow on the temple, felling him to the earth."

This set off "a general row." But DeMott lay still, and when his pals turned to lift him he didn't move. He was dead, from what the coroner decided were a cranial contusion and a broken neck. All were stunned. Gripped with grief, Stevens paced slowly to the police station. News of the fight sparked fury across town. Those who had lost bets threatened some "sporting men" from New York who had won. Disputes continued for days: about the race, and about DeMott's death.

Tempers erupted anew when the *Tribune* reported that the referee and two of the four judges had "made affidavits that the race is foul, and that their decision was rendered through intimidation." Referee Gausmann dissented: "I was not intimidated by any threats, saw no pistols or knives drawn, and rendered my decision in favor of the Samuel Collyer, of New-York, as, in my opinion, she won the race and money fairly and squarely, and I rendered my decision to the best of my knowledge and belief of the rules [of] boat racing."[20]

Still angry in September, the *Collyer* crew resented rumors they had defeated the *Field* by a foul. And they were especially irate that the $6,000 prize was being withheld. The Biglins wrote to the *Times* that they "respectfully appeal to their brother oarsmen of the United States, to evince their detestation of the conduct and actions of the Poughkeepsie crew," and threatened to sue.[21]

The Biglins ultimately triumphed at Poughkeepsie, yet had no time to savor their victory. A week after the *Collyer-Field* race, John rowed his new single, the *Charles B. Elliott*, to a close second behind Josh Ward in a two-mile race at the Worcester Citizens' Regatta. John finished second to Josh again at Cornwall-on-Hudson in August. And in September 1865, the Biglin four met the Wards in a match race their syndicates had set on the Hudson at Sing Sing, a town best known for its state prison (origin of the phrase "up the river" for being jailed). Eager to defend their American championship, John and Barney joined John Eckerson and John Blue to row the new Elliott four, *New York*, in a five-mile race for $2,000. Overnight, trains and steamers conveyed thousands of "sporting characters" from cities up and down the Hudson, John Morrissey notable among them.[22]

"The adjacent hills were filled with eager spectators," reported the Sing Sing *Republican*, "and the rigging of the schooners, tugs, and steamers in the harbor were darkened by expectant boys." An accident with their new shell left the Biglins to row an old and leaky practice boat. Their race was "closely contested throughout," but still the Wards led from start to finish. Clearly, had the Biglin crew been able to row its new shell this race may have ended in victory.

Biglin and Ward Fours race on the Hudson at Sing Sing, September 25, 1865
FRANK LESLIE'S ILLUSTRATED NEWSPAPER, OCTOBER 14, 1865, 53

Compounding their loss at Sing Sing, a week later the Biglin four met another close defeat at Pittsburgh. Pulling against a local crew that included champion sculler James Hamill, they were just five seconds slower over five miles. Still, later that day John won the Pittsburgh regatta's race for singles.[23]

Perhaps now distracted by their growing families and ever more responsible work, in 1866 the Biglins' races were erratic and results were mixed. In Worcester for the Citizens' Regatta, the three brothers and John Eckerson finished second to a record-setting four stroked by Dennis Leary, in a race that the Ward brothers failed to finish. At Pittsburgh in August, John and Barney raced with Eckerson and Blue in Elliott's *New York* against a local crew that again included Hamill. Both shells fouled, and referees called the contest a "draw." At Poughkeepsie in October, John was trailing badly in his single and withdrew near the finish of a five-mile race won by John McKiel, with old foes William Stevens second, Gilbert Ward third, and John McGrady fourth. But days later it was McGrady who withdrew when he lost to Biglin over five miles off Elysian Fields in Hoboken.[24]

In September 1867, in the only race the Biglins were able to arrange that year, John and Barney rowed three miles in a four with Blue and McKiel on the Connecticut at Springfield, finishing second to a Boston crew.

Too Damned Good

After John Biglin beat McGrady, in November 1866, he would not race a single for nearly two years. He had steadily enriched himself and his backers so buoyantly that they frightened any competitors. No other professional rowers would accept the Biglin syndicate's challenges for a match race. In 1865, for example, Biglin made more than $6,000 from racing. As the *New York Times* later noted, he "was very successful as a single sculler . . . and about 1867 or 1868 there was no one willing to compete with him in this line."[25]

With no sculling contests of his own to train for in 1867, John Biglin aided other professional oarsmen by helping set up or supervise their races. John played a critical role, on the Hudson at Newburgh, in

September. Biglin was there for the "Great Five Mile Rowing Match for $4,000 and The Championship of America," as Currier & Ives titled its popular color lithograph.

When James Hamill from Pittsburgh raced Walter Brown from Portland, Maine, on September 9, betting was the richest in US history—especially since both men were so evenly matched. Hamill had bested the legendary Josh Ward five times for the American championship, but had just lost twice to England's champion Henry Kelly on the Tyne, and then to Brown that May at Pittsburgh. The *New York Times* described Hamill as "a short, 'chunky' man, five feet six inches high," weighing 150 pounds. "His head is large and round . . . and he has the *physique* of a prize-fighter" with muscular arms and chest. Brown was "a lithe, wiry, muscular fellow," five feet nine in height, weighing 152 pounds, a boat-builder with "a face full of intelligence, frank and open."[26]

The Currier & Ives image portrayed this race as a serene affair, with the two oarsmen glancing about from their singles on a placid river. In fact, it was anything but. An "immense and promiscuous crowd" had gathered that weekend, expecting a historic contest. Then strong winds and choppy waters forced a day's postponement, leaving fans no choice but to head for the saloons. Still, up from New York City, excursion steamers kept chugging in, dropping at dockside what the *New York Times* called "a great many of the worst rowdies and thieves." Trouble began before dawn on race day when a drunken spectator aboard a steamer tumbled over the rail and drowned. Police collared pickpockets by the score, and "roughs from New York" brawled in the streets for hours. By race time, crowds lined the riverbanks, and the water was dotted with large and small craft.

Not included in that genteel lithograph were the two escort boats—six-oared barges that sped just behind the scullers. There to avert any interference, John Biglin stood in the bow of Hamill's boat while Brown's judge, Charley Moore, steered his. "Biglin and Moore flourished each a pistol," rowing historians Crowther and Rule recorded, "and every moment one or the other was threatening to shoot as the opposing barge happened to come too close to the rival sculler."[27]

"Amid such a volley of curses the two rowed on." Brown grabbed the lead, and when a few hundred yards ahead he moved in front of Hamill to give him his "wash"—the swirling puddles left astern by each stroke that can make a trailing rower pull unevenly. Brown rowed a long "English" stroke while Hamill had less body swing and dipped his oars more rapidly, "a peculiar movement to him, which has gained for him the title of the 'Little Engine.'"

Chugging away, Hamill closed the gap, and led as they neared the mid-course stake boat. When only one stake boat was used, the rower reaching it first had right-of-way. The follower was supposed to turn outside the leader, or fall behind. "Hamill attempted to make a close turn, and the strong ebb-tide took him hard on the [stake] boat and he could not get loose." Not slowing or yielding, Brown rammed Hamill's shell and sank it. Hamill couldn't swim, and had to be hauled aboard a pilot boat. Then Brown rounded the stake boat, paddled down the course to the finish, and claimed victory. This set off a rhubarb among judges and fans. The riled crowd surged onto a dock and sank it. After the referee gave the race to Hamill, on a foul, shouts and fights erupted anew.[28]

Still finding no one to race, John Biglin worked at his firehouse, then with brother Barney coached the Pittsburgh sculler Henry Coulter for his June 1868 race against Hamill, for $2,000 and the American championship. But after Coulter's left oar broke from its oarlock, the *Aquatic Monthly* reported, he had to "leave his opponent to row over the course and take the greenbacks."[29]

BACK IN THE MONEY

At last John Biglin earned greenbacks on his own in September 1868 by beating William H. Hays in a three-mile race off Elysian Fields. Bets were scarce with Biglin the strong favorite, but the *New York Times* reported that before the race "the saloons did a pretty good business, and kegs of lager disappeared rapidly." Awaiting the start "some of the old veteran oarsmen dodged about through the crowd, growling upon the degenerate state of boat racing, and how seldom it was that a man could see a square race in these days." Cynically, they mused that Walter Brown would likely beat Coulter in their upcoming match for the American championship "because he could not make anything by losing."

Biglin soon gained a boat-length on Hays who "appeared to be considerably excited and pulled in a very wild manner," the *Times* reported. Next Hays fouled Biglin by moving into his lane. Then Hays corrected course, only to meet "a lot of small craft" in his way, "as they always will do, and created considerable annoyance." Biglin, "without exerting himself" won by three lengths.[30]

Adding to those veteran oarsmen's gripes about fixed races that day came a more serious threat to professional rowing. A second race was to feature the popular New York scullers McKiel and Blue, "but it was postponed, as a great many of the friends of the men were anxious to witness the base-ball match between the Atlantics and Athletics. . . ." In legend and in history, baseball had its roots in New York City and shared with rowing the popular venue of Elysian Fields. Of the two, rowing presaged baseball as a popular sport and a lucrative line of work for able athletes. According to baseball historian John Thorn, "rowing was America's first modern sport, in that competitions were marked by record-keeping, prizes, and wagers, yet also provided spectator interest for those with no pecuniary interest" and baseball soon followed the same model.[31]

Through the 1860s professional rowers remained national sports heroes. In 1867, for example, there were forty-eight different professional match races and regattas in the United States, a number that reached sixty-five in 1869 and exceeded 150 by 1872. As one Boston lad recalled the scene on the banks of the Charles, "It was here that, on regatta days, all the rowing celebrities congregated, and here such men as Josh Ward, the Biglin Brothers, Hammill [James Hamill], Walter Brown, and many others were revealed to us. Merely to catch a glimpse of them I have squirmed between the legs of a crowd and all but crawled over their heads; but these were state occasions and occurred, alas, like angels' visits."[32]

In 1869 John Biglin won every race he entered, apparently all on the square. (Throughout a rowing career that included more than one hundred races, Biglin was accused of cheating only once or twice.) Fairly, Biglin won races at the Battery, off Elysian Fields, and on the Harlem. During 1870, John Biglin enjoyed two victories. The Biglin four with John and Barney, American sculling champion Walter Brown, and T. C. Butler, won a three-mile race at Boston's City Regatta, beating various crews by many boat-lengths. And in September John rowed to a dead heat on the Harlem against John Blue. Then came trouble from Ellis Ward, the rowing family's youngest son. Ellis, then only twenty-four, beat Biglin (age twenty-eight) racing singles on Kill-Van-Kull off Staten Island, and bested him again on the East River. Their rivalry would continue for years.[33]

THE BIGLIN STYLE

In the pantheon of skilled professional oarsmen, the Biglins were best known for their aggressive racing style, which all but startled the other crews. This employed, in part, a technique that Barney Biglin described years later when interviewed in 1906. At England's Henley Royal Regatta that year, the Belgian rowing club Sport Nautique de Gand, from Ghent, had won the Grand Challenge Cup for eight-oared shells by pulling a remarkably high stroke-rate. Afterward, a newspaperman printed this revealing encounter:

> *Barney Biglin, world-wide known as one of the greatest professional oarsmen that this country ever claimed, was plowing along Broadway at a ten-mile gait one day last week when he was hailed by a friend, who said: "That Belgian crew must be a dandy, Barney!"*
>
> *"Capital crew beyond a doubt," said the old waterman, adding: "But I can't understand why there should be so much surprise in England because the Belgian crew manages to get great speed out of its so-called short, jerky stroke. What else could they get out of it? In these days oarsmen marvel over a crew hitting up the stroke of forty-four, working like a pump-handle, as I saw one of the newspapers refer to the Navy Academy crew that went to [the annual Intercollegiate Rowing Association Regatta at] Poughkeepsie.*
>
> *"Why, man alive, when we were winning championship races so fast that we could not count them we used to hit it up to fifty or even higher during spurts. This, too, on a stationary seat. We always made it a rule to start off at a fifty-to-a-minute clip. The result was that we'd shoot away from the stake boat so fast that our opponents were dumbfounded. The fifty-to-a-minute stroke consisted chiefly of arm work*

and fore-arm work at that, but it enabled us to get so far ahead that we could take a rest, so to speak, while the opposing crew was catching up. The moment it did catch up we invariably hit it up again, each time refreshed by the let up between our spurts. Some times we'd let an opposing crew get right abreast of us before we'd give it the famous fifty again. That's the way we won all our races."[34]

The Biglins rowed more than half their hundred-plus races on fixed seats, so Barney's description explains a favored technique that won them early success. But on sliding seats they had to pull longer strokes at a lower rate, and when doing that they were still masters at alternating power bursts during the stroke with poise on the recovery. Another key to their success was John's physical strength. Reporters wrote often about how the Biglins "got down to work" when winning races by applying their strength and stamina for mile after grueling mile.

CHAPTER 4

The Rise of Professional Rowing

BASEBALL HISTORIANS REVERE AS THEIR SPORT'S FIRST GREAT HISTORY *The Book of American Pastimes*, published in New York City in 1866 by Charles A. Peverelly. His book chronicled four popular sports. Baseball (186 pages) was then becoming the country's "national pastime" and Peverelly titled its chapter "The National Game." Cricket (36 pages) was losing followers in the United States, thanks mostly to baseball's rise, and to how British traditions dwindled as immigrants from other lands swelled the population. Peverelly described yachting (104 pages) as an admittedly patrician pastime, praising the sport for its recreational appeal and the boats for their graceful beauty. But he devoted the most attention (218 pages) to rowing.[1]

Peverelly celebrated rowing as a sport at once strenuous yet graceful, expressing for him an essentially American ideal: fusing body and mind, power and poise, work and play. As he declared,

> *No recreation, no method of exercise, no out-door or in-door sport, offers less temptations and more advantages than rowing. In truth, excellence as an oarsman is wholly inconsistent with dissipation or excess of any nature. Regular habits, constant exercise, open-air life, and plain food, are essential to every man who aspires to endurance, skill, and rowing fame. There is no more certain way of fitting the mind and heart for vigorous labor and the reception of careful culture than by putting the body in perfect condition.*[2]

Boathouse Row, on the Schuylkill at Philadelphia *THE SCHUYLKILL NAVY OF PHILADELPHIA*, 1938.
THE DRAKE PRESS, PHILADELPHIA.

At the time Peverelly's book appeared, professional rowing was North America's most popular and lucrative commercial sport for human competitors, with the first professional baseball game still five years off. Rowing by professional athletes had expanded through the 1850s and 1860s, flourishing especially after the Civil War. Rowing thrived in North America as two similar but ever more separate sports: one professional, the other amateur. These distinctions were not yet rigid or widespread, their definitions still evolving. Clubs in several cities formed a "Navy" to lay out racecourses and run regattas. (Still active today is Philadelphia's Schuylkill Navy, defining force in amateur rowing since the 1850s.) Rowers established amateur associations across the continent: on the Pacific coast and along the Mississippi and Ohio in the United States, and around the St. Lawrence and Atlantic ports in Canada. Just as they do today,

Cartoon showing the professions and their financial success *FRANK LESLIE'S ILLUS-
TRATED NEWSPAPER*, JULY 16, 1881

companies sponsored races, assuring their product's name would brand these public affairs. So did amusement parks by water. So did railroads, by staging regattas at lakes that were distant from cities and profiting as they moved the thousands of fans to and from the races.

DOUBLE YOUR MONEY?

Besides these annual fixtures, rowing fans anticipated match races set between professional rowers and crews. Moneyed speculators eyed professional rowers as tempting investments. Typically, a patron bought or made for a professional oarsman a racing shell, which then bore his name. Rich individuals also financed rowers' training and travels. In return they shared their prizes. (In a match race for, say, $500, "a side" each rower's backers put up $500, winner take all. So if your man won, you doubled your money.) Big-name rowing sponsors included publisher Frank Leslie, *New York Herald* publisher James Gordon Bennett Jr., casino magnate John Morrissey, and railroad tycoon William "Billy" Vanderbilt.

Enjoying these two-to-one odds, investors and gamblers often bankrolled rowers by forming syndicates. This gave them exclusive rights to schedule races and publicity, arrange steamship and train rides for fans, charge admission to grandstands and viewing areas by the finish, sell food and drink, and—sweetest of all—organize the pari-mutuel betting pools. Some syndicates incorporated, as when Toronto businessmen formed The Hanlan Club to arrange and invest in the Canadian champion's career.[3]

Betting on races spread nationwide during the 1860s, thanks chiefly to the telegraph. By 1870, telegraph lines spanned North America and cables linked Canada and the United States to Europe. A race rowed anywhere could be bet on everywhere. But despite its expanding audience, professional rowing could not thrive as other sports did—by revenue from paid admissions and by advertising. Baseball parks charged admission for all who attended the games, and festooned their fences and walls with ads. By contrast, sponsors of professional rowing races had little control over access to the miles-long courses on lakes and rivers, nor could they erect paid ads on public lands. Most rowing courses were open to anyone.

BETTING AND CHEATING

Instead, it was gambling that made professional rowing so lucrative—and so unsavory. Spectators could buy into betting pools run by the rowers' sponsors. Or they could wager with the "sporting men" who swarmed at regattas, set their own odds, and took bets. These professional gamblers clustered at other events as well (thoroughbred and trotting races, boxing matches, baseball games), but they were essential to a financial structure that let professional rowing prosper for years. Ultimately, it was their betting that first enriched professional rowing, then for decades sustained it, and finally drove its demise.

Thanks to the professional rowers' aggression and spunk, fouls were frequent, and seldom accidental. Fouls even helped some rowers' strategies to win—or, by design, to lose when betting against themselves. The easiest way to foul was to crowd a competitor's water by easing into his lane, or to cut him off when rounding a turning stake. Like some of today's NASCAR fans, who go to auto races anticipating crashes, or like some pro-hockey fans who relish the players' fights, professional rowing fans expected and enjoyed fouls—unless, of course, the crew they had bet on was disqualified.

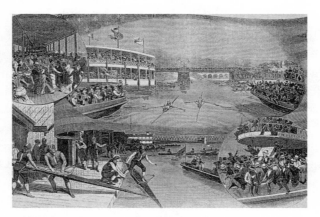

Regatta of the Harlem Rowing Association, June 26, 1875 *FRANK LESLIE'S ILLUSTRATED NEWSPAPER*, JULY 17, 1875, 336. FERNANDO MIRANDA Y CASELLAS, ILLUSTRATOR.

"I used to make more money throwing races than winning 'em," boasted professional sculler Fred Plaisted. Born in 1849 near Portland, Maine, in Saccarappa (now Westbrook), Plaisted had shipped out on a clipper when but a lad of thirteen. He won his first prize money three years later, taking $500 in gold for a race "up the bay" at San Francisco. He went on to pull more than four hundred races during a long and colorful career. But Plaisted's lifetime record is unclear because he rowed so many races under assumed names, to deceive bettors about his skills.[4]

Odds for the betting pools at the Harlem Regatta *FRANK LESLIE'S ILLUSTRATED NEWSPAPER*, JULY 17, 1875, 336. FERNANDO MIRANDA Y CASELLAS, ILLUSTRATOR.

Plaisted was a powerful and talented oarsman who went on to become a champion professional rower on the East Coast, at times in Biglin crews. Those races seem legitimate, and on their own John and Barney Biglin rarely raised suspicions of misdeeds. But during one suspect singles race, at Elysian Fields in November 1868, with odds in their favor both John and Barney fouled out.[5]

Rowers also bribed the men at the start to hold an opponent's shell just a bit longer than necessary. They had their judge claim fouls the referee could not see. And they arranged for boats or floating debris to drift into their competitor's lane.

In fact, cheating could occur even before the starter's pistol: by sabotage. Rowers could partly saw a rival's oar, hoping it would crack during the race. They could push a toothpick under the leather collar that rings an oar. This skewed the oar's smooth rotation in the oarlock and misaligned the blade when it was "squared" to drop in the water at the catch. An oar that isn't truly perpendicular in the water creates two problems. If a blade is angled toward the stern, it splashes up to "wash out," moving less water than a squared blade surface to propel the boat. Far worse, if a blade is angled toward the bow, it doesn't glide through the water but digs deep to "catch a crab" that can halt the shell's motion. A crab caught in a single or a pair can flip the shell. In an eight the crew's combined weight and momentum can lift a rower whose oar has crabbed off the seat and overboard.

With bettors and investors conspiring, a common way to profit unfairly was to "fix" or "sell" the race: Competitors scheming to "throw" a race agreed in advance who would win. As professional rowing gained both popularity and public mistrust, "sporting men" and bookies came to expect just such a fix, and bid for tips to buy in on it. Prizes swelled to more than $10,000 a race but were seldom as important to rowers and their backers as the betting proceeds.[6]

Then too, besides sabotaging a boat, a rare but most efficient way to cheat before a race was simply to poison your opponent.

Sometimes just competing brought rowers enrichment. They demanded a percentage of the grandstand gate, or a share of the railroad and steamship receipts earned when hauling spectators to and from races. "Hippodroming" was a term first used when jockeys at horse tracks or runners in public arenas made a race seem closer in order to boost the betting. Eventually, "hippodroming" became a frequent complaint against some professional rowers, although only in their last and foulest days, in the 1880s, did they find themselves actually racing inside arenas—not on water, but aboard various wheeled contraptions.

BOATING INNOVATIONS

The late 1860s and early 1870s were glory days for professional rowers. But just as responsible for the oarsmen's speed on the water were the craftsmen who designed and built their delicate racing shells. Within a few years, three innovations enhanced the sport in ways all still essential today: sliding seats, hands-free steering, and boats made not from wood but with laminated layers—first paper, today plastic.

As anyone who has tried a rowing machine at a gym well knows, coordinating your legs, back, and arms through a stroke can be tricky—and, if not performed in just the right sequence, can injure the back. Harm occurs most often when rowers use their arms and legs together—not sequentially. This conflicts muscle groups at the base of the spine. Instead

W. Brown.
Sliding Seat.
No. 107.439.
Patented Sep. 20. 1870.
A
Fig. 1
B
C
A
Fig 2
A
Fig. 3
Witnesses
Frank G. Parker
Jas. H. Curtis
Inventor
Walter Brown
N. PETERS, PHOTO-LITHOGRAPHER, WASHINGTON, D. C.

Walter Brown's sliding seat, 1870 PATENT APPLICATION, WILLIAM MILLER COLLECTION

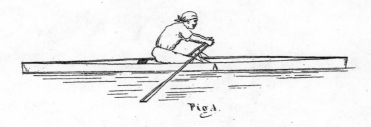

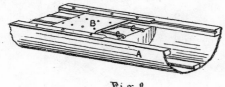

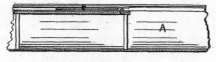

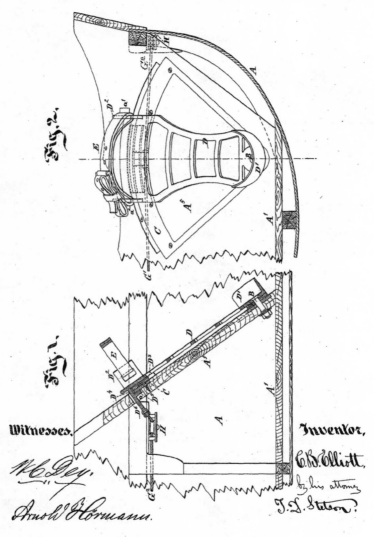

Charles Elliott's steering device, 1874 PATENT APPLICATION, WILLIAM
MILLER COLLECTION

of an all-out effort, think of rowing and its sequences as music. Like music, rowing involves contrasts: pulses and pauses, sounds and silences, rushes and rests. Power on the oar must contrast with poise on the slide during the recovery.[7]

When Walter Brown coached Yale in 1870 he first introduced his crew to sliding seats for that year's race against Harvard. Results were nasty. "They were not on rollers, wheels, or rods, as later perfected, but the seat itself slid on greased slides," wrote rowing historian Thomas C. Mendenhall. "One crew member reported that not only did the grease spread over everything but his seat jumped its slide in the race with most painful results." Harvard tried sliding seats in 1872 and beat Yale by more than a minute. Sliding seats first proved helpful to crews at Henley that year, and were standard for the Oxford-Cambridge Boat Race by 1873. With time it became clear that rowers on sliding seats pulled longer strokes powered mostly by their legs.[8]

Charles Elliott perfected a second innovation favored by the Biglins in pairs and fours: a hands-free rudder. His patent revolutionized racing shells without a coxswain by freeing the bow rower to steer with minimal distraction. Rowers strap their feet into "foot stretchers" to anchor them as they slide on seats, and Elliott rigged one of the bow rower's stretchers to pivot at the heel. With cords attached to the stretcher's toe, moving one foot left or right aligned the rudder. Elliott's steering device was quickly adopted and is used universally today.[9]

Meanwhile, on the Hudson at Troy, Waters, Balch and Company had developed a new and winning innovation by making lighter-weight racing shells from laminated paper. Elisha Waters began as a druggist, then found he had to make his own sturdy cardboard boxes to ship his goods, then found his cardboard made stiff and spiffy detachable collars for men's shirts. Elisha and son George produced paper cartridge boxes by the millions for the Union army. They later made paper cans for oil, and even constructed soaring domes of paper for a few innovative buildings. But the two are remembered best for what George Waters did when Josh Ward gave him a cast-off rowing shell that leaked. Taking materials at hand, Waters glued paper sheets to the hull and sealed them with varnish. The leaks stopped, and George imagined constructing an entire shell from paper.

This he did in 1867. Made by layering long, seamless paper sheets from bow to stern, and sealing them with a special glue-resin, the paper hull proved both stiffer and lighter than shells commonly built with Spanish cedar. He also added sealed air chambers inside the hull for buoyancy. Finally, he varnished the shell to a smooth and gleaming finish.[10]

Just as laminated fiberglass and carbon fiber replaced cedar for racing shell construction during the 1960s and 1970s, so did paper a century before. By the company's count, their paper shells won fourteen races in 1868, twenty-six in 1869, and fifty in 1870. In 1875, New York's *Daily Graphic* called their Troy operation the "largest boat factory in the United States," and the American champion sculler Charles Courtney boosted their popularity by racing in paper singles, and by coaching crews at Cornell rowing paper fours and eights. Other colleges also tried them, but over time the paper suffered from cracks and became waterlogged. Ironically, it was George Waters himself who both launched and sank the paper boat era. When building a paper shell for Syracuse University, in 1900, a blowtorch he used to seal the finish sparked an explosive fire. A Waters descendant later wrote, "The factory was burned to the ground and was never rebuilt. This is the story of the passing of the paper boat. I always thought it deserved a better fate."[11]

TWAIN ON THE RIVER

Mark Twain enjoyed a life growing up on the Mississippi that included paddling canoes, poling rafts, and rowing boats. As an adult he was a riverboat pilot. But only later did he discover the business of professional rowing, viewing it with curiosity—and his usual suspicion. There were specialty journals for rowing enthusiasts in nineteenth-century America. But it took a stylist like Twain to humanize this rich and lively sport for general readers, capturing not just the results of a high-stakes race but also the stress and doubt and elation the whole affair created for the spectators and gamblers. Twain did this masterfully in a dispatch to the San Francisco daily newspaper *Alta California* in October 1868.

Twain interrupted work on his manuscript for *The Innocents Abroad* to recount a trip from his home in Hartford, Connecticut, to Springfield, Massachusetts, to watch the Ward brothers race a crew from Saint John,

The Paris Crew from Saint John, New Brunswick, which won the international four-oared race at the Paris Exposition in 1867 NEW BRUNSWICK SPORTS HALL OF FAME

New Brunswick. The prize was "$1,500 a side," winner taking all. Surveying the bustling Connecticut River scene, Twain wrote,

The conversation of the crowd about me seemed to promise that I had made this journey to little purpose, since all the talk was to the effect that the idea of anybody attempting to conquer the Ward brothers on the water was simply absurd. Everybody appeared to think that the St. John's gentlemen would be so badly beaten that it could hardly be proper to speak of the contest as a race at all. My sympathies always go with the racer that is beaten, anyhow, and so I began to warm toward those New Brunswick strangers in advance. The cries of "Two to one on the Wards!" "Ten to one on the Wards!" "Hundred to five on the Wards!" I felt like resenting as so many personal affronts.

Watching the crews pull to the line, Twain "had never seen such grace, such poetry of motion, thrown into the handling of an oar before." At the start "the two shells almost leaped bodily out of the water. They darted away as if they had been shot from a bow. The water fairly foamed in their wake."

But at once Twain sensed trouble, watching as the Wards

made frantic exertions to increase the advantage but it was soon evident that, instead of gaining, they were losing. The race was to be a very long one —three miles and repeat. When the shells were disappearing around a point of land, half a mile away, the St. John's were already a trifle ahead. The people in my vicinity made light of this circumstance, however. They said "them Ward's" knew what they were about. They were "playing" this thing. When the boats hove in sight again "them Ward's" would be in the lead. And so the betting against my martyrs went on, just as before.

Still, Twain felt the crowd's unease, and heard as

finally, somebody suggested that appearances seemed to indicate that the race was "sold." It had its effect. The most enthusiastic shortly began

The Paris Crew from Saint John, New Brunswick, races the Ward Brothers at Springfield in 1868, a contest Mark Twain described with amusement *FRANK LESLIE'S ILLUSTRATED NEWSPAPER*, NOVEMBER 7, 1868

to show a failing confidence, and to drop anxious remarks about the chances of the race having really been betrayed and sold out by the Wards. But, notwithstanding all this talk was so instructive, the next twenty minutes hung heavily on my hands. There was nothing in the world to look at. . . .

Like many a rowing spectator, Twain discovered firsthand at Springfield how during those miles-long races most of the action transpired up- or downstream, far from sight. His thoughts drifted to daydreaming when, suddenly, Twain and his dispirited companions heard shouts:

"Here they come!"
   "Whoop! St. John's ahead!"
   "For fifty dollars it's the Wards!"

"Fifty to twenty-five it's the Wards!"

"Take them both!—hundred to a hundred it's _____"

"Three cheers for—Oh, the suffering Moses, the St. John's are ahead!"

It was easy to distinguish the [St. John four's] pink shirts, now, flashing back and forth. On they came, dividing the water like a knife, and the [Ward's] white shirts far in the rear. In a few minutes they came flying past the judge's stand, every man of them as fresh and bright and full of life as when they started, and handling the oars with the same easy grace as before. A cheer went up for the gallant triumph, but there was little heart in it. The people on the shore were defeated, in pride and in pocket, as well as the opposing contestants. The Wards came in rather more than a hundred yards behind—and they looked worn and tired. The race was over, and Great Britain had beaten America. Time, 39:38. There was but one consolation, and that was, that in a six-mile race on the same water, last year, the Wards made it in 39, thus beating the present time by 38 seconds. The Wards went into the contest yesterday in inferior condition. Their mainstay, Joshua, had been sick and was still unwell. However, these boys behaved in an entirely becoming manner.

They said that they were badly beaten, and fairly beaten, and they wanted no excuses made to modify their defeat or diminish the brilliancy of the St. John's victory.[12]

Here Twain took in stride the many shouts that the race had been "sold," because by then corruption for money in rowing was well-known. What Twain and many bettors at Springfield may not have known, however, was that while the Wards had easily bested a Saint John four there the year before, this one was the so-called Paris Crew of elite oarsmen who had defeated English, French, and German rowers on the Seine during the 1867 World Exhibition.[13]

CHAPTER 5

Women and Minorities

MEN AND BOYS DOMINATED ROWING THROUGHOUT THE NINETEENTH century in America, and another century would pass before women took to the sport significantly. But once they did their ranks grew so steadily in recent decades that today women rowers outnumber male competitors in the United States and Canada. Even in the early days, a few notable women did row for money. Despite sexist humor, widespread doubts, and risible garb, their efforts gained them more respect than ridicule.

Rowing historian Thomas E. Weil Jr. has noted that women appeared as rowers in various illustrations for two reasons: to display their charm and novelty, and to lampoon their efforts at a sport long the domain of men. As early as 1833, Philadelphia's *Saturday Evening Post* reported on a race in London when Thames fishermen's wives and daughters rowed for a purse of several gold sovereigns. In 1859, vignettes from *A Cambridge Scrap-Book* featured plates showing men rowing races on the Thames at London along with a view titled "A Scratch Pair." In rowing jargon, a "scratch" crew is one that includes anyone available to hop into the boat, often with no chance to practice. But in this illustration two women are clawing one another with their sharp nails.

In 1865, the English satirical magazine *Punch* illustrated a "Novel Sculling Match" with a jocose reference to "The Bumps," the annual races at Oxford and Cambridge in which shells on the narrow rivers row in single file and try to catch and bump the boat ahead, thus passing and advancing in the overall standings. In the *Punch* view a man stands in a boat between two women, each facing the other while reaching her oars for the catch. "Now Girls," says he, "whichever Side bumps the Shore

First Wins! So, One, Two, Three, and Away! And if you like, I will be the Prize!"[1]

A sketch appeared a year later in *Punch* forecasting a "Boat-Race of the Future" with two women's fours drifting to the start. Before a sizable crowd on shore, the rowers and coxswains all wear caps, long-sleeved blouses, and jackets, plus bulky full-length skirts. In 1870, the satirical magazine *Judy* (an upstart competitor to *Punch*) featured a full-page wood engraving on its cover with two young women rowing a double-scull skiff or wherry on the river. They are steered by an older woman in the stern, who holds a parasol. Like their counterparts in *Punch*, these ladies all wore bonnets and skirts.[2]

In North America, a women's regatta was reported at Waltham, just up the River Charles from Boston, in 1860—although it seemed more a social occasion than a sports contest. At the time, men rowed socially in colleges and clubs, often being fiercely competitive, while for women their sports were more for entertainment than for exercise. *Godey's Lady's Book* illustrated in 1866 "Boating on the Lake. New Employment for the Ladies." An engraving had two women rowing a wherry, while a gentleman passenger, wearing a straw boater, holds a parasol. As usual, women rowers wore bulky skirts and big hats. And in 1868, *Wilkes' Spirit of the Times* reported, "Five ladies pulled a [rowing] match for the championship of Lake Chinkapin, and an old maid, named Miss Lavinia Proudfoot, came in the winner amid the wildest cheering of the multitude."[3]

While women also raced for prize money during the 1870s—in upstate New York on Lake George, and at Detroit—there are few other press accounts of their competitive rowing in the United States. Filling this gap were women who tried to row just for fun, sometimes for a medal or a flag, while also seeking self-improvement. The few women's races that occurred were seen as spectacle and amusement rather than sport, and, above all, as fresh occasions for betting.

MONONGAHELA MAIDS

Pittsburgh was a popular rowing center in the mid-nineteenth century, home to several national sculling champions, and among the first North American cities to draw women to the sport. In July 1870, some twelve thousand spectators lined the Monongahela River to view what the *New York Times* headlined a "Girls' Boat Race." The river was "crowded with boats of every description" including "a large number of women present apparently not the least interested spectators of the strange scene. Bald-headed men and boot-blacks were alike waving their hats enthusiastically and cheering the pretty female contestants."

Those attending rowing regattas had many ways besides betting to lose their money, and before this race "enterprising venders of patent medicines, and the irrepressible 'Cheap John' [hawker of shoddy goods] were at various places discoursing to large and attentive crowds." Special trains were packed on the run from Pittsburgh to Glenwood Grove, a popular riverside picnic ground, and many onlookers had to hire carriages to reach the course, or to plod there on foot.[4]

The *Times* account reported how crowds swarmed down to the river where "the beautiful sculls lay quietly near the bank, while the fair contestants were arranging their pretty rowing costumes." Miss Lottie McAlice, "a plump girl of sixteen, looked really beautiful in her jaunty red jacket and white dress." Since childhood McAlice had rowed her Irish-immigrant father across the river to work each morning, and she was admired for pluck and dedication to the sport. "Among the rough oarsmen that swarmed about the river the wildest excitement prevailed, and the tumult and cheers of the immense multitude would have been enough to shake the nerves of the best oarsmen. But the girls had made up their minds to row, and their coolness was an exemplification of the wonderful power of woman's will."

Lottie McAlice, winner of a women's sculling race near Pittsburgh in 1870 *THE DAYS' DOINGS*, SEPTEMBER 24, 1870

For both the novelty of this grand event and the rowers' appearances, the press noted that when the fair ones slipped into their shells,

Miss Lottie certainly looked charming as she balanced herself in her frail bark, dipping the oars gracefully, and maintaining a composure that showed that she was mistress of her boat. Her beautifully-rounded shoulders showed to great advantage as she inclined her body slightly forward, apparently ready and anxious for the start. Maggie [Lew] quietly sat in her boat and managed it gracefully, looking, as did her rival, like a queen of the oar.

At the word "go" McAlice pulled away, "shooting her boat out like an arrow." But Miss Lew's "cool, steady manner" roused bellowing cheers. The *Pittsburgh Weekly Post* reporter compared McAlice's style to that of the local professional heroes James Hamill and Henry Coulter, and Lew's to the champion sculler Walter Brown. At the mid-course stakes where they turned, Lew "pulled away pluckily" striving to catch McAlice in the home stretch. At the finish, "a scene of the wildest excitement ensued; the steam-boats in the river set up a lively whistling, and cheer upon cheer was given by the vast multitude, while hats and handkerchiefs were waved by the enthusiastic crowd." Lottie McAlice's prize was a lady's gold watch and chain valued at $150, and $2,000 in cash.[5]

Unlike the men's professional rowing races, the women's were rarely suspected of being fixed. Yet for this race the *Times* still assured readers that while "a large amount of money changed hands," "the losers consoled themselves . . . with the idea that they had been fairly beaten and were not the victims of any gambling schemes. The matter was a topic of conversation everywhere in the city, and a great variety of opinions were expressed. But the general verdict of the immense crowd that witnessed the race was, 'all satisfied.'"[6]

Its civic pride abounding, the *Pittsburgh Weekly Post* boasted how reporters from Chicago, Cincinnati, New York, and abroad had covered this women's race, along with artists for Leslie's and Harper's periodicals. A fetching line sketch of Miss McAlice, standing among trees in an ankle-length skirt and cradling crossed oars, appeared in *The Days' Doings*, a generally scurrilous weekly published in New York that boasted "Illus-trating Current Events of Romance, Police Reports, Important Trials, and Sporting News." Most often this paper portrayed women in peril—woozy on hashish or thrashed by drunken husbands. But on this occasion it simply acclaimed Miss McAlice as an athlete to be admired.[7]

Harlem Hijinks

Two months later, in September 1870, the *New York Times* front page headlined a "Novel Aquatic Spectacle" when reporting about a race on the East River by five young women during the ninth annual Empire City regatta. This women's event was included for the first time in the day-long regatta that had become a popular feature among sports and social clubs in the city, and at the time included races for both amateurs and professionals. Reprinted nationwide, the article ran to twenty-five sentences, but only three mentioned the race itself. Instead, readers learned that Miss Amelia Sheehan "was dressed in a loose white flannel shirt, cut Marie Antoinette style in front, with a short red petticoat and panta-lettes." Her head

> was covered with a jaunty, tight skull-cap, made of white muslin and trimmed with blue ribbon, her hair falling down in two long braids at the back. The costume was a very picturesque one, and dis-played the large and splendid physique of the wearer to fine advan-tage. . . . Her comely, fair complected face, and the magnificent [way] with which she maintained in her boat, won her many admirers. She seemed accustomed to handling the oars, and used them in a very expert manner.

The *Times* went on to report that Miss Olivia Roberts, daughter of boat-builder and professional rower Stephen Roberts, was "a blonde" who wore a light dress. But, over hers Miss Kyle donned "a red Zouave jacket" and sported a "small blue turban." The two others, Miss M. Walton and Miss Annie Williams, wore "ordinary street dresses." Not until this *Times* article's closing sentences do we learn about the rowing: "The race was rowed in seventeen-foot boats, the course being three miles in length.

It was won by Miss Sheehan, in 23 minutes. Miss Walton was second. Several other races were also witnessed, in which males competed." The awards ceremony was followed by a cotillion.[8]

Noting the success of women rowers in Pittsburgh and New York, the *Times* nonetheless questioned if this might become "a movement" in future. "Rowing is doubtless a good exercise for developing the muscles and giving strength and tone to the system, but scull-races hardly seem appropriate for women. Grace Darling and Ida Lewis seized their oars and went forth on the merciful mission of saving life, and all the world honors their achievements." Both women were heroic lighthouse keepers: Darling in Bamburgh, England, and Lewis in Newport, Rhode Island. "Rowing matches, the only aim and purpose of which is the winning of popular applause, are scarcely calculated to confer any very valuable celebrity upon those ladies who may engage in them."[9]

For the Empire City Club's tenth annual regatta, in September 1871, "ladies" pulled two of the six races. Men who raced won cash, but women took home a gold watch and chain. "The third race was for ladies only, in

Women's Doubles Race on the Harlem River in 1871 *FRANK LESLIE'S ILLUSTRATED NEWSPAPER*, OCTOBER 14, 1871, 69

Woman sculler in peril on the Harlem River in 1871 *THE DAYS' DOINGS,*
OCTOBER 28, 1871, 212

seventeen-foot able working boats. There were five entries. Miss SHEAN
[Amelia Sheehan] came in first, and was declared the winner. . . . The fifth
and last race was for ladies only, rowing two pairs of sculls, in seventeen-
foot working boats, the same course as in their other races. The race was
closely contested. Miss HARRIS and Miss CUSTARCE won by about
three lengths."[10]

While the *Times* coverage of the third race was concise, other news
outfits were more graphic. After its straightforward coverage for the 1870
women's race near Pittsburgh, *The Days' Doings* reverted to more familiar
lurid ways, turning this singles contest into melodrama. Falsely, the paper
reported a "disgraceful attempt to foul the boats" and printed a woodcut
showing a woman sculler wearing a jaunty straw boater hat, while two
boatloads of men (one brandishing a whiskey bottle) pulled alongside. A
man is pictured reaching for her arm, while another grabs at her boat.[11]

In early October 1871, *Frank Leslie's Illustrated Newspaper* printed
an exciting—and accurate—woodcut of the fifth race with women rowing three double-sculls on the Harlem. Despite their full dresses, flowing

Women rowers celebrate
at a Harlem River Regatta
in 1871 *THE DAYS' DOINGS,*
OCTOBER 28, 1871, 213

hair, and flouncy hats, these rowers are clearly straining to win. Following the ladies, a boatload of men supervised the race. One gripped a rifle, ready to foil any interference.

Sexism persisted in rowing coverage in 1873 when "Why Not?" was a picture caption in *Harper's* magazine. Shown were two comely young women in tight bodices, but with bare arms, rowing a pair coxed by an older woman. "Why can't the Ladies belonging to the different Colleges have a Regatta of their own next year?" the caption continued. "Let the First Prize be a Husband with a Fortune, and we think the Winning Boat will make the Quickest Time on Record." A year later, *Harper's New Monthly* printed a wood engraving of two women in full skirts and bonnets, each holding an oar as they sat gazing at each other on the thwart of a broad-beamed boat. Steering from the stern was a young man.[12]

Compared with how avidly the popular and the specialized press covered men's competitive rowing in the nineteenth century, these reports and illustrations about women were scarce and scattered. Indeed, one reason women's rowing may have failed to expand is the raucous, often drunken, crowds at most regattas. A simpler reason may be that despite all the women's enthusiasm, those stalwarts found their feminine attire simply too bulky for so grueling a sport. Whatever the causes, professional races for women all but disappeared by the late nineteenth century. In one fleeting press report, from 1888, Mollie King, an "oarswoman of Newport, Kentucky," challenged any "female" in Covington, Cincinnati, or Newport to "a two mile race for stakes" on the Ohio River. There is no record that her offer was met, or that other women later challenged and rowed there for money.[13]

A FEW GOOD OARSMEN OF COLOR

Young women weren't the only athletes in the nineteenth century who found it difficult to row for money. Rowing was also rare for African Americans, but with a few notable exceptions. Most successful and famous was F. A. "Frenchy" Johnson, who raced and defeated the era's best oarsmen and helped them as a trainer and coach.

Before the Civil War, slaves in the South were forced to row by their owners, who bet wildly on the races and sometimes sat in as coxswains. With Emancipation came the freedom to compete when and where they chose to do so, and for those who excelled the prize money was appealing. When blacks did race, newspapers usually noted parenthetically that they were "negro" or "colored" yet seemed to make no other distinctions. True, in the vernacular of the day one Canadian paper described Johnson as "dusky" and "the Ethiopian," while an American magazine celebrated him as "the colored hero of the spoons" (a slangy term for oars). On the other hand, a few cartoons of the time, both in England and America, depicted black rowers as buffoons, comically capsizing their boats and cheating to win. Yet in thoroughbred racing black jockeys were commonly admired as participants, so it is no surprise that in rowing too athletes of color were part of the sporting scene.[14]

Black rowers surely had trouble joining many of the country's amateur rowing clubs since race, ethnicity, and social status often set membership. Still, in both the United States and Canada rowers of color persevered. At Buffalo in 1872, the black professional sculler Robert Berry, from Toronto, defeated Pittsburgh star Henry Coulter. Berry was well-known in professional rowing circles, racing Edward "Ned" Hanlan and other Canadian scullers. But when the popular Canadian artist Florence Rogers painted a famous regatta where both Hanlan and Berry raced, she omitted Berry from her picture.[15]

Two black amateurs also gained some press attention. At an annual regatta on the Hudson at Newburgh in 1877, Henry Jameson finished second behind Frank Ten Eyck (from a famous Hudson Valley rowing and coaching family) in a three-mile race for boys under twenty. A protégé of "Frenchy" Johnson was mentioned in the popular sports weekly *Turf, Field and Farm*, in 1879, when it profiled Frank H. Hart from Boston in an article about his success in a long-distance walking (pedestrianism) competition at Madison Square Garden. Hart had been born in Haiti, and when living in Boston took a fancy to amateur rowing on the Charles, thanks to encouragement and coaching by Johnson, who gave Hart one of his shells. Hart "made a good showing" at a regatta on Silver Lake near Plymouth, in 1878, but soon quit rowing for pedestrianism, a sport in which he won first money at many six-day contests, and in 1879 gained the Champion Belt of America.[16]

After "Frenchy" Johnson became the best-known black professional sculler in North America, a *Binghamton Times* (New York) reporter wrote he "is not, as his name might be supposed to indicate, at all Frenchy either in nationality or nature, but is a native of Virginia, having formerly been a slave." Born in Germantown (Fauquier County) in 1851, Johnson left the South for Boston, where he began rowing on the Charles in 1876. At the time he was a protégé and assistant to professional sculler Charles Courtney. Johnson won second prize at Boston's July Fourth Regatta that year in two-man Whitehall boats. By Boston's 1877 Regatta, Johnson was "becoming a general favorite among local oarsmen," and finished "a good second" to Fred Plaisted: both in ahead of such stars as James Ten Eyck from Peekskill, John McKiel from New York, and George Hosmer from Boston. Technically, Johnson also beat Canadian champion Ned Hanlan in that race because Hanlan was ejected for fouling both Johnson and Plaisted. The Binghamton reporter wrote that Johnson "seems well-educated and conducts himself in a becoming and gentlemanly manner."[17]

Johnson enjoyed the respect of Charles Courtney, whom he raced and beat at Silver Lake in June 1877, then lost to him at two races in upstate New York. Later that year, at Newburgh, in a professional race for single sculls, Johnson grabbed the lead and held it to the end, defeating such leading scullers as James Ten Eyck, George Hosmer, John McKiel, George Faulkner, and John Biglin (who a press report said finished clearly "out of the race"). The *New York Herald* then described Johnson as "a negro oarsman who during the last three years has won half the races in New England."[18]

When Johnson entered Boston's July Fourth Regatta again, in 1878, he defeated Ephraim (Evan) Morris from Pittsburgh, and later that year won twice in singles at Silver Lake: finishing first against James Riley from Saratoga and James Ten Eyck in June, then over Riley, Ellis Ward, and Courtney in August. By his rowing prowess Johnson was so widely known that a notorious New York shoplifter named Mary Wilson chose "Frenchy Johnson" as her alias.[19]

By 1879, Johnson and Courtney had bonded, first while racing one another but also by training together. Johnson won a regatta at Pittsburgh that year, and in a three-mile race on Lake Ontario at Charlotte, New York, Courtney beat him by just half a length. Johnson beat James Dempsey from Geneva, New York, at Seneca Lake, but that year Johnson was mostly working as trainer for Courtney's first match-race with Canadian champion Ned Hanlan.[20]

At Jacksonville, Florida, in January 1880, Johnson won $1,000 against James Lee from New York City. Then, while still training for his own contests that spring, Johnson helped Courtney prepare for a second Hanlan race.[21]

Wallace Ross, from New Brunswick, and Johnson agreed in 1880 to a match-race on the Charles at Boston, but Johnson jumped the gun and ignored the referee's call to re-start. When Johnson finished first and was declared the winner, angry spectators protested, and the referee called off all bets to calm the crowd. Later that day, Ross ran into Johnson at a Boston tavern and took a swing at him, starting a fight. Police finally broke up the brawl, and the incident was forgotten. In a double, with Frank Hilley from Boston, Johnson won $200 at the city's 1880 July Fourth regatta.[22]

Both Johnson's robust health and his rowing career seem to have expired soon after. When English sculler William Elliott visited the United States, in July 1882, and bid several professionals to race him, *Turf, Field and Farm* complained that "the idea of challenging poor, sick Frenchy!" to row was an insult. By year's end, the paper reported that for medical treatment "Frenchy A. Johnson, once well-known as a professional sculler, and the friend and admirer of Charles Courtney, has been sent to [a hospital in] Lowell by the Lynn, Mass., Gun Club, of which he is a member. Consumption [tuberculosis] is the oarsman's ailment." From there Johnson moved to Florida, where, according to the *New York Clipper*, the famous "colored oarsman and trap-shot" died on March 19, 1883.[23]

CHAPTER 6

The Biglins Challenge the World

BY 1871 THE BIGLINS HAD ROWED MORE THAN FIFTY RACES FOR MONEY against crews from the United States, plus the random Canadian boat that appeared at Boston's City Regatta. But they had yet to race for an international title, and craved to do so.

After American independence, Canada had remained in the British Empire and through cultural ties continued to be influenced more directly by England than the United States. This was true especially for two popular professional sports: cricket and rowing. Canada had become a thriving scene for rowing and its intrinsic betting as early as the 1850s. With international triumphs by the Paris Crew from Saint John in the 1860s, and by the sculler Edward "Ned" Hanlan from Toronto in the 1870s, Canadians enjoyed a proud global rowing heritage. In turn, Canadian rowers began inviting Americans up to race, for prizes they could call North American championships.

HALIFAX

Canada's first international regatta for professional rowers was staged at Halifax, Nova Scotia, in 1871. The prize was $3,000 for a race in four-oared shells and what sponsors boasted to be the "Championship of the World." The Biglins vowed to be there: on their sliding seats, with their flexible rudder, and eager to race formidable crews from Canada and England. The most powerful boat to enter was the Tyne crew from Newcastle in England, stroked by James Renforth. In 1868 Renforth had defeated Harry Kelly from London to become the world's sculling champion, and Kelly was also in this boat. John and Barney Biglin enlisted two

Pittsburgh men, Henry Coulter and Joseph Kaye Jr., and by early that August their four was training hard on the Harlem River. Three times a day they rowed the Halifax distance (six nautical miles). They strode through long walks. And they limbered up with gymnastic exercises. This training regimen complete, the Biglin four packed their gear onto a train to Boston. From there, on Tuesday, August 22, they boarded an overnight steamer to Halifax.[1]

The world of rowing was shocked the next day by news that James Renforth, while winning a race in the Tyne four at Saint John, had faltered and lost his grip on the oar. Of course, spectators knew what happened, and were quick to yell and jeer, sure this meant the race was fixed. "Fraud!" they cried along the shore. "Sold Out!" "Shame!" But maybe not. Renforth muttered, "I have had something!" and slumped back into Kelly's lap. The crew lifted him from the boat, and rushed him by cab to their hotel nearby.

"What will they say at home?" Renforth asked. A teammate thought he'd been poisoned. Another rubbed his arms and legs with hot flannels. Renforth lost feeling in his limbs. Brandy and therapeutic bleeding didn't help. He swooned, and died. He was but twenty-nine years old. Debates raged about the coroner's inquest: Was he poisoned? Was a poison smeared on his oar? Was this an epileptic fit, something he had suffered before? In the end, the most likely cause was heart failure, although pulmonary apoplexy or congestion of the lungs was also reported.[2]

When the Biglins disembarked at Halifax they learned the grim news. Sad. But also, exciting. Renforth's crew was odds-on favorite, considered then to be the best four in the world. Now what? His mates agreed to race in Halifax, but saw the odds shift to favor the Biglins.

In Halifax the Biglin Crew posed for William Notman, Queen Victoria's official photographer in Canada. In his studio Notman stood the Biglins on a bearskin, holding oars and wearing nautical tunics and white tights. But for a second, more risqué photo he posed them without oars or shirts, stripped to their shorts.[3]

Neither posing nor rowing bare-chested seemed a public concern, although journalists did note that at the start of the fours race both the Biglin and the Tyne crews had stripped to the waist. The Biglins were

The Biglin Four in Halifax in 1871. Clockwise from the top: Barney Biglin, John Biglin, Henry Coulter, and Joseph Kaye Jr. PHOTO BY WILLIAM NOTMAN, MCCORD MUSEUM

The Biglin Four in Halifax in 1871, without oars PHOTO BY WILLIAM NOTMAN. FRIENDS OF ROWING HISTORY WEBSITE

pleased with their new Elliott shell, *America*. But they were flustered when they drew lane six, the farthest into the harbor. There, one paper noted, the two outside crews "were in the trough of the sea during the whole course" while the two English crews had the inland lanes. Both were from Newcastle-upon-Tyne. In *Queen Victoria*, Renforth's Tyne crew, with a substitute for their lost comrade, all wore black armbands. *Coaly Tyne* had noted scullers James Taylor, Joseph Sadler, Robert Bagnell, and Thomas Winship.[4]

A drunken spectator rowed onto the course, delaying the race. And while awaiting the starter's pistol the Biglins faced "a veritable gale." Then came the start. As they had so often, the Biglin crew jumped out ahead, stroking at forty-four per minute. They left the Tyne and Taylor fours straining to catch up. But steadily, the English boats vied for the lead, and by the mid-course turn the Biglins found themselves fourth. They had often won by coming from behind, but now faced a dire problem: Adding precious seconds to their time, in their lane the Biglins had to pull around two stake boats, while the other crews rounded just one.

Yet on the Biglins charged, and rallied in the home stretch by taking high-stroke spurts. They were gaining on the leaders when they swept past the frigate HMS *Royal Alfred* as her sailors, manning the yards, "cheered lustily." Then came more trouble. A timber from the *Alfred* had slid over-board and drifted onto the course. The Biglins' *America* struck it, poking splinters into the bow and checking their speed. Still they surged along, pulled hard spurts, and finally drew up to tie the Tyne crew for third place—behind the Taylor four and one from Nova Scotia that included Canada's champion sculler George Brown.

Once ashore, Coulter spotted the *New York Tribune* correspondent and complained that ramming the timber had cost them three or four lengths, and the race. The Biglins filed a protest, citing both the extra stake boat and the timber; but their charges were promptly denied.[5]

Here the Biglins were at last close to a world championship—and yet so far. If they had not drawn the windiest lane, had not rounded two stake boats, and had not hit that timber, victory may well have been theirs.[6]

SARATOGA

Home from that close and compromised finish at Halifax, the Biglins set to training for their second international regatta. This one was at Saratoga Springs, a spa in upstate New York where boxer, gambler, and former congressman John Morrissey had built a thoroughbred racetrack and casino. He now sought to enhance the resort's betting options with a regatta on Saratoga Lake, and was the umpire for an international four-oared race. Here the Biglins would meet several known rivals: the Tyne and Taylor crews they had just raced in Halifax; their old foes the Ward brothers; and, a Poughkeepsie boat stroked by John's old sculling rival William Stevens. Again, the winner would be world champion.

"The Biglin crew are as perfect representatives of the metropolitan muscle man as the Wards of rural bone and sinew," the *New York World* reported, while "the white skins of the Englishmen contrasted queerly with the brown pelts of the Biglins." (In this apparent slight, the *World* noted the Biglins' swarthy Irish features.)[7]

Taking a break from his artful attacks on Tammany Hall's "Boss" Tweed, the cartoonist and illustrator Thomas Nast was on hand to depict the Saratoga regatta for *Harper's Weekly*. This he did grandly, with a panoramic, full-page sketch. In it gentlemen in top hats and ladies twirling parasols stand above crowds crushed along the lakeshore. But only barely

"International Four-Oared Boat Race on Saratoga Lake," by Thomas Nast *HARPER'S WEEKLY*, SEPTEMBER 30, 1871, 908

shown, in the distance, are pencil-thin shells streaking toward the finish. Nast omitted the regatta's seamier side, especially the clustered gamblers the *Times* described as wearing a "glittering display of diamonds" common to New York sporting men. The *Times* also noted that "blacklegs [cheating gamblers] and swindlers of every description, were plentifully scattered around, and roulette, the little joker [a form of bid whist] and the three-card trick appeared to be doing a good business."[8]

The Wards led at the start of this four-mile race, but soon the Tyne, Biglin, and Taylor crews pulled even. Nearing the stake boats at two miles, the Biglins veered off course, drawing with them the Tyne and Taylor crews. When righting their courses toward the stake boats the Biglin and Taylor crews nearly clashed oars. This cleared the Wards to turn first, and from there they charged to the finish. The Tyne crew was second, while third place caught the Biglin and Taylor fours in a dead heat. Umpire Morrissey asked the Taylor and Biglin crews to re-row the race for the $750 third prize. But in each boat was a man competing in the singles match that afternoon. Most considerately, Morrissey gave both crews third prize.[9]

Ward Brothers pose as "Champions of the World" in 1871. Left to right: Benjamin, Ellis, Henry (Hank), Charles, Gilbert (Gil), and Joshua (Josh) Ward with manager Dick Risdon. FROM *WARD BROTHERS, CHAMPIONS OF THE WORLD* BY IRENE WARD NORSEN

After this Saratoga race the Wards declared themselves "Champions of the World," although it was their competitors' mishaps on the course that assured them this title. Had the Biglin four not veered away, and then not nearly collided, it is possible this second international championship might have been theirs.

In that day's four-mile singles race, John Biglin (rowing the notably named *John Morrissey*) finished third behind English champions Sadler and Kelly but ahead of Ellis Ward. Now world champs, the Wards returned home to Cornwall-on-Hudson and announced they would no longer race as a four-oared crew.[10]

John Biglin had no such plans to retire, in a four or any other boat. Two weeks later, on the Harlem, he finished third in a double-scull race, but won that day in singles against James Ten Eyck.

The *New York Times* reported how the Biglins "are not satisfied with the result of the Halifax or Saratoga regattas. They have, under the circumstances, challenged the Ward brothers, or any other crew in the United States, to a five or six mile race for $1000 to $5000 a side." Josh Ward declined, saying simply that the brothers have "renounced rowing as a four." He would have accepted the Biglin challenge just after racing at Saratoga, he said, "but it is too late now."[11]

CHAPTER 7

Spectacle on the Schuylkill

THE BIGLINS WERE IRATE THAT MISHAPS DURING BOTH THE HALIFAX and Saratoga races had scuttled their quests for a "world championship." Still chasing that dream, Barney published letters in English and American newspapers in December 1871 that challenged England's Taylor four to another race: for £1,000 (then about $6,000, now about $115,000) at Saratoga, Springfield, or anywhere else on the East Coast.

Beyond big prize money, the Biglins' wealthy investors promised foreign crews ample travel expenses. Barney also joined with John to propose a five-mile pair-oared race for £500 ($3,000) "against any two men in Great Britain" around the time of a race in fours. They offered potential competitors "a series of international regattas, for valuable prizes" assuring a visit "both pleasant and profitable."[1]

Curiously, the Biglins' challenge for an international championship pair-oared race on American waters was bold, and quite odd. After all, they had never raced a pair, indeed, had hardly rowed one at all. Also, this would be the first professional pair race in North America, while in England these powerful but precarious two-man shells had been popular for decades.

PAIR-OARED CHAMPIONSHIP

The Biglins were disappointed when weeks passed and there came no reply from England, or even from Canada. Undeterred, John and Barney opened the field to any Americans and, in February 1872 signed articles of agreement to race two esteemed rowers from Pittsburgh. The national champion sculler Henry Coulter had defeated James Hamill and John

McKiel, and in 1871 had raced in the Biglin four at both Halifax and Saratoga. His pair partner was Lewis Cavitt, a prize-winning amateur eager to turn professional. Coulter called him the "toughest man he ever saw." Terms were set for a five-mile race with one turn, on the Schuylkill, for $2,000 and the Championship of North America. The date set was May 20.

Training was "necessarily severe," reported the *Philadelphia Press*, with each crew out in earnest for weeks before coming to town. Every day, Coulter and Cavitt had rowed twenty to thirty-five miles, walked another twelve to fourteen miles, and jumped rope. "This latter exercise is a comparatively new one," the *Press* noted, "and has been found very beneficial in developing the muscles of the arms and legs."[2]

The Biglins had practiced hard for a month, on the East River and along Newtown Creek, rowing fifteen miles a day and walking just as far. Once in Philadelphia, the *Press* reported that "Their rowing since their arrival here has been much admired for the grace and ease manifested in every motion, and the betting has been decidedly in their favor from the first, not only on the part of New Yorkers, but also by a number of our Philadelphia sporting men." The paper called the Biglins "both dapper fellows, about medium height, well formed, and with a very determined cast of countenance. . . ."[3]

Grace and ease are essential in the sport of rowing because it requires, in *yin/yang* fashion, both power and poise. Each stroke must have finesse, with the mental calculation to time and take it efficiently—and, in a pair, to do so in flawless unison. Each race must also engage a sustained physical effort unmatched in other sports. While a weightlifter may hoist several hundred pounds once or twice in the course of a contest, during a five-mile race rowers perform similar exertions for half an hour, pulling the oar from toes to chest thirty to forty times a minute. Perched above the water in a delicate shell, rowers must fuse balletic aplomb with exhausting effort. Also essential is their need to maintain constant balance, aligned above the keel as the light shell glides through water. It may well have been just this complex balance—combining both poise and power—that Thomas Eakins found so appealing when he tried to capture the Biglins' movements on paper and canvas.[4]

Crowds lined the Schuylkill by midafternoon, but strong winds and rain showers postponed the race until just past 6:00 p.m. Then the starter raised his arm to fire a pistol shot. The Biglins seemed surprised by the signal, and the Pittsburgh crew pulled quicker strokes to gain a lead. The Biglins recovered and slowly drew even. Then one of their oars "crabbed" by digging too deep, ruffling their balance and pace. But by exerting their legendary power the brothers recovered, pulled on, and by the first mile eased their shell ahead. Next the Pittsburgh crew rowed through the wrong bridge arch, a detour that cost them three boat-lengths. They also appeared less coordinated in their swing.[5]

With the Biglins now clearly ahead, gamblers along the shore rushed to shift their bets. "One hundred to eighty on the Biglins," the *Press* reported a sporting man from New York shouting. "What! No takers! Where's the Pittsburghers? Well, then, a hundred to seventy five; a hundred to seventy—to sixty—to fifty! There, that's odds enough, surely!"

"I'll take that 'air, old hoss," yelled another. "Just you put up or shut up!"

"I'll hold the stakes," offered a tipsy companion. "But who'll hold me?"[6]

At the race's halfway point the Biglins spun their shell confidently, Barney in the bow pulling them around while John the stroke gently backing down. The Pittsburgh pair by this point was just approaching its red-flagged stake. From there, the *Press* noted, "The Biglins 'got down to their work' in true earnestness, and turned the lower stake boat three lengths ahead. . . ." They settled into a powerful yet snappy stroke, driving through the last two-and-a-half miles with stamina and style. Stronger, smoother, and altogether calmer, the Biglins widened their lead from the turning stakes to win by several lengths. Whistles, horns, bells, and cheers echoed up through the park for a full quarter-hour. Thanks to the telegraph, the race made page-one headlines from Halifax to Seattle, and in faraway foreign capitals. With this decisive race, John and Barney Biglin became the pair-oared Champions of North America.[7]

PART TWO

JOHN AND BARNEY

CHAPTER 8

John as Coach and Curmudgeon

AFTER THEIR TRIUMPH IN THE PAIR-OARED SHELL AT PHILADELPHIA IN the spring of 1872, the Biglin brothers each tried a new line of work: Barney became a politician, and John became a coach. Both had coached rowers informally, at clubs around New York City, but for John here was a new and lucrative career—another way to win.

COACHES CASH IN

More than any other team sport, rowing requires exacting symmetry. Individuals must time their blade-work with crewmates to all pull at the same moment with the same pressure. They must swing their bodies in unison, fore and aft in line above the keel. They must even breathe as one. "Rowing attracts a particular kind of guy," said University of Pennsylvania and US Olympic coach Ted Nash, himself a medalist. "He's got a strong determination to see himself improve physically and technically over time." That intense motivation animates each rower in a quest for perfection. But from outside the shell only a coach can unite the crew as a single force.[1]

That guidance strengthens a crew physically, technically, and emotionally. Rowing historian Thomas E. Weil Jr. notes how the "seeming ease of the rower is an illusion compounded by the extraordinary grace and efficiency of motion of a good crew. In fact, rowing requires the most intense simultaneous expenditure of effort and endurance in team athletics." As Weil explains,

Added to the repetitive full pressure use of every major muscle group and the heroic testing of aerobic and lactic limits is the need to perform

in perfect synchronicity with every teammate on every stroke, to be
exquisitely aware of the boat's pace and timing, to adjust one's blade
and stroke to the vagaries of wind and wave, and to do all this while
perched on a moving seat in a craft that may be rocking from side to
side.[2]

Only an outside expert can see and correct both individual form and collective movement. Professional rowers and crews hired a trainer or coach to help prepare for their races: often another oarsman or teammate with whom they split any winnings. But not the amateurs. Following the English custom, North America's colleges at first had their crew captains act as coaches. This proved awkward when rowing four- and six-oared shells with no coxswain because the captain had to turn his head to watch the timing and angle of his crew's oars, a motion that easily upset the boat's rhythm and balance. Also, crew captains were often the stroke, setting the pace from the stern seat. Placing the captain/coach in the bow didn't help much because bow rowers were also busy: first looking about to see the course ahead, then steering the shell.

All that changed in the 1870s once crews raced in eight-oared shells. Eights needed a coxswain, or "cox," who sat in the stern, opposite the stroke, and by facing forward could see the course and watch his rowers and the other crews. The cox also steered the shell by tugging hand-held cords to adjust the rudder. Shouting through a megaphone strapped to his forehead, the cox advised and cajoled his teammates. As the sport became more popular and more competitive, however, it was clear that only an outsider might decisively improve a crew's performance.

The earliest American college to break from the English amateur, self-coaching tradition was Yale. Seeking a fresh approach after it had lost to Harvard in their first four races, Yale hired William Wood, a professional sculler from New York City, to be its physical-education instructor. Wood aimed to harden his crew for the 1864 Harvard-Yale regatta. Months before the race, Wood had his oarsmen rise at 6:00 a.m., don heavy flannel suits, then run and walk for miles. Twice daily his crew rowed four miles at racing speed, and worked at weight-lifting in the gym.

Yale won handily that year, and again in 1865, showing that physical conditioning was every bit as important as a crew's rowing technique. Harvard followed Yale's lead when preparing for their 1866 regatta by having its rowers run and lift weights throughout the school year. And, to improve technique, Harvard sent its former stroke, William Blaikie, off to Oxford to learn the English rowing style, which had a lower rate and shorter body swing. Based on his coaching experience, Wood published a *Manual of Physical Exercises* in 1867. Like Wood, Blaikie was a fitness advocate who later coached Harvard (as a devoted alumnus, not for pay) and who wrote the popular book *How to Get Strong and How to Stay So*.[3]

When in 1869 Harvard challenged Oxford it was hailed "the race of the century," drawing seven hundred fifty thousand spectators to the same twisting four-mile course on the Thames at London rowed for the annual Oxford-Cambridge Boat Race. Such an international contest was then rare, the only comparable event being the regatta at the 1867 Paris Exposition won by the Saint John four.

The Harvard-Oxford four-oared race was publicized widely, and nationalistic feelings were intense, in part because of a dispute then about Britain's aid to the Confederacy during the Civil War. Fifteen reporters from American newspapers rode the press launch, and thanks to the telegraph and the new transatlantic cable, the next day's *New York Times* filled 80 percent of its front page with lively reports of the race, plus a detailed course map. New York's *Herald* printed nearly two pages about the race,

The Oxford-Harvard four-oared boat race on the Thames at London in 1869 *FRANK LESLIE'S ILLUSTRATED NEWSPAPER*, SEPTEMBER 11, 1869, 408

and sports historian Melvin L. Adelman concluded that between 1820 and 1870 no other sporting event received more coverage on any one day in the American press. Spectators included the Prince of Wales, Prime Minister Gladstone, novelist Charles Dickens, philosopher John Stuart Mill, and international singing star Jenny Lind. Oxford won, but only because Harvard's captain had refused to follow the Boat Race practice that allowed the lead boat to leave its lane and strike the shortest course through the river's many bends.[4]

Blaikie had served as starter for that race, and wrote a nineteen-page account, with seventeen illustrations, for the popular *Harper's New Monthly Magazine.* This article sparked interest in amateur rowing that burgeoned in both colleges and clubs nationwide. For their race on the Thames both Harvard and Oxford had foresworn hiring professional rowers as their coaches, a practice mostly followed in North America as well. The notable exception was still Yale, which hired the champion professional sculler Walter Brown to train its crew for the 1870 Harvard race. But this investment proved fruitless when, at the turning stake, Yale rammed Harvard's shell and lost on a foul.[5]

In the United States in 1869 only three colleges were rowing competitively: Harvard, Yale, and Brown. By 1871, a Rowing Association of American Colleges (RAAC) was formed by delegates from Harvard, Brown, Amherst, the Massachusetts Agricultural College (now UMass-Amherst), Bowdoin, Williams, and Troy Polytechnic (now Rensselaer Polytechnic Institute). The RAAC organized its premier regatta on the Connecticut River at Springfield in July 1871.

This was the country's first intercollegiate contest for more than two crews—but just barely. In the end, most new RAAC members scratched, leaving only Harvard, Brown, and the Massachusetts Agricultural College, known as the "Aggies." The state-run technical college had been founded just eight years before, and it had a practicality the older and more elite schools lacked. To launch their rowing program the Aggies hired as coach the renowned professional Josh Ward. Himself a national champion sculler, and a rower in his family's powerful four, Ward imparted his skill and tenacity to the young farmers, and worked them hard. As a coach, observed Springfield's *Republican,* "there is no better in the country."

This proved prophetic in their three-mile race when the Aggies beat the favored Harvard crew by thirty-seven seconds, and Brown by more than a minute. Josh Ward had bet heavily on his novice crew, and left Springfield a much richer man.[6]

The Aggies' win shocked other college crews, both because a public school had bested the nation's most prestigious private university, and because it seemed that by hiring a professional rower as coach anyone might learn tricks of the trade. Rowing historian Thomas Mendenhall noted that "Harvard's defeat by the Aggies while Yale never even appeared was a source of great delight to all the small colleges, who resented the pretensions of both Harvard and Yale on the water."[7]

Other colleges rushed to follow the Aggies' lead. For the second intercollegiate regatta in 1872, the Aggies kept Josh Ward as their coach, Amherst College hired John Biglin, and Bowdoin College enlisted George Price from the Paris Crew. By the third regatta in 1873, eight of the eleven competing colleges would have professional rowers as their coaches.[8]

John Biglin had already tried his hand at coaching when in November 1871 he boarded a train for Washington, DC, along with his firehouse colleague and rowing partner Dennis Leary. Washington's Analostan Boat Club had hired Biglin while the archrival Potomac Boat Club engaged Leary. Both boathouses adorned the Georgetown waterfront, and their brief rivalry was already intense: This year's regatta was their third, after Potomac had won the first two. The race was set for three miles, with one turn, in six-oared gigs, which are shorter and wider than racing shells. Biglin worked his boys hard, stressing coordination and especially self-control. This time Analostan triumphed, whipping Potomac by almost two minutes in the twenty-five-minute race. To celebrate, Analostan threw a dinner aboard the yacht *Arlington*, and as they glided on the Potomac the club presented Biglin with an Ed. Fabre-Perret gold watch, engraved from the "Six of 1871."

As a coach Biglin was tough and tight-lipped. In 1872 he trained New York Rowing Club (NYRC) crews on Newtown Creek, and that October journeyed to Baltimore where a NYRC four raced the Ariel Boat Club on the Patapsco River. A journalist overheard him give his boys this "last injunction" before they shoved off from the dock: "Not too fast." Again it was self-control Biglin was after: poise and power. After turning the mid-course stake, "both shells sped on amid almost breathless excitement, some saying the 'Ariel is ahead,' and some claiming the lead for the New York Club," the *Aquatic Monthly* reported also rather breathlessly. The crews were so close that for a few minutes all betting ceased. Then, steadily, the New Yorkers edged ahead, their stroke slow and constant as Biglin had urged, to win by three lengths.[9]

AMHERST

John took up college coaching in 1872. Amherst College was eager to improve its own informal rowing program, and especially keen to beat those "farmers" from its triumphant hometown rival. If the price of victory involved paying professionals, well, so be it, vowed college president William Augustus Sterns. On campus, Biglin appeared gruff and ill at ease with his crew, which the local paper had dubbed the "intellectuals" to distinguish them from the "Aggies." In one photo the Amherst

John Biglin with the 1872 Amherst College crew AMHERST COLLEGE ARCHIVES AND SPECIAL COLLECTIONS, ATHLETICS COLLECTION

College crew sat self-consciously, their oars propped against a tree-trunk, while arrayed on the lawn were Indian clubs, barbells, and croquet mallets. And behind them, leaning over a fence, John cast a suspicious eye at the camera.[10]

A brusque and severe mentor, John Biglin applied his own intense practice regime to the college boys, insisting that before lifting an oar they first exercise daily in the gym. Biglin chose athletic young men weighing in the mid-150s, expecting them to "burn off" ten pounds by race day. Using a diet he obeyed himself, Biglin's boys ate coarse foods (cracked wheat, oatmeal, hominy) and drank plenty of milk. He forbade pies and pastries, insisting they eat potatoes and onions. To this menu he added mutton, which was most pro-rowers' preferred meat. Then, a week before the race, Biglin switched his crew to eggs and stale bread. He replaced the milk and coffee with weak tea. And he ordered his boys to enjoy "all the pale ale they wanted."[11]

On the Connecticut River, Biglin pushed the Amherst boys hard, sculling alongside in his single, shouting stroke-by-stroke to instill them with his own disciplined style. He taught a strict cadence and smoothly coordinated swing that the *New York World* likened to "pulling with the steadiness of an engine piston." Biglin also taught the Amherst College six a racing technique he and Barney had perfected: start with a fast-paced "wicked spurt," then slow for a "rest" while the other boats catch up, then spurt again. Above all, Biglin inspired a firm confidence that freed them to ignore the lofty public expectations for the two favorites—Harvard and the Aggies—and to simply row their own race in their own steady way.[12]

Testy and glum, Biglin shunned publicity throughout his rowing career. When he had to speak with reporters it was always to play down his own and his crew's chances. This he did at Springfield, saying only that the Amherst College boys were "pulling as fast and as well as any six on the Connecticut." Hearing this, a Boston paper's correspondent suspected "It is but fair to say that he invested a large portion of his spare cash on them in the pools." The betting pools for multi-boat races set odds on the three top crews: as in a thoroughbred race to win, place, or show. Among the three favorites a $5 bet on Harvard paid back only $5 if they were to win, but a $4 bet for Bowdoin paid $5 if they won. Crews considered too weak to finish in the top three were all lumped as "the field," and with Biglin's expectations so low Amherst College found itself there. Betting on "the field" had long odds but big rewards. For this race, a bet of $3 or $4 on any crew in "the field" paid $50. Through others, the *Springfield Daily Republican* later noted, Biglin bought all the "field" bets "he could lay his hands on."[13]

Predictably, the college race began with Harvard and the Aggies as odds-on favorites, and Harvard's six took a quick lead. But soon enough the *New York World* correspondent saw in the style of Walter Negley, the Amherst College stroke, a "nerve and self-poise" that seemed to stir his teammates. "His movement was absolutely without flaw, and it acted like music on the rhythm of the whole Amherst stroke. His vigor and determination inspired everyone in the boat" so that even in the race's third and final mile—with rowers gasping for breath, lungs and limbs aching through each stroke—"it seemed as if no more lithe and charming oarsmanship had ever been shown by a college six." Watching on shore, Biglin's assessment was curt: "I never see'd prettier rowing than that."[14]

Amherst had charged along the course at thirty-eight strokes a minute, but late in the race began an "extraordinary spurt" to forty-five, "a pace that astonished and bewildered" Harvard. "At every touch of the gleaming oars in the water their boat leaped forward like a race-horse nearing the goal," the *Republican* reported. At the finish, "a cry of mingled astonishment and admiration welled out over the stream. The crew that

The 1872 Intercollegiate Regatta at Springfield with the Amherst College crew winning *FRANK LESLIE'S ILLUSTRATED NEWSPAPER*, AUGUST 10, 1872, 329

was expected to gain the goal last passed it first," and in record time. At the finish it was Amherst College, Harvard, Amherst Agricultural, Bowdoin, Williams, and Yale.[15]

The *Boston Post* reported, "The Amherst men bore their honors with a sense of dignity and self-confidence, and looked as if they thought, 'We knew it all the time but didn't care to say so!' Biglin . . . was on the bank . . . and after the first gush of joy had subsided a little he attracted the attention of a crowd of Harvard men and astonished them by drawing from his deep coat pocket a double handful of pool cards, on all of which was the tell-tale word 'field', where Amherst had been consigned by the betting men." Later, Biglin joined a riotous party at the Amherst quarters where "the excited friends of the crew crowded around him upon all sides, covering him with congratulations, but he steadfastly refused to make a speech."[16]

When news of the race reached Amherst, some students dashed to the campus and "rang the bell vigorously," reported the *New York Clipper*. President Sterns rushed up, saying, "What are you ringing for?"

"They've beaten!"

"Who's beaten?"

"Why, our crew!"

"Ring her then, 'til the old thing cracks," Sterns urged gaily.

Columns about this stunning Amherst victory ran in newspapers nationwide. Some revived the debate about American versus English rowing styles; others questioned how useful professional coaches could be to amateur crews. The *Brooklyn Eagle* praised Amherst's "slow, easy stroke." By contrast, the best authorities "have already declared that the stroke of Harvard and Yale is too quick and consuming to last. It is the pace that kills."[17]

At Harvard, reported the *Clipper*, the losing crew, "though a trifle sore," was now "convinced that if they had had the services and advice of an experienced professional trainer . . . [they] would have been victorious" and "are desirous of securing John A. Biglin, as mentor for the University race of 1873."[18]

DARTMOUTH

For America's third annual intercollegiate regatta in 1873, again featuring races in six-oared-shells, many of the leading professional rowers were on hand to coach the students. The Amherst Aggies had rehired Josh Ward, who rowed about with a cigar stub in his teeth, rhythmically blinking his eyes—left, right, left, right—on down the course. Yale had hired champion sculler James Hamill to oversee its freshmen. Columbia had Hank Ward, Wesleyan had Fred Sinzer, Trinity had John Blew, Bowdoin rehired George Price from the Paris Crew, and Cornell had Henry Coulter. Ellis Ward hoped to repeat last year's Amherst College win, and agreed to train both its varsity and freshman crews. Harvard may have wished to hire Biglin, but he accepted a rich offer from Dartmouth: $100 a week, plus expenses, for twelve weeks (a total then twice a middle-class family's yearly income).[19]

Biglin recruited rowers the *New York Tribune* called "raw beef and bloody bone giants" for the new Dartmouth varsity crew, but the Springfield paper found "his disposition, especially when in training, is decidedly savage, and his manner hardly civil" even to his generous employers. One reporter described Biglin "as hard as iron and as tough as a man could be, never tiring and probably never realizing that the big six-footers, whom he selected, could not endure as much as he himself could." The Springfield paper said that "three rows and three walks per day have not been unusual" for Dartmouth, which logged at least twenty miles daily on the water and up to thirty miles on foot. But when "the natural result followed, and some of them showed signs of breaking down," Biglin did allow a "letting up" that seemed to restore them.[20]

During Biglin's coaching there were "some pretty hot times between crew and trainer," Dartmouth records reveal, and the *Tribune* reported a "burst-up" by the crew against their "overtraining." After one day that included an eighteen-mile walk and two pulls in the six, Biglin ordered the varsity to take a third row after supper. He "took the bow [seat] and put them through ... a rush for six miles. They are powerful men, but that 'used them up.'" Four of the five students "vomited on leaving the boat, and most of them have been more or less 'under the weather' ever since." In his typically secretive way, to conceal his training techniques and progress from the press and other coaches, Biglin had Dartmouth practice near their Hanover campus, and only brought them to Springfield a few days before the race to learn the course.[21]

Before the regatta "Few collegians were present, and the betting was wholly confined to the professionals" who were also racing that week, the *Springfield Daily Republican* assured readers. (John Biglin and Ellis Ward were to race their singles.) But the paper added, irresistibly, "Yale was the favorite in the freshman race, at $7 to $5 for Harvard and $4 for Amherst." Despite their prohibition, some betting pools were being sold on the university races whenever "no police were on hand." Milling about, as usual, were "large numbers of low browed and ill dressed sporting men."[22]

Springfield was packed as college men arrived by train and tram to cheer their crews. Food was scarce, lodging cramped and costly. Students slept in huddles on hotel-room floors, on park benches, and once the gaslamps dimmed they even stretched out on the green-felt tables in pool halls.

"The local authorities have taken the most praiseworthy steps to preserve order and morals during race week," a priggish *New York Times* correspondent reported in a page-one dispatch. "Several faro-dealers from New-Haven and Hartford have been summarily squelched, and sent back to wicked Connecticut. During the whole of to-day, until the contests have been decided, the bars are to be closed. Every effort has been made to stop the selling of pools, and whatever the students may do among themselves, it is certain that public betting has been reduced to a minimum...." Well, perhaps, because the *Times* reported that "inquiry *sotto voce*" sustained private gambling all day long.[23]

Keeping the young hordes from betting proved as futile as keeping them sober. "The regulation about closing the bars during this [regatta] day has occasioned a little grumbling, but not much," the *Times* revealed, "because it is seemingly well understood that if any one wants something stronger than water all he has to do is to ask for sandwiches, and he will be shown into a back room well provided with dark-colored bottles."[24]

Merchants closed Springfield's largest stores at noon, freeing clerks and customers to enjoy the regatta and share its festive mood. All afternoon fans jammed aboard special trains that steamed from the city toward the course downriver. By road, too, the spectators migrated. "Every moment saw the arrival of some queer farmer's wagon," stated the *Times*, "fresh from the market . . . and now holding the farmer's ample spouse and smiling daughters."[25]

When the varsity race began Harvard, Amherst College, Yale, Wesleyan, and the Aggies all rushed out. But well into the race, with excitement "at its zenith," Amherst College and the Aggies edged past Columbia. Dartmouth, Cornell, and Bowdoin "tested each other's muscle and endurance in earnest and severe rivalry, sometimes one having a slight lead, and then the other," the *Aquatic Monthly* recorded. Clustered shells and churning oars animated the river until, at the line, Yale pushed by victorious. Ellis Ward enjoyed some consolation when his Amherst College boys, after clashing oars with Columbia, recovered to row Wesleyan to a dead-heat for second place. Harvard was third. And John Biglin's Dartmouth giants—exhausted by their tenacious trainer—finished a distant seventh.[26]

Afterward, resentments lingered against the professional coaches for their aggressive training techniques. But Biglin wasn't the only rough taskmaster. Columbia rowers found Hank Ward's training too harsh, and Henry Coulter's work with Cornell was later scorned by the *Times*. His training at Springfield "overdid the business, like all the blundering professional muscularians who go by a system of rigid laws without understanding the principles that underlie them."[27]

Indeed, for the fourth annual intercollegiate regatta, at Saratoga Springs in 1874, nine crews raced. But all agreed not to hire coaches, at least for a year or two. So it was just for fun that John Biglin appeared on Saratoga Lake and rowed in a six-oared shell with the Ward brothers. Their coxswain was former Harvard rower and coach William Blaikie. Manned by these celebrity professionals the six "came gliding swiftly" ahead of the college crews, stopping at the finish to watch the races.[28]

As coaches John and Barney also gave informal lessons in New York, conducting what one newspaper called an "athletic school" that was "patronized by the best and wealthiest citizens of the metropolis" and "a large number of amateur oarsmen [owed] their proficiency to the tuition received from the Biglins."[29]

CHAPTER 9

John as Competitor and Champ

WHILE THOMAS EAKINS TOILED IN HIS PHILADELPHIA STUDIO THROUGH the summer of 1872, striving to portray in sharp and startling ways John and Barney Biglin as paragons of professional rowing, their younger brother Philip was back home in Manhattan—publicly slighting them. At DeGramo's Hall on Fifth Avenue, Philip joined men from more than two hundred American boat clubs to found a National Association of Amateur Oarsmen. Upset by professional rowing's mercenary nature and rampant betting, the group debated for two days about just who was an "amateur," hoping to redeem a sport that was seeming ever more commercial and corrupt. This convention marked the first direct national reaction against professional oarsmen and the big business their syndicates had created.[1]

Philip Biglin was a delegate from New York's Friendship Boat Club, which boasted having the largest boathouse on the East River. After the convention rejected a motion to make the Bible's ten commandments required standards for governing all amateur rowing races, it did manage to define an "amateur" as someone who would not accept money for rowing—from sponsors of the race, a percentage of the gate, kickbacks from rail and steamship lines, cash prizes, or any other source. A further compromise, unlike the practice in England, decided men "employed in or about boats" were deemed amateurs, allowing watermen and rowing coaches in the United States to continue to compete.[2]

Betting was another matter, and an *Aquatic Monthly* correspondent who called himself "Devoted Oarsman" was firm when arguing,

> *I protest against the incorporation of the ten commandments in the boating statutes or the enforcement of any special moral obligation on an amateur oarsman. There must be no law prohibiting an amateur from making bets, if he chooses to bet, openly and honestly, that he may not be compelled, as is the case at present, to add the additional sin of deception and falsehood to that of betting.*[3]

Amateurs also rallied against professionals in Canada where, in 1880, a Canadian Association of Amateur Oarsmen was founded. Besides frowning on gambling, the Canadians also aspired to forsake alcohol and smoking.[4]

And rowing wasn't the only sport with pro-am tensions. Historians Elliott Gorn and Warren Goldstein report that in 1871 "a group of baseball traditionalists based mostly in New York tried to form an amateur alternative to the money game" by proposing to "discountenance the playing of the game for money, or as a business pursuit." This revolt held little appeal among baseball's burgeoning fans, players, investors, and club owners; so the sport expanded as both amateur and professional.[5]

When denouncing professional rowing, Philip had in mind his brother John, since Barney was by then chasing new ambitions. Barney had issued challenges for more races in the pair-oared shell, and in the four. But no other crew in England or North America would accept, which freed him to focus on politics.[6]

For his part, John had rowed fifty-seven professional races before winning the pair-oared championship in 1872. In years to come he would row thirty-six more.

JOHN AND ELLIS AS RIVALS: NYACK AND SPRINGFIELD

Throughout the summer of 1872, John Biglin spent less and less time at his firehouse on East 40th Street and more at Elliott's boat shop in Greenpoint. From there John rowed his single up and down the East River, and to avoid barges and tugs often pulled into Newtown Creek. Ignoring the creek's stench, he was bent on perfecting an already famed physique, and eager to profit from his syndicate's next big investment: a match race in September against archrival Ellis Ward for $1,000 and the Championship of America.[7]

Hailed by the *Aquatic Monthly* as the 1872 rowing season's major professional race, newspapers kept fans informed by reporting the latest betting odds with each fresh edition. The Biglin and Ward families were widely known to be aggressive but usually fair competitors, and with only a few nasty exceptions they remained honest practitioners in an increasingly crooked sport.[8]

For professional rowing matches some newspapers printed special issues that sold as souvenirs. (Papers of the day were also beginning to report on games played by new professional "base-ball" teams, but in many fewer column inches.) Most early money was on Ward. He had beaten Biglin in two singles races at New York in September 1870, but then finished behind him the next summer at Saratoga. Still, Ward had bested other scullers at Boston's July Fourth Regatta in 1871 and again in 1872.[9]

When the Biglin-Ward race day finally dawned—a sunny Thursday on September 19, 1872—passengers who pushed aboard steamboats in Manhattan saw on chalkboards by the gangways that odds for Biglin were improving, but still favored Ward. The fans quaffed lager and bet as the steamers chugged upstream. Just past the soaring brown-rock Hudson River Palisades, where the river broadens to form the Tappan Zee, the boats discharged their animated cargo on the western shore, at the village of Nyack. This parade of steamers was joined ashore by special trains hauling thousands more fans on rail lines along both riverbanks. By early afternoon the shoreline below Nyack thronged with spectators, and fishermen used their wide-hulled boats to snag a new catch: passengers eager to see the oarsmen close-up.[10]

About to turn twenty-six, Ellis's "entire rowing career, for so young a man is a grand record," the *Aquatic Monthly* noted, "and his participation in the memorable four and six-oared races of the Ward Brothers will always form a bright page in American aquatic annals."[11]

Nothing so nice could be said of John A. Biglin. Five years older than Ellis, John had rowed competitively for more than sixteen years: in workboats, doubles, fours, and pairs, but most often in singles. A *New*

York Clipper editorial about this Nyack race called Biglin a "tough, sinewy specimen of human mechanism." Journals and books at the time dubbed professional rowers "engines" and "machines" and "watch springs" and "pistons"—all marvels of industrial technology. Some accounts even called their sweat "steam" and a rower with power in reserve had "plenty of steam in his boiler." Biglin's muscles were reported to stand out on his brawny arms "like whip cords." He had trained in his intense way, and though always wary of the press did admit to a reporter that he "never felt better" in his life.[12]

Odds held for Ward all morning. But the *New York Times* revealed how "the friends of Biglin were quiet and modest in expressing their opinions previous to the race, but also confident, and took the odds offered by the wealthy and enthusiastic admirers of Ward freely."

Hawkers on the shoreline sold sepia photo cards: John, in a velvet-collared coat, glares, his lips pursed under a shaggy moustache; Ellis, in white tie, glances aside and pouts. (If these images could speak, John would snarl and Ellis would sigh.) Excitement jumped when the steamer *Eliza Hancock* chugged into view bearing Ward and his party from the cross-river town of Sing Sing, where for days they had been training.[13]

"The scene in Nyack Bay was one of the grandest boating displays ever witnessed upon the Hudson," boasted the *Aquatic Monthly*. To discourage public disorder Nyack had closed its saloons, although out along the course "refreshment" tents selling beer and spirits never emptied.

When the Hudson turned "perfectly smooth" at 4:00 p.m., the men were called to the line by Nyack's steamboat dock. Ward "looked well, and acted perfectly cool. He weighed 148 lbs. . . . was dressed in blue knee-breeches, white merino shirt, and wore red colors on his head. His shell was called the Argonauta." As Biglin launched his shell "it was universally remarked that he looked in perfect condition, and was rowing in unexceptionable form. He weighed 163 lbs., and was clad the same as Ward, excepting the colors on his head, which were blue." Biglin named his boat for fire commissioner and state senator James W. Booth, a patron.

At the cry "Go!" Biglin's strong strokes plucked his shell away from Ward's to gain a boat-length, both men rowing a rapid thirty-eight strokes a minute. For nearly a mile Ward labored to catch up, and while their shells surged bow-to-bow Biglin seemed more relaxed. He moved with a steady swing on his sliding seat, while Ward seemed awkward on his: thrusting with his legs for each stroke, then lunging his torso back toward the stern, instead of gliding more gently aft so the boat eased forward before his oars grabbed water at their next catch.

Biglin was a length up after rounding the stake boat, yet Ward battled on as the two aimed upstream, meeting the river's current and an ebb tide. Here Biglin could flaunt his legendary strength. Journalists called his mighty strokes "lifters" because they seemed to hoist Biglin's shell from the water, and these he pulled while also upping the rate. That surge set Biglin two lengths ahead, and he clearly "rowed within himself" said the *Aquatic Monthly*, with a phrase still used to describe the poise and confidence that unite conditioned stamina with a practiced style. Now commanding the race, Biglin "could decrease or increase the clear water between himself and his competitor at his will," and he zipped over the line nearly four lengths up on Ward, in a near-record thirty-nine minutes five seconds. This race again proved Biglin the undisputed single-sculling Champion of America.

After the race, both rowers "laid their boats alongside each other and cordially shook hands," then, once ashore, Ward granted that Biglin had simply out-rowed him. He had "no cause for complaint." Betting had favored Ward for weeks before the race and all that day, his backers giving $100 for every $50 or $60 that Biglin's fans invested, and these wagers were paid "with no resistance." By now, news accounts needed to assure readers that bets were settled amiably since so many professional races ended in suspicion and rancor.[14]

Clearly sensing the sport's drift to more crooked ways, *Aquatic Monthly* editor Charles Peverelly deemed this race "as fair a one as was ever pulled," then added, a bit wistfully, it

> *demonstrated John Biglin to be a little the better man with the sculls; enough better to win a match race this season, and it may be for one or two seasons to come; but in time Ellis Ward's youth, like blood, will tell in his favor, and if the men continue to row in rivalry, on some*

fine sunny day Biglin will realize, as truly as Ellis did at Nyack, the sensations and discouragements of the proverbial stern chase.[15]

Embracing this view, Ward still presumed his youth an advantage, and in the spring of 1873 instructed his financial backers to challenge John Biglin's syndicate to another race. Both Ward and Biglin had coaching duties for the third annual intercollegiate regatta at Springfield in July, so they agreed to race there.[16]

Contrasting the Hudson's broad and rustic Tappan Zee, the Connecticut River at Springfield was a sluice that gushed through a bustling industrial city, its banks crowned by the New York, New Haven & Hartford Railroad's tracks on the east, and by the dust-clouded Hartford Road along the western shore. The course ran from the river's bend just south of town for two-and-a-half miles downstream to a turning stake, between Longmeadow and Agawam, then back to the start.[17]

John Biglin arrived with brother Barney as his judge. The telegraph flashed rowing news around the country, yet the richest details appeared in local papers and every day the *Springfield Daily Republican* published plans for the Ward-Biglin rematch. The night before the race the paper printed odds in Biglin's favor, and also noted that Barney had "distinguished himself . . . by stopping a pair of runaway hack horses in front of the Exchange Hotel."[18]

Appraising the professional rowing match, the *Republican* called John Biglin "undoubtedly the best general oarsman in America, unless we except 'Josh' Ward, whose style as a professional is almost perfect. . . ." Ellis's older brother, Joshua, had become Champion Single Sculler of the United States in 1859 when rowing a five-mile race at Staten Island in a record time that held for years. In 1862, Josh lost twice to James Hamill. But he beat Hamill in 1863, and bested John Biglin that year at Troy. Then at Worcester, in 1864, Josh beat Biglin in singles and in doubles, throughout his career perfecting a rigorously efficient rowing style.

Now that Biglin had again become national champ, the reporters studied him attentively. "As a physical specimen he is about as near perfect as can be found, every muscle standing out distinctly, his shoulders are broad, limbs large but not gross, and his whole form very neat and compact," observed the *Republican*. "In aspect," reported the *New York Tribune*, "Biglin is a picture of the rudest power. He is heavy and bull-necked, large in the chest and abdomen."

The *Tribune* was kinder to young Ellis, praising his "graceful and athletic figure," while the Springfield paper wrote that he "is a slimmer built and lighter man. . . . about the same height, and his muscles, though not so large as Biglin's, appear to be harder and tougher. His manner is very quiet and gentlemanly, and his whole appearance pleasing." He had the same "honest appearance" and manner as his brothers, "but has less of their dry humor."[19]

On race day, Tuesday July 15, 1873, the *New York Times* reported "crowds of betting men are coming in by every train, and as they lounge around the hotel corridors and doorways, soon begin their business by offering, in hoarse and discordant voices, to bet against one man, or back their favorite. . . ." About 5:00 p.m. Biglin set his shell on the river and began "darting around among the craft at the start, now and then giving one of those powerful strokes that always seem as if they were going to send his wherry out of the water. . . ."

Taking "a very good start," Ward edged ahead, pulling a rushed and ragged forty-two strokes a minute. "Biglin struck in at 40, and while Ward seemed to be straining his well-knit frame to its utmost, Biglin, though rowing a powerful and telling stroke, was clearly not exerting all his immense strength." Biglin regained that lost half-length, pushing Ward to quicken his "beautiful and already very rapid stroke a little." This spurt put Ward up by a length and a half.

The two shells sped by the Amherst College quarters, where Biglin heard Ward's young crew shout: "Give it to him, Ellis!" Biglin, in reply, gave *them* a few of his "lifters" to close the gap. Then "an unexpected catastrophe drew every eye upon the leading boat and brought consternation to the hearts of those who had wagered their shekels upon its occupant." Barely a mile from the start, Ward swayed abruptly, glanced side-to-side and seemed stunned. "Before the surprised lookers-on could even guess at its nature the oars fell from his nerveless grasp, his body dropped forward, his head between his knees and he sat as if dead."[20]

"Ellis Ward Breaking Down" *THE DAILY GRAPHIC*, JULY 17, 1873, 109

Biglin pulled in an oar to avoid fouling Ward, and, half joking, shouted: "O, come on, Ellis, we'll row along easy." Slumped and pale, Ward had no breath to reply. With vertigo and temporary blindness Ward was hauled aboard a steamer and ferried ashore. His doctor said the vertigo "was caused by a congestion of the lungs, brought on by over-exertion while suffering from a cold." Biglin rowed on, stopping to answer spectators' anxious questions about Ward. He glided to the stake, then turned upstream, intent to complete the distance, and finished in forty-six minutes. He won $1,000 and, again, the Championship of America.[21]

SAINT JOHN AND HALIFAX

After two strong wins against Ward, America's singles champion John Biglin craved wider fame and riches. His syndicate penned a contract to race Canadian champ George Brown, for $1,000 a side and the Championship of North America. Their race was set for September 1873 in Halifax. En-route, Biglin stopped at Saint John for a regatta on the Kennebecasis River. There he faced a fleet of local scullers that included Robert Fulton, the robust stroke from Saint John's famous Paris Crew.

When stiff breezes postponed the scullers' race, angry crowds set to their typical mayhem. "As usual on all such occasions," griped the *Morning Freeman*, *the place swarmed with booths and shanties in which liquors were dispensed to the thirsty in exact proportion to the amount of money they were willing to spend, and without the slightest regard to the consequences of over indulgence. As usual also there were present numbers whose sole business it seemed to be to get drunk as speedily as possible, and almost simultaneously with the arrival of the first train, drunken men and boys were to be met on all sides, some lying insensible on the road side or in clumps of bushes, others straying around in search of more rum, and numbers promenading up and down the roads with an evident desire to provoke quarrels.*

Biglin's race the next day drew huge (if groggy) crowds—then stormy complaints. Biglin planned to take it easy at Saint John. Appearing slower than expected against Fulton, he aimed to lower his odds against Brown—making a win against him next week all the richer. Barney was along, as

Refreshments tent at the Saint John Regatta in 1873 *THE CANADIAN ILLUSTRATED NEWS*: VOL. 8, NO. 15 (OCT. 11, 1873), 232.

John's coach and judge, joined by a gang of New York "sporting men" who set three-to-one odds on Biglin.

Fulton and Biglin led the other scullers off the start and hung together a while. But by the turning buoy Biglin enjoyed a slight lead. One reporter noted that he "had a pleasant smile on his face, and ... seemed to be rowing with the confidence of a man having the prize within his grasp." But just yards from the finish Fulton yanked a quick and mighty stroke to edge across the line first. Shocked and irate, Biglin dropped his oars, flailed his arms, and roared oaths at the judges. "What! Given the race to Fulton!!!" They all declared Fulton the winner, although a local paper noted that Biglin "could have won, and knowing that he could he purposely, for reasons known to all boating men, 'played' with his opponent. Too late he found that Fulton is not a man to be played with in this manner, and that the splendid 'spurt' which he [Biglin] intended should bring him in ahead, was useless." Barney and his New York pals were especially

John Biglin protests his loss to Robert Fulton at the Saint John Regatta in 1873 *THE CANADIAN ILLUSTRATED NEWS*: VOL. 8, NO. 15 (OCT. 11, 1873), 232.

mad because they had expected John to pull off a close win and instead lost thousands of dollars.[22]

Stiff winds in Halifax Harbor postponed the Biglin-Brown race, again "increasing the evils of drunkenness and consequent disorder" as "all along the shore drunken fights were common." At their start the next day, Biglin snatched a quick lead. But by the mid-point turn Brown was a few seconds ahead. "Biglin pulled a splendid stroke the last mile," but a reporter noted he was "evidently too nervous in his motions to accomplish anything. Brown kept up his long, powerful strokes, sending his boat in toward the goal in beautiful style" and winning their five-mile race by five lengths.

Biglin and his backers agreed it was a fair race, although Barney regretted losing $1,400 and his New York compatriots even more. Brown "is the best man" he ever rowed against, Biglin declared. "I have rowed fourteen match single scull races, and Brown is the only man who has fairly beaten me." For Biglin it was also his most prestigious singles race— and grandest loss—because afterward no English rowers would accept Brown's challenges, making him "Champion of the World." Still craving that title, Biglin offered to race Brown on the Schuylkill. But Brown's backers declined, saying it was too late in the season. Biglin was furious. This was the second world-championship race he had lost at Halifax: first in the four, now in his single.[23]

Biglin's 1874 season was hardly better. He finished second in a single at Boston's July Fourth City Regatta, and second in a double with the popular Boston-Irish sculler Patrick Reagan. In early August on Narragansett Bay for the Oakland Beach Regatta, by Warwick, Biglin trailed Evan Morris and James Ten Eyck from Peekskill in a four-mile race. He then enlisted Morris, Ten Eyck, and Charles Engel for a "Biglin scratch crew" that turned short of the stake, was disqualified, and swamped as fours from Boston and Portland won first and second.[24]

Biglin's luck improved in October when he met Ten Eyck again, on the Hudson at Nyack, racing him three miles for the Championship of New York State and $1,000. "A large crowd of sporting men assembled" giving their odds to Biglin, who rowed the *James W. Booth*. He won by a length "showing no signs of exhaustion after his exertions." This race was big news in sporting (and betting) circles. Papers reported it nationwide, few more avidly than the *Omaha Bee,* which filled two front-page columns.[25]

JOHN AND ELLIS AS RASCALS: RED WING AND ROCKAWAY

John Biglin and Ellis Ward were renowned for their many big-money races in single sculls. But in 1875 both marred their fine reputations by rare public deceits. That May, the *Brooklyn Eagle* complained how

> *honest contests are the exception rather than the rule, few races being rowed on the square. . . . The knaves of the oar in this fraud business lose thousands of dollars in order to gain a few hundreds by what they consider "smart" tricks. To such an extent has the evil of "hippodroming," or "selling" or "throwing" races affected professional rowing, that it has driven all the patronage of the admirers of the sport from the professional arena to that of the amateur. . . .* [26]

Regrettably, Ellis Ward soon proved how easily the realms of professional and amateur rowing could be blurred. About the time of that *Eagle* editorial Ward tried a new form of knavery, off in Minnesota. He wandered west from his home on the Hudson, claiming to be an itinerant carpenter named John B. Fox (Fox was his middle name). Ward disembarked at the Mississippi River town of Red Wing, where he told local boat club members he had "rowed a little once on the Susquehanna River." But when townsmen saw Ward perform in a shell they rejoiced, and urged him to race in the upcoming state championship regatta. A grocer hired Fox, although some folks were suspicious. "Now and then the new clerk would shift a case of prunes or unpack a box of tinned peaches," one townsman recalled, "but most of the time he could be found loitering along the river front." For weeks, Fox gladly helped coach the local rowers, and trained hard in a single.

Ward had imported his own deception, but his hosts more than matched it. When a crew from Stillwater sent photos of its burly rowers, among them lumberjacks, Red Wing put a rowing costume on the town blacksmith, who had never been in a boat before but gladly flexed his bulging muscles. Then Stillwater sent a scout to assess its competition. But once he was recognized, the Red Wing rowers threw a sloppy performance for his benefit. Their charade succeeded. Word spread fast: Red Wing's oarsmen would be sure losers. This led crews from Stillwater and St. Paul to rate themselves the odds-on favorites, and they were eager to place bets when their steamboat chugged into town. Hundreds of cheering fans rushed ashore, their arrival livened by a peppy cornet band.

"Prominent citizens caught the gambling fever," wrote one historian. "Money was wagered freely. Respectable citizens who had never hazarded a cent in all their lives, stood along the levee with their pockets bulging with bills. Nearly all the money in the Red Wing banks was drawn out for betting purposes" and one "old-timer" claimed deposits in the First National Bank fell to $50.[27]

In the Regatta's first race, for two miles in singles, Fox grabbed a lead over a St. Paul sculler who was then state champion. Fox sped on. At one point he quit rowing to splash water on his arms and face to cool off. And he sucked a lemon until his opponent caught up. Then, rowing along easily, Fox won by a boat-length.

Next, Fox rowed as stroke for the Red Wing Boat Club four. Their crew won handily, leaving fans from Stillwater and St. Paul broke. The steamboat's captain had shared their excitement, and lost so much he couldn't afford to buy the coal needed for the return trip—until a Red Wing man offered $1,500 from his hefty winnings to cover costs.

Performing in town were the Tennessee Jubilee Singers, a student choir that had toured the eastern and midwestern United States. The Singers appeared to raise money for Fisk University, an institution founded in Nashville after the Civil War to educate African Americans. Their concert favorites included gospel and spiritual melodies, Stephen Foster tunes, and patriotic pieces like "The Battle Hymn of the Republic."

One choir member recognized Fox as professional rower Ellis Ward. When challenged, the *New York Times* reported, the Red Wing rowers professed ignorance that "the stranger was Ward, and that he was undoubtedly put upon them by 'betting sharps' for their own gain. Thousands of dollars were won in this way, and the feeling in St. Paul and other places against Ward is said to be one of intense indignation." This scheme became national news when the *Times* headlined,

ELLIS WARD'S LITTLE GAME.
HE RUSTICATES IN MINNESOTA UNDER THE
NAME OF FOX—CASUALLY PARTICIPATES
IN AN AMATEUR REGATTA AND WINS
EVERYTHING—A DISHONORABLE ACT.

The paper stated its "deep regret that Ward should blot an honorable career in aquatic sport by the despicable act of becoming the tool of gamblers to fleece innocent sportsmen." Minnesota historian Merle Potter later named as conspirators the grocer who hired Fox, a hardware merchant, and a Red Wing grain dealer. But, in time, Ward's "dishonorable act" was forgotten. Like many a professional oarsman, he went on to become a legendary coach. Beginning in 1879, Ward was hired as the first rowing coach at the University of Pennsylvania, and he continued there with winning results until 1912.[28]

A month after news about Ellis Ward's guile in Minnesota, John Biglin prompted angry press on his own for a suspicious "performance" in a three-mile singles race at Rockaway Beach, in Queens. When racing for $1,000 and the Championship of New York State, Biglin was the bookies' three-to-one favorite. But he enriched colleagues who bet against him by feigning an accident as he rounded the mid-course stake boat. Ten Eyck rowed on to win by half a mile.[29]

After Biglin's surprise loss the *Eagle* headlined its coverage of the race "A Specimen of Professional Fraud." The sub-head was as harsh: "A Lesson for People who Bet on Professionals." When the race began, "betting was then $100 to $30 on Biglin. Scores of Biglin's admirers laid their money out freely. In the meantime several very quiet, innocent looking countrymen were taking the odds every time." Once begun, the "first mile was simply an exercising gait. It was apparent that Biglin did not care to win." By this time, "His admirers had no time to hedge, for Mr. Biglin, in water smooth as glass, managed to get foul of the stake boat, then pulled his shell so clumsily as to fill it with water. An amateur could not have gone through such a performance; it required the skill of a professional."

Calling the race "a disgrace" that "will do much toward lessening the confidence of the public in professional oarsmen," the *Eagle* reported how a spectator with no money on the race "characterizes it as a '-----fraud,' and the men who were parties to it as 'no good.'" The paper reported "another gentleman said that there was no doubt it was twenty dollars to five that Biglin could win the race if he wished to. Biglin has given himself away for a very paltry sum." Still, John's passion for rowing endured that fall, and he continued to race in singles and pairs.[30]

CENTENNIAL CONSPIRACIES AND CONFLICTS

In 1876 the United States celebrated the centennial of its independence from Great Britain with a glorious exposition in Philadelphia's Fairmount Park. The three sports chosen for international competition during this extravaganza were yachting in New York Harbor in June, rowing on the adjacent Schuylkill in August, and riflery at Creedmoor, Long Island (now Queens, New York), in September. Americans were easy winners at yachting and riflery. Their results at rowing were mixed, despite ambitious schemes by the Biglins and the Wards.

In February 1876, the *Aquatic Monthly* was confident about rowing prospects for the Centennial Regatta: "Uncle Sam ought to be represented by at least three crews, hailing, respectively from the Empire, Keystone and Old Bay State. The first-named could be culled from the Wards and Biglins; the second from Evan Morris, [William] Scharff, Coulter, etc., and the last from the best of the Fort Hill and North End crews, so well known in the famous Charles River regattas." A Biglin four had been organized by their boat-builder Charles B. Elliott, and was well funded by his syndicate of investors. In March, the *Monthly* reported the crew was training "every fine afternoon" on Newtown Creek. But early on came dissension when Frederick Engelhardt quit in a blowup with the often-grumpy John Biglin.[31]

That Spring Biglin was eager to race in more than the four, and challenged to row a pair-oared race against "any two men in America" for up to $2,000. He planned to race a pair with Fred Plaisted, or even brother

Barney. Plaisted was a famous professional known on both the East and West Coasts. The legendary Faulkner-Reagan crew from Boston took Biglin's challenge for a pair race, and sought another in a four.[32]

Biglin continued training daily in a pair with Plaisted, while also trying other rowers for two empty seats in Elliott's four. *Turf, Field and Farm* reported that they sought competitors, but "when nothing offers to race against they try speed with the tug-boats which frequent the creek." The *New York Times* reported, "The stroke oar, Biglin, applies himself to his work in true scientific style . . ."

> *The crew's present head-quarters are at Barnett's Boat-house, on the right [Brooklyn] bank of the creek, a short distance below the Union avenue bridge. . . . At present the practice hours of the crew on New-town Creek are from 10 to 11 in the morning and from 3 to 4 in the afternoon. Hundreds of spectators watch their progress daily, and on Sundays, when swarms of shells of all dimensions are also out, the banks are lined with crowds of sightseers.*

Up the Hudson at Cornwall, the Wards were also out training intensely for Philadelphia, and in Saint John the Paris Crew was hard at work.[33]

Boston's City Regatta in July offered a preview for Philadelphia. The Biglin four's rivalry with Boston's Faulkner-Reagan crew drew a huge crowd and rampant betting. (John Biglin stroked, with Fred Plaisted, Tom Elliott, and J. Flannery.) The six-mile race with three turns began as Faulkner's boat sprang away and led for a quarter-mile, over-stroking the Biglins by thirty-eight-to-thirty-four a minute. When the Biglins "hit up sharp to 37" they "walked easily by, opening a long gap of four lengths," reported *Turf, Field and Farm.* Desperately, the Faulkners spurted to thirty-nine and to forty, but couldn't catch up. The Biglins led around the first stake, and widened their lead while "rowing easily and well within themselves."

Odds that had favored the local crew swung to the Biglins, and even as a stiff wind sprang up, turning the water "very rough and lumpy," the Biglin four kept adding distance. But with the wind came trouble. Suddenly "a portion of the wash-boards on their shell gave way, and immediately their ship commenced to fill." The *Times* concluded, "Had it not been for this accident, the Biglin crew undoubtedly would have won. . . ."[34]

Dauntless after this fateful race, the Biglin and Faulkner crews boarded a train to Providence, eager for another rich contest on the Seekonk River. *Aquatic Monthly* editor Charles Peverelly noted "great interest in this race from the fact that the Biglin crew have been sharp rivals of the Faulkner men for several years, as far back as 1860," and from the mishap on the Charles earlier that day. He described the afternoon race with his usual jaunty style:

> *The gun had thundered its call to the four-oared shells while the boys' paddles were making the spray fly, and presently they came out, manned with lean but brawny men, the foremost oarsmen in the country. The famous Biglin crew of New York took position on the west, bareheaded under the fierce lighting in a "sun-bath" which would have stricken the average man in death in almost fifteen minutes. The equally well-known Faulkner-Regan [Reagan] crew of Boston hung on the east, and the Shawmut crew of Boston between.*
>
> *At the start "John" gave his men a tremendous stroke, 41 or 42 to the minute, and held it up for nearly a mile, when he eased it up one or two strokes, still going at 40 up around the mile and a half stake and down the course home, putting on a burst of speed as he passed Regatta Point that made the boat leap almost clear of the water and finishing in 18:32, which was remarkable considering the strength of the wind.*

Just as remarkable was the Biglin four's victory margin. They finished more than forty boat-lengths ahead of the Faulkner-Reagan four. Exuberant at what Peverelly had witnessed, he proclaimed: "No such oar-handling as the Biglins' has been seen on our waters, and it is plain they will cut out a large job for somebody at the Centennial regatta at Philadelphia. . . ."[35]

Back in New York, Biglin told Charles Elliott that he wished to race a single at Philadelphia—as well as a pair with Plaisted and the four. Elliott balked, then refused. Biglin kept up daily practice in the four, leaving the city to train in "Connecticut, on a secluded piece of water where they were free from the curiosity of friends and strangers," noted the *Times*. There, Biglin was visited by Nathan C. Meeker, a Centennial official who had arranged rowing events at Philadelphia. Having Meeker's support, it seemed the Biglin four was the American favorite. Adding to its report on the crew's training, the *Times* declared, "That they may be successful is the hope of every American."

The betting public expected that Biglin and Ward fours would race at Philadelphia, and "sporting men" set odds eagerly. For American rowing fans here was another "race of the century." Then greed intervened. By Peverelly's account, Elliott's syndicate decided John Biglin should not race his single, as "they desired him to concentrate all his energies and focus on victory in the four-oared championship." Ten days before the race, Biglin confronted Elliott, and quit.

In another surprise, Biglin then turned to rivals Josh, Gil, and Ellis Ward. Surely, he proposed, such a crew would prevail! The Wards agreed to join him, and Peverelly then hoped these four champs would win for America. But the Wards haggled with their sponsors, holding out for more money. Days passed, the Biglin-Ward crew missed the filing deadline, and in the end no Biglins or Wards raced a four in Philadelphia.[36]

There were more surprises on the Schuylkill. Fred Plaisted stroked the Elliott syndicate's New York four (minus John Biglin) and they lost in the first round to an English crew. In another upset, Saint John's vaunted Paris Crew lost to a "Fisherman's Crew" of burly seamen from Halifax. Racing in pairs, Boston's Faulkner and Reagan easily beat Josh and Gil Ward, who "splashed and dragged their oars along the water in poor style." In the professional singles race that John Biglin couldn't row, Canadian Edward "Ned" Hanlan from Toronto deftly bested all comers. Racing scullers who included Plaisted, Hanlan was seen "pulling around leisurely, occasionally stopping to allow his competitors to come up with him," and won by five lengths, becoming the World Singles Champion.[37]

In fact, Hanlan won so decisively *Spirit of the Times* surmised he must have cheated. Perhaps, the paper fancied, he had concealed a set of bellows in his shell that were compressed by his feet and puffed him along the course.[38]

Afterward, a *Brooklyn Eagle* reporter asked John Biglin why he had quit the New York four. He gave two reasons, not mentioning the main one—his dispute with Elliott about also racing a single. First, said Biglin, his boat-mates failed to match his own stamina, and could only row a mile and a half before they were winded. "He further said that he would stick by the crew only [if] his friends in New York and Brooklyn and elsewhere in America would bet on them on his account, and he did not want to have them lose their money. 'You saw,' said he, 'that my predictions were right, the crew got winded after a mile and a half.'"[39]

Resentment against Biglin's quitting lingered, with an *Eagle* account noting he was "variously criticized and his alleged reason for leaving the crew derisively commented upon." Eager to put this aside, Biglin appeared in October 1876 for a three-mile professional race at Greenwood Lake against Fred Plaisted, Henry Coulter, and Ed Powell from Pittsburgh, John Landers from Portland, and John McKiel from Cold Spring, New York.

Turf, Field and Farm dubbed Greenwood Lake "the new Eden of rowing courses" for its picturesque setting amid rolling hills on the New York–New Jersey border. But for John Biglin the place must have seemed hellish. The *Eagle* reminded readers about Biglin's slight that his "crew could not row more than a mile and a half of the three mile course" and that Plaisted expected "to demonstrate to him the error of his judgment. . . ." Plaisted was first from the start, with McKiel and Coulter close behind, leading Biglin and Landers by a length. "Powell and Biglin were not much interested, save as to which should claim the codfish . . ."— the prize for last place. Rounding the stake, Plaisted moved out farther from Coulter and with "plenty of steam in his boiler" crossed the line well ahead of Landers, Coulter, and McKiel. Biglin and Powell were so slow they weren't timed.

But a "splendid race" was ended, until there "arose a discussion." A protest charged that Plaisted, Coulter, and McKiel had turned the stake west-to-east instead of the opposite, as the referee had directed. This gave the referee no choice but to award prizes in their order of finish to Landers, Biglin, and Powell. "After all Dame Fortune was just," opined *Turf, Field and Farm*. "For one party had the glory while the others were soothed in defeat with plasters of greenbacks."[40]

John Biglin's second-place "victory" at Greenwood Lake no doubt rankled Plaisted, and he hoped to race Biglin again at Silver Lake, near Plymouth, Massachusetts, in early June 1877. There, Plaisted faced Ned Hanlan, the new world champion, and "Frenchy" Johnson, John Landers, and George Hosmer from Boston. Plaisted gained the lead and held it halfway to the turn, then moved away from Hanlan and Johnson. But when Hanlan's oarlock broke, Johnson and Landers finished second and third. At Silver Lake Biglin rowed a pair race with William Maxwell, and they bested the popular Faulkner-Reagan crew—as well as the boats of the Connelly and Gookin brothers, all hearty Boston Irishmen.

Hanlan won a singles race on Silver Lake two weeks later. The Biglin four was to race there too, but just days before Maxwell fell ill. After suffering heatstroke during practice he had jumped into Newtown Creek to cool off. From the fetid waters he contracted a "congestive chill" that worsened, and ultimately proved fatal. Before Maxwell's death, the *Times* wrote that the creek appears to be "an excellent sheet of water for practice" and "they say that they get used to the ill-savor which comes of the factories ... thereabout." (Today the creek is ranked among the most polluted estuaries in the nation.) In Boston that July, Biglin and Engelhardt won the pair-oared race against the city's Connolly brothers, but in double-sculls they finished second to their frequent rivals Faulkner and Reagan.[41]

That August, Biglin rowed a singles race on the Hudson at Newburgh, but with little gumption. The *New York World* saw how "the great Biglin was lying on his oars" and clearly showing that "the days of Biglin and the Ward brothers are over." Winning that day's singles race was "Frenchy" Johnson.

Still, Biglin wasn't finished. By this point in his career, at age thirty-five, John Biglin couldn't beat the best younger scullers, and found he had trouble in two-man boats as well. At Newburgh, after losing miserably to Johnson, John Biglin rowed a double-scull working boat with James Hickey from New York City, but both their boat and one the Ward brothers rowed finished "many lengths behind" the younger James and Frank Ten Eyck. It was "easy to see" the *World* recorded, "that the old-time favorites were struggling as hard as they could, and Biglin set Hickey a fine pattern of a strong stroke, but it was all to no purpose." John might have fared better in the pair race, but it was postponed by rough water, and neither the Biglin-Engelhardt nor Faulkner-Reagan pairs stayed in town to compete the next day.[42]

In February 1878, John Biglin was fired from his sinecure as a weigher's foreman at the New York Custom House. An order from the Treasury Secretary reorganized the Weigher's Department as prime for civil service reforms that President Hayes began after Grant's administration. With more time to row that spring, Biglin and Frank Bell were back on Newtown Creek, training in a pair for a Silver Lake regatta in May. But for unknown reasons they never competed.[43]

John and Barney Biglin appeared at the New York waterfront in July 1879 to greet Ned Hanlan when he landed after winning the world singles championship in London. Joined by Irish actor and playwright Dion Boucicault and several politicians, they all rode off in a parade of carriages to a reception at the Fifth Avenue Hotel, followed by a gala at Madison Square Garden. A few days later, Barney, Fred Plaisted, and boat-builder Charles Elliott led a delegation that saw off Hanlan at Grand Central Depot for his return to Toronto.[44]

The Biglins were seldom competitors now, just celebrities at regattas around New York. In 1879 John again profited from Barney's Republican connections when he was named an assistant weigher at the Custom House. But in March 1880 John was fired again, this time for being "found absent from duty." Barney lost his lucrative monopoly contract to cart immigrants' baggage at Castle Garden, and the *Washington Post* saw John's removal as part of a continuing GOP purge, writing: "The Biglin brothers, in the custom-house, have been among the loudest supporters of Grant."[45]

His Last Season

John Biglin rowed his last three races in 1880, realizing, by age thirty-eight, how his days on the water were numbered. In September on Jamaica Bay, off Brooklyn and Queens, he finished a sorry fifth behind Fred Plaisted, George W. Lee from Newark, William Knoth from Canada, and Frederick Engelhardt. But he did manage to stay ahead of James Ten Eyck, and

Ohio sculler Daniel O'Leary. In the next day's "consolation race" Biglin beat Ten Eyck by two lengths and O'Leary by ten.[46]

John's final race—and Barney's, too—wasn't for prize money, a trophy, or a title. This was a grudge match in the fall of 1880 over who would win the presidential election. Republican nominee James A. Garfield was running with Barney's crony Chester A. Arthur as vice president. Accounts differ about who challenged whom to a boat race, but political loyalties were ablaze that fall.[47]

The Sylvan Club was a Democratic, young men's sports and social group organized by the Tammany Hall district-captain Charles Francis "Silent Charlie" Murphy. He ran it from rooms above his saloon in Manhattan's Gashouse District—named for its many gas tanks by the East River and their telltale sulfurous aroma. Sylvan Club rowers had raced on Newtown Creek, and were able competitors against other city boat clubs. Murphy's district was just south of Barney's, on the Lower East Side, and he trained stout shipyard hands for a Sylvan four-oared crew. Barney enlisted brothers John, James, and Philip.[48]

Gashouse District residents became gripped by the race. Workers bet heavily on Sylvan, and when the crews met on the East River off 100th Street, crowds jammed north to 129th Street and the Harlem's Boathouse Row. Betting and brawling intensified as crowds converged around The Red House, a popular tavern at the foot of East 104th Street. Then rumors swept along the water's edge: The Sylvan stroke, a powerful shipwright nicknamed "Tecumseh," was sick. He claimed he was drugged. One paper reported "a roar that shook Harlem." Sylvan and Biglin supporters set to fighting. The Biglins proposed they row over the course to win by forfeit. As English journalist Maurice Low wrote, a riot was "imminent."

"Just when the prospect was blackest Murphy stepped down to the river bank," wrote Low. "He took off his hat, coat, and collar, handed them to a friend, and calmly took his place as stroke of the Sylvan boat." Now ecstatic, Sylvan fans "began to bet again for their men, taking all the money the Biglin crowd could rake and scrape together."[49]

Murphy set a steady cadence from the start, matching the Biglins stroke for stroke. His four charged along, and when nearing the finish Murphy added a powerful spurt that drove the Sylvan shell to victory.

That night, gleeful crowds hoisted Murphy to their shoulders, parading around the Gashouse District and singing Tammany anthems. "He had won the day, and by winning it saved thousands of dollars for the poor men who had wagered on his crew," the *New York Times* later recounted. Murphy went on to replace Richard Croker as Tammany Hall's chief sachem in 1902, and dominated New York City's Democratic politics for more than two decades.[50]

John Biglin seldom took up an oar after that race, and by the next summer a *Brooklyn Daily Eagle* piece about Newtown Creek reported: "A once famous oarsman, John Biglin, who has made the place a head-quarters for many years, was there yesterday, and rowed up the water in a row boat. He does not exercise on the creek this season, and but little anywhere. The new oarsmen springing into notoriety from year to year seem to be pushing the once famous scullers to the wall." John sometimes dropped in as an honored guest at regattas around New York. He also joined a "Sinn Fein" Irish social club.[51]

In 1883, a Pittsburgh newspaper listed Biglin as a competitor—with longtime Boston rival George Faulkner—in a "veterans" race, but there is no record that he actually attended the regatta. That year the last of John's six children, Polly Adelaide, was born, but as time passed he became estranged from his wife, Catherine, and she moved off to the Bronx to live with their son, John Jr.[52]

John Biglin was listed as a "Boatman" in New York's 1884 City Directory, living on East 34th Street, between First and Second Avenues. From there he moved to a handsome brownstone on Second Avenue, just south of 34th Street. According to the *Brooklyn Eagle,* John's last work (or at least paid sinecure) was as superintendent of transfer for Barney's Castle Garden baggage franchise.[53]

Early in 1886 Biglin developed a "heavy cold" he couldn't shed. With Barney he journeyed by train to Hot Springs, Arkansas, seeking medical treatment. The brothers enjoyed the town's warm mineral baths, but John's condition persisted. Still ailing, John rode back to New York and there contracted pneumonia. His health worsened, and at midnight on Monday, April 19, 1886, he died at home. He was forty-four years old.

The *New York Times* obituary hailed John A. Biglin as "once the foremost oarsman in America" and recounted his many victories. Funeral arrangements were lavish. "Crowds of people, lines of carriages and delegations of politicians and sportsmen from different parts of the country blocked Second-ave. and Thirty-fourth st.," reported the *New York Herald*. In the parlor at 614 Second Avenue, "clusters of floral gifts were scattered in profusion around the coffin." Catholic priests chanted eternal good wishes. Biglin's boat-builder Charles B. Elliott joined rowers George Faulkner from Boston and Canadian champ Wallace Ross to pay their respects—along with more than fifty other oarsmen.

"You should row a pair with your brother," the racing-shell maker and rowing mentor George Pocock—son of an Eton College boat-builder— once said, "because when you are done fighting he will still be your brother." Together in a pair, and bound by blood and their shared exploits ashore, John and Barney Biglin were especially close for years, making John's death distinctly woeful for Barney. "Among the chief mourners were the brothers of the dead man, James B., Bernard, Joseph C., Philip and William" the *Tribune* noted. "The oldest brother sadly remarked that they could never form a six-oar crew again."

Biglin's funeral cortege snarled traffic from around his home to the East River, where mourners crowded the saloons while awaiting the ferry. Once across, the procession took its way to the Calvary Cemetery, passing on its sad journey the glinting waters of Newtown Creek.[54]

CHAPTER 10

Barney and Blarney

ANYONE WATCHING JOHN AND BARNEY BIGLIN ON THE WATER SAW ONLY their splendid unison: power applied precisely, stroke by mighty stroke. Seen up close, the Biglins' lives and characters were more distinct: often diverse, sometimes disorderly. John was gruff and taciturn: a boatman and laborer and fireman. Barney was glib and mellow: a brass-molder until GOP connections made him a Custom House official. He was also a politician with national ambitions, and a businessman with greedy dreams. While John was self-absorbed in his sweaty toils, on and off the water, Barney was suave and beguiling—especially when charming cronies for his next rich favor. Barney's public life was suspect from the start, and sordid to the end.

After winning the North American championship in the pair, in May 1872, Barney continued challenging English, Canadian, and American crews. But the brothers were just too good, and no professionals dared race them. In July that year Barney stroked a four-oared gunwale boat to victory in Boston's July Fourth Regatta. This was his twenty-eighth race in an exalted rowing career as a professional oarsman. But Barney was already enticed by New York City's Republican Party politics, and this attraction first bumped him to victory at the polls in November—then to other exploits in public service and in public scandal.[1]

POLITICS AND PATRONAGE

With its opening in 1825 the Erie Canal linked the Great Lakes and America's bountiful heartland to the Hudson River and the Atlantic. The port of New York became the nation's busiest, and richest. After taking office in 1829, President Andrew Jackson installed a "spoils system" that dispensed federal jobs to his party's faithful. By the 1850s, about 80 percent of all federal revenue came from the New York Custom House, and its diverse services required more than a thousand employees.

Once Republicans gained the White House, with Lincoln's inauguration in 1861, party officials expanded and thrived on this federal patronage for nearly a quarter-century. Barney Biglin first enjoyed these spoils in the early 1860s, and prospered once he befriended a New York City lawyer and Republican leader named Chester Alan Arthur. In 1871, President Grant appointed Arthur to be collector of customs for the Port of New York, and for the next seven years he ran a patronage empire surpassing any in the nation. Arthur "was entirely sympathetic toward the spoils system," wrote historian Mollie Keller, "ignored the corrupt activities in his office, and allegedly earned several times as a customs collector what he did as a lawyer: by one account he made $50,000 a year from 1871 to 1873." That sum equaled the US president's salary, and Arthur gained it just by skimming a share of fines collected on overvalued imports. He also reaped salary kickbacks from his Custom House employees, using them to fund the state's Republican Party. The port regulated shipping and immigration, and both were booming.[2]

Arthur was quick to impose his own style of machine politics on this most bountiful fiefdom. The Custom House opened for business at 10:00 a.m., but Arthur seldom arrived until early afternoon. As his biographer Thomas C. Reeves explained, "This was caused by a fondness for late hours: night after night Arthur sat up until two or three in the morning talking politics, smoking cigars, and eating and drinking with 'the boys'"—including party boss John J. O'Brien, ward-heeler Michael Cregan, and Barney Biglin. At the time, most of New York City's Irish were Democrats loyal to Tammany Hall, but from working for Vance at his chandelier works young Biglin gained both employment and by 1860 his first Republican Party sinecure: inspector at the Custom House. This job he quit in 1863 when a better one opened: as a gauger, an excise officer who inspected dutiable bulk goods. He enjoyed this post until his own election as a Republican officeholder in 1872, and his gains from GOP patronage would still flow for decades. Aspiring to join the middle classes and improve on his curtailed education, Barney went to night school to learn some law. He even studied some anatomy, perhaps to better coach rowers.[3]

Barney had enjoyed Republican largesse for more than a decade by 1872 when he gained party support to run for a State Assembly seat from Manhattan's contentious Eighteenth District. His opponents were a Tammany Hall toady and three other Democrats. In a sense, Barney's 1872 campaign pitted Tammany's Democratic city corruption against Arthur's Republican federal corruption. As the staunchly Republican *New York Tribune* noted in a profile later in his public career, Barney could seem "a pleasant, agreeable, well-informed man of the world, courteous and most obliging, devoted to his half-dozen daughters, and apparently at peace with himself and all the world." Yet the same profile granted he also seemed "the incarnation of all that is wicked and depraved in politics, a 'tough', a shoulder-hitter, a coarse, brutal type of humanity, a robber of immigrants."[4]

Despite a reputation for political scheming, Biglin was still hailed for some noble deeds. When coaching a Friendship Boat Club six-oared gig on the East River in 1870 he saw a young woman leap from the Manhattan-Williamsburg ferry. "The danger of the feat was enhanced by the desperate resolution of the unhappy creature to drown in spite of all assistance," a police report stated. Still, Biglin dove into the swirling water and dragged her to safety. "There is not, perhaps, a man in . . . the whole country who has saved more persons from drowning than Mr. Biglin," surmised the *New York Herald*. "It was almost a daily experience with him while training for his boat races to rescue one or more, and instances are known to his friends where he has saved as many as five people in a single day."[5]

Once Barney Biglin joined Arthur's political circle, their fortunes rose like red-white-and-blue balloons. Both sons of Irish immigrants, Biglin and Arthur relished one another's company, consorting often in a Greenwich Village oyster saloon at Bleecker and Leroy Streets that became their hangout. The two enjoyed what US senator Daniel Patrick Moynihan called "the Irish era" in New York politics, when both Democrats and Republicans seized power and expanded their influence against

Chester A. Arthur, commissioner of the Port of New York and a Barney Biglin patron MILLER CENTER, UNIVERSITY OF VIRGINIA

the city's Dutch and English establishment. Beginning in the early 1870s, Moynihan wrote, the prosecution and removal of "Boss" William Magear Tweed (a Scot) as grand sachem of Tammany Hall gave Irish Democrats new opportunities to dominate City Hall for decades—until their last fair-haired hero, Mayor Jimmy Walker, sailed off with his mistress for Europe and exile in 1932.

The "Tweed Ring" had profited from the 1850s by bleeding New York City finances through bold and ever-more-audacious graft. With Tweed on the run in 1871, John Kelly became Tammany's grand sachem, the first of many Irish Catholics to enjoy that post. For his part, Biglin learned to exploit both parties. He declaimed against the Democrats' grip on city administration by Tammany Hall's patronage, but when convenient he gladly traded favors for their votes.[6]

In what seems a pre-election campaign stunt, Biglin gained public honor when the *New York Clipper* reported, "Barney Biglin, whose name is as familiar as household words to the lovers of rowing in America ... was recently presented with an elegant gold hunting case watch and chain valued at $375." An inscription read: "Presented to Bernard Biglin by his friends, as a tribute to his ability and standing as an American oarsman. New York, Oct. 12, 1872."[7]

ASSEMBLYMAN

A few weeks later, Biglin won his first election to the New York State Assembly from the normally Democratic Eighteenth District. Voters went his way by a slim plurality thanks to anti-Tammany (anti-Tweed) resentments and ballots split by four rival Democrats. Unlike brother John, who was often sulky and reserved, Barney jumped into public life and social occasions with glee: In 1873 a newspaper noted how he enjoyed July Fourth "festivities" that "wound up late" at the Friendship Boat Club. Barney was also a busy family man, now father to four daughters and a son. He and wife "Polly" would have three more daughters in the next four years.[8]

Barney and Polly lived well in a townhouse on Lexington Avenue: He was a rising political star and businessman with party connections to enrich his work; she was a gracious hostess, active in Catholic charities and a doting mother. Polly had been born to English parents in Sheffield, immigrating to New York when she was two. This heritage gave Polly higher social status than Barney, an edge she asserted by sending their daughters off to school at the Sacred Heart Convent in London, Ontario—lest they acquire their father's brogue. Barney had "married up" in society, and gained richly from Polly's elegance and charm.[9]

During Barney's first weeks in Albany, in January 1873, he was named to the Assembly's Committee on Commerce and Navigation. Barney also fell in with the New York Republican Party's political boss Roscoe Conkling, who served as the state's US senator throughout the 1870s. He was sometimes known as "Lord Roscoe" for his grip on party patronage at its epicenter, the New York Custom House.[10]

By his post as collector of customs for New York, Chester Arthur was a valued Conkling ally, and Biglin's new work in Albany on commerce and navigation united the three men's interests. Biglin was re-elected in a tighter race in November 1873, and returned to serve in Albany in the spring of 1874. This victory gained scorn when *The Nation* magazine denounced him for defeating the much admired Republican reformer William Gardner Choate. Stressing the two candidates' social and ethical contrasts, the article called Biglin "a man of extremely doubtful antecedents himself, and belonging to a class—that of 'professional rowing-men'—which has always been in very bad odor." This, the magazine charged, made him nothing but "an active gambler" deserving no public trust.[11]

Still craving a world championship, and ever the entrepreneur, Barney continued to seek a four-oared match race with English professionals. Finally, that fall the Taylor-Winship crew accepted. Barney lined up Evan Morris to stroke, along with himself, brother John, and veteran champ Josh Ward. With such celebrity competitors, reported the *Hartford Daily Courant*, "the proposed race is creating quite a stir in sporting circles." But a month later, perhaps appraising their American competition, the English four cabled to decline Biglin's challenge.[12]

When 1874's November election approached, Biglin faced a new threat to his budding political career. This time he was defending his Eighteenth Assembly District seat against a Tammany Democrat; and again the reformer William Choate, who had split from the Republican Party. In his first run for the Assembly Barney had eked out a 612-vote plurality over four squabbling Democrats. In this 1874 election season, political cartoonist Thomas Nast—who had attacked Tammany's "Boss" Tweed with relentless images depicting his greed—for the first time used an elephant to represent the Republican Party. Barney did win a three-way race, but this time by just 556 votes.[13]

Election night was best remembered not for Barney's slim victory, but for a political murder. Barney had enlisted brother John to be a poll-watcher in their neighborhood, and as John walked home he spotted Tammany pols strolling his way; among them City Coroner Richard Croker, his brother, and some cronies.

"I passed them and bid them the time of day," Biglin recalled. Just then, Croker spied James O'Brien, an ex-senator and Tammany favorite who had broken ranks to become an Independent Democrat. O'Brien was a scoundrel, disliked by politicians in all parties and hated for enlisting gangs of ruffians to harass voters and stuff ballot boxes. As Croker passed O'Brien he insulted him. The two threw punches. Their comrades joined the brawl. A pistol shot hit an O'Brien henchman. The *Times* reported "although witnessed by a large number of persons, great difficulty was experienced in obtaining the particulars, almost every person giving a different version of the affair." John Biglin became a star witness for the defense at Croker's trial, and his testimony made page-one news. Croker escaped with a mistrial and only years later admitted that a loyal friend had pulled the trigger.[14]

HAYES SWEEPS UP

The patronage and fraud that had flourished throughout both the Johnson and Grant administrations had grandly enriched Arthur, Conkling, and Biglin, along with families and friends. Understandably, all sought to maintain their privileges as the 1876 presidential election neared, and they conspired to keep Grant in the White House for a third term. The three cronies formed a "Stalwart" faction in the Republican Party, then called the "Gallant Old Party" and later the "Grand Old Party" (GOP). In the US Senate Conkling was often at odds with Maine's James G.

Blaine, who headed another GOP faction: Called the "Half Breeds," they favored boldly restructuring the entire federal civil service. Such a reform alarmed Biglin, who was then collecting two salaries at New York's Custom House, as both a clerk and a weigher, while also running the port's baggage-handling monopoly. Rutherford B. Hayes, a US representative and a governor from Ohio who gained the GOP nomination, posed more grief for the Stalwarts when he condemned the spoils system and urged that the federal civil service adopt a merit system for pay and promotions.

Soon after taking office in 1877, Hayes formed a presidential commission to study personnel practices and administration at New York's Custom House. Hayes gave Chester Arthur and his aide, Alonso Cornell, a choice: cease all Republican patronage, or resign. When they refused, Hayes named replacements. But in the Senate Conkling withheld his consent, and Hayes had to wait for Congress to adjourn before appointing his own men. The Senate did approve them, but for years Conkling found ways to undermine the administration's new merit system.[15]

ALDERMAN

In 1876, Barney Biglin feared another close election as assemblyman and ran, instead, for a seat on the New York City Board of Aldermen. Brashly he ignored Hayes's reforms and extorted campaign donations from his Custom House employees. (Later investigated, Biglin swore they were "entirely voluntary.") He won a close race that November, and, once sworn in, Alderman Biglin ingratiated himself with fellow board members by always being first to move that they dispense with reading the last session's minutes.[16]

The *New York Times* had endorsed Biglin over a Tammany Hall lackey when he first ran for the Assembly in 1872, but then covered his political career with scrutiny, and with mounting scorn. A *Times* story in 1878 exposed how, right after joining the board, Biglin had a court stenographer fired, and filled the post with two cronies. A judge who objected said he "had no control over the place, as it belonged to the Republicans and was subject entirely to their disposal."[17]

Shifting his ambitions from federal to city patronage, Biglin joined the board's Public Works Committee and began trading favors large and small. New York City was then installing a network of underground pipes to carry steam to high-rise buildings from heating plants on the East River. (The steam lines were also used to melt ice and snow, and could be tapped to drive fire-engine pumps.) Biglin tried to steer the contract to a shady political ally, Francis B. Spinola, an impudent and sleazy Democrat he had befriended when serving in Albany. The *Times* revealed that when running in 1878 Biglin "made an arrangement with Spinola (steam-pipe) by which 500 votes were to be given to him by each Tammany candidate for District Alderman."[18]

Biglin also profited by voting in a streetcar contract that the *Times* called an "outrageous swindle." He was caught packing GOP nominating conventions with his pals, and flooding certain districts with counterfeit ballots. Despite the Democratic votes from Spinola and Tammany Hall, Biglin polled a sorry fifth and fellow Republicans publicly rejoiced at his defeat.[19]

None of this chicanery distracted Barney from his abiding love for rowing. In 1878, a Columbia College four beat two Oxford crews, becoming the first foreigners to win the Visitors' Challenge Cup at the Henley Royal Regatta. When the transatlantic cable relayed this news, Biglin was eager to celebrate.[20]

His high-flown board resolution praised the win for America over the "nation from whom, a century ago, we won our political independence, and who, until this great victory . . . claimed to be our superiors in manly sports and athletic games, particularly as oarsmen. . . ." *Times* writers clearly relished quoting his orotund speech in an editorial on "Alderman Biglin's Hurrah" that proclaimed:

> *It will be long, we think, before any such florid and expansive specimen of municipal* RHETORIC *can be found in this country. . . . The American Eagle has never soared so high, nor screamed so loud, as on this occasion. . . . For when he was plain "Barney Biglin" his achievements with single and double sculls attracted the attention of two continents.*

After Columbia's crew landed in August 1878, Biglin hosted a reception at Madison Square Garden—and displayed their Henley trophy at Tiffany's.[21]

This jolly diversion aside, the *Times* kept exposing Biglin's political tricks, reporting how his "heelers" had infiltrated a Republican Hall meeting. The *Times* said Biglin's political strength "lies in his hold upon offices of trust and profit, and his protégés were on hand in large numbers."[22]

Even as an ex-assemblyman and ex-alderman Biglin still made headlines. In November 1879 the *Times* accused him of forging a signature supporting his bid to run again for alderman. The paper also published a letter denouncing the many Biglin relatives then in patronage jobs.[23]

Once Arthur's crony Alonzo Cornell was forced from his sinecure at the New York Custom House he ran for governor, defeating the Democratic incumbent. Now GOP patronage would flow from Albany as well as New York City. In 1880 the GOP nominated Arthur to run as James A. Garfield's vice president. In November they won handily.

PRESIDENT ARTHUR

In July 1881 a shock hit Arthur, Biglin, and the whole Republican Party. At a Washington train station President Garfield was shot by a mad federal jobseeker who shouted: "I am a Stalwart and now Arthur is President!" Garfield languished, and despite inept medical care he still survived.[24]

Finally, on September 19, 1881 telegrams reached New York reporting that Garfield had died. Biglin paid a call on Arthur's residence that night, and kept in touch with him after he moved into the White House. They also met for drinks during the president's many visits home to New York, often at The Gilsey House, an ornate luxury hotel on Broadway at 29th Street that was far more elegant than their old Bleecker Street oyster bar. Seated nearby at the Gilsey one day, a *New York Sun* reporter overheard Arthur ask Biglin if he would like a drink. Biglin gave his order. They raised and clinked glasses. After sipping a while, Biglin asked Arthur: "Will you have another drink?"

"Barney!" Arthur scolded, "Never ask a gentleman if he will have 'another' drink. Ask him only if he will have a drink."[25]

In Arthur's company, and on his own, Biglin became a fixture in New York Republican politics, all the while profiting from his Castle Garden baggage franchise. Some 2.8 million immigrants entered the United States during the 1870s, an influx that swelled to 5.2 million in the next decade. After the Irish and Germans came the French and Italians, then the Russians, Hungarians, Romanians, Bohemians, and Greeks. Boosting this mass migration was new technology as steel-hulled steamships replaced smaller wooden vessels driven by sail.[26]

Although consumed by politics, business ventures, and scandals, Biglin still fancied rowing, and in August 1884 he refereed a race between the professional sculler John Teemer and the Canadian champ Wallace Ross on the East River at Oak Point in the Bronx. With usual pique, the *Times* noted how "the men who bet on races were down in all the glory of plaid suits and diamonds, displaying big wads of greenbacks, and offering to wager fabulous amounts upon their favorite."[27]

That November the GOP, which had held the White House since 1861, lost to Grover Cleveland, the popular Democratic governor of New York. After succeeding Garfield as president in 1881, Arthur could never pacify the GOP's angry factions. But he did maintain Barney's loyalty, leading the *Washington Post* to list Biglin among Republicans "regarded as monsters of political iniquity."[28]

Barney's Republican allies at the time included John J. O'Brien, the party's "boss" in New York City and an outspoken lobbyist in Albany against civil service reform. To the *New York Times* O'Brien was a "choice specimen of the East Side slums." But to Barney, O'Brien was his pal and benefactor. After the 1884 election, O'Brien and a crony warily approached the president-elect at a reception in Albany. Just the year before, these two had been Governor Cleveland's bitter adversaries against his statewide electoral reforms. Now they were greeted cordially.[29]

"We have come to see you on a very important matter, Mr. President," O'Brien began.

"Very well, gentlemen, I am pleased to meet you," said Cleveland.

"It's about your Cabinet," O'Brien continued.

"That's a very fruitful topic," Cleveland rejoined.

"Yes," O'Brien resumed, "we've got a man for Secretary of the Treasury."

"Who is the gentleman?" Cleveland asked.

"Well, Mr. President," said O'Brien, in a whisper, "it's Biglin."

"A very good-looking man," Cleveland replied.

"Come now," O'Brien insisted, "that won't do. We came up here to get Biglin appointed and we want a definite answer. The people want Biglin. He would make a splendid Secretary. The question is whether you will appoint him. With Biglin in the Treasury the Administration is bound to be a pronounced success. Without him, there is no means of telling what will happen."

"Well, gentlemen, your suggestion shall receive proper consideration," Cleveland remarked cheerfully.[30]

Biglin's chances were slim. Besides being a GOP worthy, he was by then notorious for taking years of Treasury Department largesse: Custom House jobs for himself, his family, and his pals, and the bountiful baggage franchise that made him richer with each arriving steamship.[31]

Amid political tumult in 1884, Biglin suffered two deep personal losses. That March his nineteen-year-old son, William, died of Bright's disease, a kidney ailment. Even worse, in December Barney lost his thirty-eight-year-old wife. Polly had suffered a stroke in 1881, and was recovering steadily until William's death prostrated her. She seemed well enough to travel with her eldest daughter to visit the five other girls at their boarding school in Ontario, but this trip further weakened her. Around Christmas Polly lost her sight and speech, and she died a few days later. After her death, Barney intensified his political and business pursuits, but also vowed to devote more attention to his surviving daughters.[32]

POLITICAL BAGGAGE

Barney Biglin's profiteering drew steady complaints as his baggage service worsened. He faced a state investigation in 1885, a federal review in 1887, and a congressional hearing in 1890. All three proved fruitless, however, as long as the Republicans controlled patronage.

As early as 1882, Biglin had to pay off several passengers who sued him for baggage that was lost or damaged. In 1883, he faced a new challenge when John C. Jacobs, a Brooklyn Democrat in the State Senate, opened hearings on immigration services in the Port of New York—trying, as the *Brooklyn Eagle* put it, "to legislate Mr. Biglin out of his bonanza at Castle Garden." In response, Biglin and New York City's GOP boss John O'Brien took a ferry to Brooklyn where, at Kerrigan's Auction House on Willoughby Street, they paid a call on Hugh McLaughlin, the city's Democratic Party boss. (Brooklyn was an independent city until 1898.) Sitting among the oil lamps, vases, and settees, Biglin and O'Brien made their pitch: Jacobs should "take his hands off" the whole immigration matter, especially that baggage business. An *Eagle* editorial wasn't sure about how this visit to McLaughlin ended, but it was certain about the underlying problems at Castle Garden, and their cause:

> *The experience of travelers entering New York could not have been much more unpleasant had they been shunted into the city through a sewer. The Barge Office and its belongings had been made by the Arthur Administration a Stalwart stamping ground, a monopoly of pickings and of pillage for Biglin & Co.*[33]

Eventually the Treasury Department did open its baggage franchise to public bids. But Biglin, on the sly, put in an anonymous low offer. It won, but was never claimed, so Biglin regained the contract for nearly as cheap a price. After Republicans retook the White House in 1889, Biglin's monopoly grip seemed assured, despite affidavits documenting extortion by his drivers. The *New York Times* mocked his denials with the headline, "Biglin Says He Isn't Bad." Brother Philip had by then been exposed for selling immigrants unauthorized railroad tickets, but the mostly Republican Emigration Commissioners abided Biglin's service, and even agreed to reduce his annual fee.[34]

The joint Congressional Committee on Immigration found that at Castle Garden 90 percent of employees were still Republicans. In 1891, Biglin boldly arranged for his brother Joseph and a cousin to sign on as appraisers at the Custom House. A year before, this cousin had been fired for using his office "as a means of promoting the personal business interests of Bernard Biglin." He had forced merchants "to give Biglin

Barney Biglin's estate at Bellport, New York BERNARD BIGLIN

their trucking business in order to get their goods out of bond," but was still rehired.[35]

In 1892 Ellis Island opened to receive its first arrivals, replacing Castle Garden at the Battery as the landing station for US customs and immigration. Biglin groused that this raised his expenses, now requiring both water and land transport. The Immigration Service let him boost his charge for each piece of baggage from twenty-five to thirty-five cents. To no one's surprise, a few months later Biglin was caught charging fifty cents apiece.[36]

Biglin finally lost the franchise in 1908 when caught charging immigrants for transport to Grand Central Terminal but forcing them to ride the subway. In the 1890s, Barney was flush with citywide baggage business and bought a twenty-acre estate on Long Island's south shore at Bellport, where he built a twenty-room Italianate "cottage." He sold his townhouse to move into the elegant Wolcott Hotel on East 31st Street by Fifth Avenue.[37]

For three decades Biglin had dominated the New York Harbor baggage business, and had prospered deftly thanks to GOP patronage and his own predacious style. The archives of the US Immigration and Naturalization Service reveal the sorry nature of his franchise by its title in the document catalogue: "Several files pertain to investigation of fraud practiced upon immigrants by private contractors . . . Some of these criminals were contractors with Ellis Island (such as Baggage Agent Bernard Biglin). . . ."[38]

Living comfortably at the Wolcott, with pleasant getaways to his Bellport estate, Barney Biglin was eighty-three when he developed bronchial pneumonia. The illness was brief and fatal. He died on May 11, 1924, at Flower Hospital in New York City. Barney was buried in the Biglin family plot in Calvary Cemetery, next to his brother John and—as it happened—in the shadow of a looming monument to his longtime Republican patron John J. O'Brien.[39]

James Hamill and Walter Brown in their Great Five Mile Rowing Match for $4,000 and the Championship of America at Newburg Bay, Hudson River, New York, September 9, 1867 CURRIER & IVES 1867

Max Schmitt in a Single Scull (1871) by Thomas Eakins THE METROPOLITAN MUSEUM OF ART

Thomas Eakins sculling in *Max Schmitt in a Single Scull*
THE METROPOLITAN MUSEUM OF ART

Perspective drawing for *The Pair-Oared Shell* (1872) by Thomas Eakins
THE PHILADELPHIA MUSEUM OF ART, PURCHASED WITH THE THOMAS SKELTON HARRISON
FUND

The Pair-Oared Shell (1872) by Thomas Eakins THE PHILADELPHIA MUSEUM OF ART, GIFT OF MRS. THOMAS EAKINS AND MISS MARY ADELINE WILLIAMS, 1929

The Biglin Brothers Racing (1872) by Thomas Eakins THE NATIONAL GALLERY OF ART. GIFT OF MR. AND MRS. CORNELIUS VANDERBILT WHITNEY, 1953

The Biglin Brothers Turning the Stake (1873) by Thomas Eakins THE CLEVELAND MUSEUM OF ART, HINMAN B. HURLBUT COLLECTION

Perspective Drawing for the Biglin Brothers Turning the Stake (c. 1873)
THE CLEVELAND MUSEUM OF ART, MR. AND MRS. WILLIAM H. MARLATT FUND

John Biglin in a Single Scull (c. 1873) watercolor THE METROPOLITAN MUSEUM OF ART, FLETCHER FUND

John Biglin in a Single Scull (1874) oil YALE UNIVERSITY ART GALLERY, WHITNEY COLLECTIONS OF SPORTING ART, GIVEN IN MEMORY OF HARRY PAYNE WHITNEY, B.A. 1894, AND PAYNE WHITNEY, B.A. 1898, BY FRANCIS P. GARVAN, B.A. 1897, M.A. (HON.) 1922

JOHN TEEMER.
ALLEN & GINTER'S
Cigarettes.
RICHMOND.   VIRGINIA.

Tobacco company Allen & Gintner trading cards featured professional
rowers. THOMAS E. WEIL JR. COLLECTION

Tobacco company Allen & Gintner trading cards featured professional rowers.
BILL MILLER COLLECTION

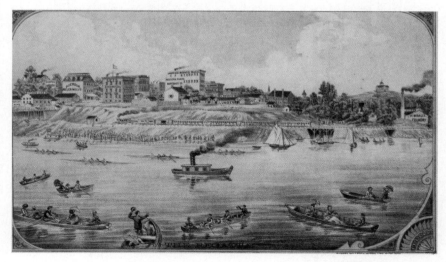

An 1882 regatta at Lawrence, Kansas, drew amateurs and professionals from the
East Coast and even London's Thames Rowing Club   KANSAS HISTORICAL SOCIETY

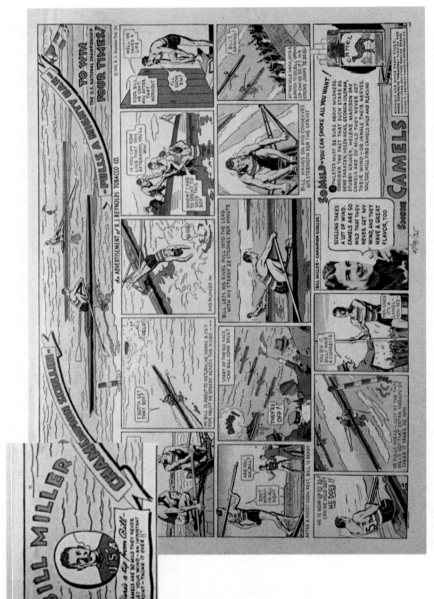

(detail)

Champion sculler Bill Miller in a 1935 Camel cigarette ad from the *Philadelphia Inquirer*. *PHILADELPHIA INQUIRER*, COMICS, MAY 19, 1935. BILL MILLER COLLECTION

Part Three

Ruin and Revival

CHAPTER 11

Courtney v. Hanlan

IN THE HISTORY OF PROFESSIONAL ROWING, TWO YOUNG MEN ARE remembered for raising the sport to national and global acclaim by their ambition and talents, then for compounding its disgrace and downfall by their greed and guile. Yet with the professional sport they helped ruin now long forgotten, both are remembered today: Charles Courtney as a revered college coach, and Edward "Ned" Hanlan as an international sports celebrity. Like Ellis Ward, Courtney became a legendary college coach after his dubious rowing career. But if Ward's deceit when posing as an "amateur" in 1875 was a shameful one-time mistake, Courtney's malign antics throughout the decade he raced for money earned him censure then and a sullied reputation now.[1]

Charles Edward Courtney was a powerful oarsman whose special skills earned him a distinguished record as an amateur, which makes his scandals as a professional seem feckless and all the sorrier. His parents emigrated from Ireland, met and married in Salem, Massachusetts, then moved in 1840 to Union Springs, a village on Cayuga Lake in upstate New York. Charles was born there on November 13, 1849, the sixth of their seven children. He grew to be a strapping six-foot lad who made the town's bustling waterfront a favorite place to play, and then to work. "I could row a boat when I was seven and go anywhere on the water," he recalled, "and we had races between the boys about every evening after school."[2]

Charles was only six when his father died, forcing the family to survive by his mother's hard work and her children's odd jobs. Charles earned money around the boatyards, and built his own rowboats both for sale and for fun. He quit school to learn carpentry, and with brother John set up a business in town: Window sashes, stair casings, and wooden-spoked wagon wheels were their specialties. A skilled cabinet-maker, Charles invented a self-propelled cart for children he called the "Irish Mail," and he built a rowing machine he used for practice in his shop.[3]

On a dare, nineteen-year-old Courtney took a homemade boat and oars down the lake to a water carnival at Aurora, in August 1868. Courtney was amazed to see that racing shells could be made of paper, and awed by their trim lines and light weights. The *New York Times* later told how spectators "came upon a rudely constructed canoe, cumbersome and with a pair of oars beside it, seemingly out of place among the sleek, shining, glistening racing shells. They laughed, most of them," as it was Courtney's handmade craft, and he felt "overcome with shame."

But "at the pistol, Courtney jumped out ahead with his awkward contraption." He held the lead, surprised more than anyone, and afraid that his rivals' "newfangled" boats would in some baffling way catch him. They never came close. "Much to their disgust and to the delight of the crowd, I crossed the line when they were still desperately trudging along somewhere down the course, and my first race was won." At Buffalo, two years later, Courtney saw the professional sculler Henry Coulter race, and decided to buy himself a racing shell. It was in a single that Courtney's strength and style gained him fame. He won a race at Ithaca in 1872. At Syracuse in 1873 he bested two scullers up from New York City, winning a three-mile race by a quarter-mile.[4]

But it was at age twenty-three, in 1873, when Courtney first discovered what riches he might gain by consorting with professional gamblers—an alliance his defenders later blamed for his villainous behavior and undoing. Courtney was then earning a dollar a day in his Union Springs carpenter shop when a friend from town landed a summer job at the opulent Grand Union Hotel in Saratoga Springs. There the friend touted Courtney's rowing feats, and organizers of a September regatta invited him to race. Neighbors and a generous doctor helped Courtney buy a new racing shell, for $126 (about $2,500 today), and he was eager to compete.

Courtney boarded the train for Saratoga with just $15 in his pocket; this, he assumed, would cover expenses for more than a week while training and racing. So at the Grand Union Hotel he was stunned when room and board cost $3.50 a day. "I nearly dropped," he later recalled.

> *I went into the dining-room and I was never so scared in my life. I had never been as far away from home, and I felt so awkward and green that I imagined every one was looking at me; I simply couldn't eat, hungry as I was. If I reached for a fork, I stuck my fingers into the butter, the soup was so hot I burned my tongue, and in reaching for a glass of water I knocked over the celery dish and things were a mess. The waiter glared at me. I thought the best thing for me to do was to bolt; so out I rushed, feeling that I had made myself a laughing stock. I walked along the lake and, about the time I cooled down, came to Moon's Hotel. That looked good to me and in I went.[5]*

Wandering by Moon's at the north end of Saratoga Lake proved a lucky stroll, for it was there Courtney met "an old friend," John Morrissey, "who immediately took me under his wing." At first, this friendship seems a mystery. Courtney was a small-town carpenter, awkward and naïve on his first visit to this glamorous spa. Morrissey, by contrast, was a celebrity: an Irish-born bare-knuckle prizefighter and New York City gang leader who had been twice elected to the US Congress. He was best known as a wealthy gambler with investments in more than sixty clubs. Morrissey had founded the popular racetrack at Saratoga Springs in 1863, opened the casino there in 1866, and in 1871 had begun staging regattas on the lake for professional and amateur rowers. Yet while this was Courtney's first time at Saratoga, he may well have surmised that Morrissey had bet on him before, knew about his powerful showings in upstate races, and was likely behind his invitation to compete there.[6]

By Courtney's account, Morrissey introduced him to proprietor Charles B. Moon, and they all sat down at the family table for a memorable dinner of partridge, brook trout, and black bass. More at ease after this reception, Courtney settled in at Moon's and turned to practicing for the amateur singles race. When not rowing, Courtney often lay on the grass behind the boathouse, "as I didn't like to be stared at as one fresh from the country" and he resented that "it had been noised around how green I was." Yet Morrissey proved to be a stout patron, who "ever after looked out for me" and "never failed to come by each day, or to send someone to see how I was getting along." Courtney worried about his skimpy finances, and, later said, "when I plucked up courage one day and told Mr. Moon how much money I had and wondered whether that would see me through the eight days before the race, he just laughed, and guessed it would be enough."[7]

Relieved, Courtney trained hard for a week, but was still "pretty nervous" as he eyed the twelve other scullers along the starting line for their two-mile race. His first few strokes were swift, "as if it were a hundred-yard sprint," and he shot out so fast spectators shouted "Whoa, whoa!" and laughed. Courtney said he "thought they were making fun of me" and "rowed all the harder." Still holding a wide lead near the finish, Courtney relaxed enough to look about. He spotted a lady and a young man in a boat, and heard him call to offer a glass of lemonade. "You have time enough," he shouted. This jollity only drove Courtney to pull harder, and he won by a quarter-mile in fourteen minutes fifteen seconds—a minute under professional Josh Ward's course record. "They all thought it was a wonderful performance," Courtney remembered, "but I had a minute up my sleeve even then, if the water had been smooth." For his efforts Courtney received a handsome engraved silver pot, and soon discovered even bigger rewards.[8]

When Courtney asked to pay his bill Mr. Moon said, "Well, young man, come with me into the sitting-room and we'll settle up." Courtney recalled, "we went in and he sat down at a table and pulled out a roll of bills and counted them. 'There!' he said, 'I won three hundred dollars on this race—you take half of it.' He insisted upon my taking the money, and he didn't charge me a cent for board besides, and then he hitched up his horses and took me and my boat back to Saratoga." Before leaving, Courtney met a Union Springs man who said "he had placed a little on the race, and as I had done all the work I ought to have a share in the result. He had won six hundred dollars and gave me half of it. I felt like a Rothschild. I never had so much money before."[9]

During his nine years as an amateur, Courtney rowed eighty-eight races. He won them all, including the international single-sculls championship at the Centennial Regatta in Philadelphia. When he turned professional the next year he went on to win forty-six more races while losing only seven. But it was *how* he won, and *why* he lost, that fouled his reputation. On the water and off, Courtney was unpredictable. Always quick to take offense, he was suspicious and shy. He haggled over contracts and race details. To skew the betting odds he exploited and faked his physical condition: sometimes concealing, sometimes feigning, illness. He dickered over details, proposing when—or even if—he might compete. He contrived "accidents" to confound his foes and excuse or avoid defeats. At first, these quirks were taken as signs of Courtney's rustic roots or

Charles Courtney stereograph for the Centennial Regatta at Philadelphia (1876) THOMAS E. WEIL JR. COLLECTION

prickly personality. But these faults grew so outrageous that finally a *New York Times* reporter questioned his sanity in print. Then, in an editorial, the paper unloaded. It branded him a "welcher" (one who didn't pay his debts) and a "miserable imposter" whose "appearance anywhere among decent people is an insult."[10]

How could such a bumpkin be so good at rowing and yet so bad as a notable competitor? Even Courtney's supportive friend and biographer, Cornell physical-education professor Charles Van Patten Young, had to shake his head. In Young's biography of Courtney he concluded: "The probable explanation for some of the actions of which he was guilty during this period was that he not only became intoxicated with success, as he himself intimated, but was early seized upon by professional gamblers, who took advantage of his inexperience and callowness and used him for their own ends."[11]

Courtney's last contest before turning pro typified how weird troubles marred his rowing career. In July 1877, he was to race the professional sculler James E. Riley from Saratoga, at the resort town of Greenwood Lake, New York. This race was technically "amateur" because there was a trophy but no prize money at stake. Yet the gambling on it was intense, and Courtney later admitted that he only participated after being secretly promised half the grandstand receipts and a quarter of the railroads' excursion fares. The *New York Times* was keenly skeptical about the race, reporting, "New York City had sent a large delegation of her 'toughest' citizens. Thieves, swindlers, gamblers, and ruffians of every sort were to be met with on every hand."[12]

Courtney was the odds-on favorite by race day. He seemed poised and relaxed at his hotel as he tucked into a hearty lunch of mutton. But when he ordered an iced tea it was later noted that the hotel manager insisted on mixing it himself. Courtney took a swig. "My God!" he said, "that's the worst tea I ever drank, I feel very bad!" He rose from his chair, reeled, vomited, and staggered upstairs to his room. There he complained of stomach pains, sweating, and chills.

With Courtney ailing all afternoon, Riley rowed over the course and claimed victory. But the *New York Times* exposed a broader scheme, noting how betting parlors in Hoboken had shifted odds quickly from

Courtney to Riley even before that noontime meal. "Within an hour or two of the time fixed for the race . . . Riley became a prime favorite, and as high as two to one was wagered that he would win. The lowest class of turf gamblers and 'sports' laid their money heavily on Riley, and with a confidence and boldness which, to outsiders, seemed incomprehensible." At day's end, "Among the 'inner circles' of the betting fraternity," the *Times* revealed, "the feeling was general that Courtney was bound to be defeated by some means—fair if possible, foul if necessary—and the result, therefore, surprised no one."[13]

Some critics accused Courtney of faking the poisoning because he feared losing. This charge he stoutly denied. But suspicions lingered, and only grew as Courtney opened his ignoble career as a professional sculler a month later. Then he rowed at Saratoga for the Championship of America against Riley and Fred Plaisted. Special trains hauled the rowers' many fans to town, and Saratoga promoter John Morrissey added $500 to the $100 each contestant's backers contributed. Crowds lined the lakeshore, and publisher Frank Leslie, whose mansion stood near where races started and finished, that day hosted aboard his steam yacht William H. "Billy" Vanderbilt. Billy had just become the richest man in America after the death of his father, industrialist and railroad tycoon Cornelius Vanderbilt. A sportsman who spent freely on yachts and thoroughbreds, Billy also bet on professional rowers, and he staked prize money for their match races.

Courtney won the three-mile race, finishing three lengths ahead of Riley. But his victory was clouded because Plaisted's manager had bet on Courtney. A fix was suspected when, with a mile to go, Plaisted stopped rowing. A *Times* reporter later investigated to find that Plaisted had nearly fainted and collapsed, and was truly ill when he quit the race. But this incident only served to foreshadow Courtney's many suspect races as a professional.[14]

Courtney beat Riley twice more that fall, although doubts about his honesty expanded. When back home on Cayuga Lake, in the spring of 1878, Courtney lost a race to James Dempsey, a blacksmith from nearby Geneva. Suspiciously, and despite flat water, Courtney's shell upset and he had to swim ashore. The two soon arranged a rematch on Seneca Lake at

Geneva, rowing three miles for $1,000. Again Courtney was the bookies' favorite. Again there was a mishap. This time, while turning the stake at mid-course, he somehow caught an oar on what he later claimed was an underwater wire. Again he capsized. No wire could be found, and the referee called for a new race. In the rematch, on Skaneateles Lake, Courtney won with ease. These races made it clear: Courtney could win when he wished to, or lose at will.[15]

More than a month later, and still carping about pains in his side from that mishap with the "wire," Courtney appeared at Silver Lake, near Plymouth, Massachusetts. Acting "discouraged and depressed" he complained about being sick since before he left home. Still, Courtney was expected to win, and he told a *New York Times* reporter he would "pull because he had promised that he would, and because his mother, who was formerly a New-England girl, was particularly anxious to have him row in Massachusetts and create a favorable impression here." Crowds trailed Courtney to his boathouse. As he launched his paper shell the fans cheered loudly "and to gratify the spectators he took a short spin up the lake and close in shore, where all could see his magnificent stroke." Courtney was rowing against his colleague and sometime trainer "Frenchy" Johnson. Also in this race were the wily professionals Ellis Ward and James Riley.

Johnson and Riley led to the turn. When trailing on the home stretch, Courtney—in now predictable form—stopped rowing. He casually told the referee he was "dizzy" though admitted being "not in the least tired." Johnson won over Riley, setting a new record. Then Courtney "came rowing slowly down the course past the crowds and to the boat-house, amid a dead silence, only broken by an occasional disparaging remark, as the great oarsman, looking neither to the right nor the left, pulled up to the float." Sympathetically, the *Times* reporter wrote that Courtney "is certainly a very sick man mentally, and, as I honestly believe, physically as well," and shared his regret how "it has of late become so customary for a foul or accident of some sort to occur in Courtney's races...."[16]

THREE RACES, THREE DISGRACES

Courtney's quirky ways only worsened when he entered three infamous match races against Edward "Ned" Hanlan from Toronto, himself a crafty competitor known for suspicious behavior and surprising outcomes. Hanlan had won with ease the professional single-sculls races at the 1876 Centennial Regatta, becoming world champ. The next year he beat Wallace Ross from New Brunswick for the Canadian championship, and a year later took the American title from Pittsburgh's esteemed sculler Evan Morris.

Unlike Courtney, a six-footer with a long even stroke, Hanlan was just under five feet nine inches tall. He maximized his power by compressing—then expanding—his body in energy bursts. As one of the first professionals to master the sliding seat, this gave him extra reach and pushed the full force of his brawny legs into every stroke. "His ability to co-ordinate the strength of his whole body enabled him to defeat much larger opponents," noted *The Canadian Encyclopedia*.[17]

"Hanlan's lower-class Irish background did not endear him to Toronto's snobbish upper- or middle-class British sportsmen who were

Woodcut of Edward "Ned" Hanlan *THE MODERN OARSMAN* BY ED. JAMES, 1878

dominant in the organization of rowing," wrote sports historian Don Morrow. Hanlan was born on July 12, 1855 to an immigrant family. His father was a fisherman who also ran a hotel on Toronto Island in the harbor, and it was there young Ned first learned to row a fishing skiff, "either in pursuit of angling or in the business of illegally smuggling rum across Lake Ontario to his father's hotel." Ned was also known as a brawler and hard drinker with a quick temper. But setting class distinctions aside, Toronto's elite formed The Hanlan Club in 1876 to organize his finances and arrange his races, leaving him free to practice and compete. Like Courtney, Hanlan could be cunning and aggressive when racing, and at Boston's City Regatta in 1877 he was barred after fouling Fred Plaisted and "Frenchy" Johnson at the turning stake.[18]

For the first of their three unsavory races, Courtney and Hanlan met at Lachine, on the Island of Montreal in the Saint Lawrence River, in October 1878. Widely publicized, the race stirred an emotional following as a proxy struggle between the United States and Canada. Their five-mile race for $6,000 (plus a side bet between them for another $4,000) began with Courtney grabbing the lead. Both men pulled mightily, and the odds shifted minute-by-minute. Nearing the finish they were even, when across the course drifted wooden barges. Courtney stopped, then pulled on, while Hanlan darted around them to cross the line a boat-length ahead. But the barges weren't the only suspect features of this race: The *New York Times* reported that Courtney was clearly the stronger oarsman, and the "sorrowful conclusion" by his closest friends was that "he had sold the race."

One story given for a fix was that Courtney owed $2,000 on a mortgage, and this amount was his kickback for losing. A *Times* investigation refuted that rumor, blaming Courtney's loss solely on those mysterious drifting barges. The quick shift in odds for Courtney before the race, the *Times* explained, swelled from a betting frenzy that began in upstate New York, then spread by telegraph nationwide. Also, that mortgage was not due for two years. Yet, even the supportive *Ithaca Tribune* reported, "the general belief here is that Courtney sold yesterday's race," citing as evidence his erratic steering and low stroke-rate—never above thirty-two in the last mile. All this Courtney denied, blaming his loss on "rough water." The *New York Clipper* reported "an alleged dishonorable bargain" among the rowers and their backers "whereby the Union Springs sculler had bound himself to lose the race whether able to win it or not."[19]

Press reports and rumors sustained a belief that the two oarsmen had schemed with their syndicates for Hanlan to win this first race, Courtney a second, and then either one to take a third. This three-race plot Courtney finally admitted to years later, and it helps explain how weirdly their second meeting occurred and, perhaps, also the third.

Before he could face a rematch with Courtney, Hanlan rowed two other races that proved to be shady. In the first, on the Tyne at Newcastle in June 1879, Hanlan won the English championship easily (by eleven lengths) against William Elliott. Too easily, it was soon revealed. An item on "Professional Crookedness" in *Wilkes' Spirit of the Times* reported that Elliott's backers had "weakened" before the match, and Hanlan himself secretly put up the last forty pounds of the two hundred that each side was to contribute. If Elliott had forfeited, Hanlan would have won nothing. But with Elliott rowing, Hanlan could "win all the money which a confiding and patriotic English people will bet on their champion." Even Elliott's backers put their money on Hanlan "for enough to pay for their time and trouble," leaving the betting public the losers.[20]

Clearly, Hanlan was a preeminent sculler—when he chose to be. Beginning in 1880, he won the world sculling championship seven times; first on the Thames, then on the Tyne, and once at Point of Pines outside Boston when besting John A. Kennedy, America's second challenger.[21]

Hanlan was feted in New York when returning with the English championship in July 1879. A three-mile flotilla greeted his steamer as it chugged into Toronto Harbor, and a Hanlan Gala Day honored him at the city's Horticulture Gardens. Wasting little time, the Hanlan Club set a match on Kempenfelt Bay near Barrie, Ontario, against the infamous James Riley in August, for what one newspaper would headline "An Aquatic Burlesque." Hanlan took the lead and held it to mid-course, but near the finish Riley was gaining on him. Abruptly, Hanlan stopped rowing. Riley stopped too, and refused to cross the line first. Riley had bet on Hanlan, and could not afford to win this race. Another account mentioned that at mid-course Hanlan had halted when an unknown sculler crossed his path, nearly colliding. "Most of the spectators," the *New York Times* reported, "are of the opinion that the stranger was there on purpose," giving Hanlan an excuse to stop because he'd bet against himself. When the judges declared a draw, Hanlan refused a re-row and forfeited the prize money.[22]

Both the public and the professional gamblers awaited a Hanlan-Courtney rematch, and in 1879 two wealthy gents offered a $6,000 prize for the race. One was Billy Vanderbilt; the other was James Gordon Bennett Jr., enterprising publisher of the *New York Herald* and an avid sponsor of sporting events. Besides running thoroughbreds, Bennett was first to introduce polo and tennis matches to the United States, and he had won the first transatlantic yacht race in 1866. Hanlan and Courtney accepted the Vanderbilt-Bennett challenge, but from spring to summer the two sponsors bickered over details about the race, and finally withdrew their purse.[23]

To the rescue came Asa T. Soule, head of the Hop Bitters Company in Rochester. He matched the proposed $6,000 prize and set a race in western New York on Lake Chautauqua, for October 1879. Hop Bitters was a popular patent medicine touted as "The Invalid's Friend and Hope." Compounded from hops, mandrake, buchu, and dandelion, the mix promised to cure nervousness, sleeplessness, female complaints, and drunkenness, along with all diseases of the stomach, bowels, blood, liver, kidney, and urinary organs. Hop Bitters was a grand commercial success, no doubt for another ingredient: It was 12 percent alcohol.[24]

The course was to start and end at the lake's Fair Point by the Chautauqua Institution's busy campgrounds, run west to Mayville, and after turning stakes by the town's waterfront return to finish where it began. A rail line was laid along the lakeshore for an excursion train to follow the action. Gamblers and prostitutes and con men invaded Mayville. The New York City odds-makers Quimby & Forse set up "sentry boxes" on street corners to sell bets. A beer garden opened by the lake. And from his pulpit a Presbyterian minister warned, "The seven plagues of Egypt swarm about us and Hell's foul rays are focused upon our unhappy village."

For his part, Soule was delighted that his investment had become the nationally celebrated Hop Bitters Prize. Courtney even named his new paper shell *Hop Bitters*. A wily businessman, Soule boasted to a journalist that he squeezed commissions from the railroads, excursion and sightseeing boats, the builders of grandstands, owners of hotels and boarding-houses, and "all the games, straight and skin" [crooked] that flourished in town.[25]

A few days before the race, Courtney went to William Blaikie, the former Harvard oarsman and New York attorney who had agreed to be referee. Courtney revealed that Hanlan's friends had urged a fix, for Hanlan to win, and had threatened his life if he reneged. After this, Courtney carried a pistol. At first the odds favored Hanlan. But with two days to go, panicky telegrams clacked in from betting parlors across the United States and Canada. As the *New York Times* explained, "All of a sudden word came that the pool-selling had stopped everywhere . . ." in San Francisco, Denver, Chicago, Cincinnati, Pittsburgh, Philadelphia, Hoboken, New York, Boston, and Halifax. In cipher and in slang the telegrams were the same: "Give us the tip" or "How is it fixed?" or "Who is to be the winner?" or "Hurry up your pointer" or "Lots of money ready when we hear what the steer is." Something nasty was afoot, with more intrigue to come.[26]

Courtney awoke the morning of the race to learn that during the night his racing and practice shells had been sawed in two. Both were custom-made paper boats. He rejected offers of cedar shells by Hanlan, and by his trainer "Frenchy" Johnson. The season was late, and Courtney claimed that another paper shell could not be made for two weeks. Given this situation, he withdrew. Hanlan expected to collect the prize money and rowed over the course; but Soule refused to pay, insisting on a two-man race.

Again the press was quick to spot a conspiracy. There was one rumor that Courtney had reneged on the alleged three-race deal, and was determined to win at Chautauqua, prompting Hanlan's men to ruin the shells. Another rumor was that they had sawed the shells because Hanlan was drunk the night before, and in no condition to race. But deal or no, Courtney also drew suspicion of the deed: to avoid a race he might lose. Arguing about who cut the shells thrived for years, and "Who Sawed Courtney's Boat?" became a catchphrase, a folk song, and an unanswered riddle.[27]

Missing no chance to scorn corruption, the *New York Times* was quick to declare:

> *The moralist who has watched with dismay the steady growth of that class of crimes commonly known as "athletic sports," will be little surprised at the recent outrage committed at Chautauqua by certain rowing malefactors. It had been advertised for some time that two of the most prominent oarsmen in the country were to publicly engage in the swindling game known as a rowing match . . . for a stake of $6,000. An immense crowd assembled, and bets were made to an estimated extent of $700,000—no less than $370,000 being bet in pools alone.*[28]

The paper reminded readers, "This is the fourth time that some unforeseen accident has prevented him [Courtney] from winning a boat-race, and it is to be hoped that this time he has made enough to enable him to live without further pursuing the profession of failing to row races."[29]

Outrage came from other papers as well, the *Syracuse Courier* complaining about "a widespread feeling of disgust. . . ." Charles S. Francis, editor of the *Troy Times* who had been a skilled Cornell oarsman, wrote grandly, "It seems as if never since the firing on Fort Sumter did an event so arouse the anger of the American people. In every city, village and hamlet, wherever a telegraph wire or a newspaper penetrated, the storm of indignation raged." Insults and rumors lingered. Courtney revealed a letter from Soule promising him $2,000 whether he won or lost. To that, Hanlan produced a letter from Courtney offering him $3,000 to throw the race.[30]

The "Chautauqua Lake Fizzle" dismayed both rowing's fans and financiers. But as tempers eased, and time passed, both Courtney and Hanlan praised Soule. He, in turn, declared his continued support. The two oarsmen were famously headstrong, but for Courtney at his crankiest nothing topped his third race with Hanlan. Courtney haggled for months with Soule and Blaikie. He also bickered with Hanlan over how to split the railroad receipts. But finally a date was set, for a five-mile race on the Potomac at Washington, DC, on May 19, 1880. The Hop Bitters Prize

Cartoon showing *"Courtney, fully prepared for emergencies, goes to meet Hanlan."* FRANK LESLIE'S ILLUSTRATED NEWSPAPER, MAY 22, 1880

was still $6,000, and qualms about Courtney shenanigans ran stronger than ever. His predictably erratic conduct raised new worries, among both the "sporting men" who bet on rowers for a living and the two rowers' many ardent fans.[31]

Mocking Courtney's fickle ways, the *New York Times* proposed "a sixteenth amendment, declaring that in no circumstances shall a proposition be made to or accepted by Mr. Courtney to row a race with anybody." The popular *Frank Leslie's Illustrated Newspaper* featured a cartoon showing Courtney "fully prepared for emergencies" as he strode to meet Hanlan, bearing to the water's edge his racing shell, two oars, and a saw.[32]

Newspapers across Canada and the United States speculated about the coming race, and both rowers were welcomed as celebrities when they arrived at Washington. Matthew Brady, the famed photographer who had chronicled the Civil War and often portrayed President Lincoln, sat Hanlan for a portrait—but was rebuffed by Courtney, who complained about not feeling well. Courtney moved into the Riggs House at 15th and G Streets NW and Hanlan set up headquarters at Willard's Hotel at 14th Street and Pennsylvania Avenue NW. The opulent Willard lobby filled with admirers, and swarmed with gamblers. The hotel even staged a gala boat-race party.

This third Courtney-Hanlan race was an extravaganza, until it became a farce. Hats and cigars were sold banded with the oarsmen's names and pictures. Banners sold in the men's racing colors: cardinal red for Hanlan, blue for Courtney. Pickpockets disguised as priests worked the crowds. Congress adjourned early. Schools let out for the afternoon, and government clerks were excused from their offices. On the course the US Signal Corps prepared to hoist red and blue balloons at relative heights every quarter-mile to display the scullers' positions. Navy launches patrolled the river, manned with armed guards to ward off any interference.[33]

Spectators clambered onto grandstands lining Georgetown's waterfront, where the race would start and end. The shoreline downstream to the turning stake by Long Bridge (near today's 14th Street Bridge) swarmed with eager fans. A crowd estimated at one hundred thousand included President Hayes, many Cabinet members, and the British ambassador—along with political notables, business tycoons, and show-business celebrities.[34]

William Blaikie was to referee the cancelled Chautauqua Lake race, and for months had persevered to arrange this rematch. Long resigned to dealing with Courtney, Blaikie was relieved once the contract had been inked. But he was then hardly surprised to learn, on the eve of the Washington race, that Courtney suddenly complained about a "headache." Some of Courtney's friends told newsmen he was ill, but others assured he was well rested and vigorous.

Was he ailing, or again faking to skew the odds? Blaikie had his suspicions, and later told a *New York Times* reporter,

When I went into Courtney's room on the morning of the race, Courtney was lying asleep, and I found his brother wiping his head with a sponge. I told him to take off the sponge and let me feel the oarsman's head. I felt of it and of my own, and I said then that Courtney's head was not as hot as mine was. But his brother declared he had a fever, and had said he was not to be called until 3 o'clock in the afternoon.

"Not until 3 o'clock?" Blaikie asked. "Why? Was he restless last night?" Courtney's brother was silent. Again Blaikie asked, "Was he restless last night?"

"Well, no-o," the brother admitted, shaking his head.

Blaikie surmised that "if either of those men had ever been the father of a child they would know that when it has a fever it will play tag all over the bed."

Returning to Courtney's hotel that afternoon, Blaikie determined: "I couldn't see that there was any feverish look about him. His eyes were not

The start of the Courtney-Hanlan race at Washington, DC, 1880. Inset: Courtney gives out after two miles. *FRANK LESLIE'S ILLUSTRATED NEWSPAPER, JUNE 5, 1880, 228*

dull at all, and there were no drawn lines or flabby looks about his face."
Next Blaikie "asked the doctor, who had been called in, to take Courtney's
pulse, and he did so. It was a little under 70. It doesn't strike me that that
is exactly a fever pulse."[35]

Blaikie had called Courtney's bluff, and at the Potomac Boat Club
two hours later, Courtney appeared lively and determined as his hosts
launched him with applause and rip-roaring cheers. To a *New York Times*
reporter Hanlan appeared "plucky" and Courtney looked "fresh and in
good condition." The crowds pressed toward the water as the rowers lined
up under the aqueduct (by today's Key Bridge) for their race downriver
and back.[36]

At the starter's pistol shot Courtney grabbed the lead, but held it
for just a furlong. Hanlan's solid and steady strokes eased his shell even.
Then it pushed ahead. For two miles they raced, until. . . . What happened
next surprised everyone, and no one. Courtney stopped rowing. He sat
and swabbed his face and neck with water. He turned his shell around.
And he pulled back up the course to his dock. There, "with hanging head
and a dogged, suffering look" he heard a cheer or two, but otherwise
landed amid silent glares. Once Courtney retreated to his hotel, disgusted
Potomac Boat Club members flung his shells and gear into the street.[37]

Headlining "A FARCE ON THE POTOMAC," the *New York
Times* accused Courtney of faking illness "for the sole purpose of influ-
encing betting." Courtney's own doctor admitted to a reporter that his
patient had been "in fine condition" before the race, "although at first he
was unwilling to announce the results of his diagnosis." The *Times* surmised: "Some declare that the man's real trouble is ineradicable cowardice,
and others believe that his course is in accordance with the terms of some
secret contract." Again, rumors dogged Courtney about betting against
himself to pay off a mortgage, which, that year, was actually due. This
third suspicious Courtney-Hanlan race left the public more disgusted
than ever with professional rowing. But for the many boisterous spectators, the allure of betting and drinking and fighting at regattas held
abiding appeal, and there were still a few pro rowers capable of even more
outrageous exploits. This rich and rowdy sport was damaged, but not yet
destroyed.[38]

CHAPTER 12

Courtney v. Courtney

CHARLES COURTNEY'S REPUTATION WAS WRECKED, WITH NO CLEAR WAY to redeem it. He nonetheless endured the scorn and maintained he was still a competitive oarsman. But who would race him now? Who would bet on him, to win—or to lose?

Clearly appalled by the spectacle on the Potomac, a *New York Times* editorial grumbled, "For several years Mr. Courtney has been more of a burden than the most objectionable grasshopper could possibly have been. The great question whether Mr. Courtney could be induced to row with this or that oarsman has been forced on the attention of the public until the mildest and best of men have even wished that he were dead." The *Times* reminded readers of the "wire" that had ruined a race for Courtney, and said sarcastically he should claim to be paid for his "personal lack of exertion" whenever he lost. Alluding to ways Courtney attracted trouble, the paper said Courtney's illness on the Potomac "has closed his career as a public oppressor," predicting: "We shall never hear of him again as an oarsman, and his only possible chance of keeping his name before the public will be for him to back himself to have more headaches or more colic within a given time than any other man."[1]

In his defense, Courtney told the *Washington Post* that he was prostrated by the heat and could not finish the race. Courtney added how he resented attacks by "many well-known sporting men," and then—hinting blackmail—he warned that "if these attacks are not stopped the history of some very interesting boating events may be made public."[2]

After leaving Washington Courtney and Hanlan refused to speak, although they were both quick to utter public challenges for another race. This nearly occurred at a regatta in Toronto, in September 1881. But Hanlan withdrew, claiming he was "out of condition," and when racing there Courtney finished third behind the Canadian Wallace Ross and the American James Ten Eyck. On Saratoga Lake in August 1882, Courtney lost to sculler George W. Lee from Newark—but a month later crushed Lee in record time on Canadarago Lake in upstate New York.

Meanwhile, Hanlan sailed for England, where he won the world sculling title on the Thames in London against Australian Edward Trickett in November 1880. He twice defended the title, beating Australian Elias C. Laycock on the Thames in 1881 and Englishman Robert W. Boyd on the Tyne in 1882. Hanlan was then celebrated as the best single sculler in the world.

EPITHETS FREELY BANDIED

Courtney and Hanlan had no other plans to race, but they did manage to stage a shouting match that drew widespread press. The setting was a regatta on the Saint Lawrence at Ogdensburg, New York, in July 1883. Both men were full of themselves. Hanlan was defending his world sculling championship against fellow Canadian Wallace Ross, and Courtney came to town as Ross's principal judge. Hanlan protested Courtney even participating, but Ross insisted. Hanlan easily beat Ross, then shouted up at the referee's launch: "Bring out Courtney here, now, will you?"[3]

"EPITHETS FREELY BANDIED" was the *New York Times* page-one headline for their bitter encounter after Courtney and Hanlan acted out their anger with theatrical flair. Tensions began when a brass band serenaded the men at their respective hotels. Courtney said he hoped the band would play at a championship race he would row "at no very distant day." Hearing about this remark, Hanlan sent Courtney a defiant note, insisting they meet.

After breakfast next morning, both men strode into regatta headquarters. Hanlan "promptly proceeded to business by offering to make a match for $5,000 on the spot," the *Times* reported in a dispatch it noted had been censored for much foul language. When Courtney stalled, Hanlan bet him another $1,000 he would not even dare take him up. Then, with still no response, Hanlan declared he would race Courtney "on any river, lake, or pond in the world—at your own door if you like. . . ." Still hearing no reply, Hanlan advanced on Courtney.

"You have a reputation of winning against everybody by fair means or foul—principally by foul means," he said. "I give you warning that I will do my best to disqualify you from ever entering a boat-race again unless you accept my offer, because you have done more to injure my profession and yours by dishonest conduct than any man living. You are a duffer [incompetent or stupid], and you don't dare to row." Finally "nettled" for the first time, Courtney spoke.

"How much did you pay for having my boat sawed at Chautauqua?"

"Nothing," Hanlan said, "and you can't prove I paid anything."

"I can come near proving it," said Courtney.

"You are a skin [a skinflint, cheat, or fraud] and almost a thief," Hanlan replied. To this, Courtney drew from his pocket a wad of bank notes, and shouted he would bet $1,000 he could beat Hanlan at Watkins (now Watkins Glen), New York, in a regatta on Seneca Lake scheduled for the next month.

"I'll bet you $1,000 that I beat you," snapped Hanlan.

"Ned," Courtney said, "you know you can't beat me and never could!"

"I can beat you the best day you ever were born," Hanlan said. "If you don't think so put up your money. But you haven't the heart to do it. I don't see how the Americans tolerate you. If you had been born in Canada my countrymen would drown you."

"Yes," Courtney replied, "you would be glad to be rid of me, because you know I'm the only man who can make you row. Why didn't you row at Toronto?"

"Because I was not in condition," said Hanlan. "I did not drink poisoned tea or saw my boat, as you did."

"You paid for both," retorted Courtney.

"You're a liar!" Hanlan shouted.

"You're no gentleman!" said Courtney. "But you can't get me to strike you, no matter what you say." Their rhubarb expanded. Again Courtney goaded Hanlan.

"Anyhow, I'd be willing to bet that you won't row at Watkins."

"I'll bet you $1,000 to $100 that I'll be there," roared Hanlan, "and another thousand that I'll beat you."

Hanlan demanded Courtney put up $5,000, half the prize for a match race. Courtney said he hadn't come there to race or set a match, and didn't have $5,000 on him. Hanlan turned away in disgust, but paused, composed himself, then let loose.

"You're afraid, that [sic] what's the matter with you; you're a duffer," Hanlan said. "I give you warning again that I am going to do everything I can to force you out of this profession which you have disgraced by your dishonest practices." Hanlan stalked out, "leaving Courtney sitting unabashed in a corner."[4]

Comparing rowers' ethics to those of the country's robber-barons, a *New York Times* editorial about this Ogdensburg ruckus said, "What a 'skin' may be we know not, but we infer from Mr. Hanlan's further observation that Mr. Courtney was 'almost a thief,' that to be a skin is to be guilty of indirect forms of larceny which escape the legal definition of that offense. Mr. Jay Gould, for example, might be described by admirers and apologists as a 'skin.'" Jason "Jay" Gould was a financier and speculator who invested in the Erie and the Union Pacific Railroads, and was reviled for trying to corner the gold market in 1869. He once put up $1 million bail to free Tammany Hall's "Boss" Tweed from prison.[5]

Despite their repeated name-calling, both Courtney and Hanlan did arrive at Watkins in mid-August. But they never raced one another. In a trial heat George Lee crowded Courtney's lane. The two nearly clashed oars, and Courtney finished third. When no foul was declared, the crowd growled with anger and regret. This loss kept Courtney from advancing to the finals against Hanlan—who won his heat easily over the able George Hosmer and Wallace Ross. Now freed from racing Courtney, Hanlan softened his tone, and "acted the gentleman" the *Times* observed. "In a speech . . . he manfully apologized to the public for so far forgetting himself at Ogdensburg as to be betrayed into the use of ungentlemanly language."

Yet Hanlan never withdrew his many complaints about Courtney's cowardice and deceit, and a week later still had him in mind. After losing a race to John Teemer at Fall River, Massachusetts, because he capsized at the mid-course buoy, Hanlan declared to a reporter: "I was not hit with a sand bag. I was not poisoned, I used no saw, but I was beaten on my merits." It was curious, though, how a champion like Hanlan capsized twice that day: the first time in a race later invalidated because of confusion at the start; the second in the race Teemer won. In both races (and as if by design), Hanlan, the odds-on favorite, managed to run afoul of the turning buoy, a common way for professionals to throw a race.[6]

OAK POINT ANTICS

By the following spring, Courtney found a new way to anger Hanlan—and most other professional rowers—with his antics before a match-race against Wallace Ross at Oak Point Park in the Bronx. A popular amusement center on the East River, the Oak Point picnic grounds were managed by James Pilkington, the champion amateur athlete who excelled at rowing, pedestrianism, Greco-Roman wrestling, boxing, trap-shooting, tug-o-war, and the shotput. Pilkington was a retired policeman whose beat on Broadway had kept him in contact with New York's social and political elite, including many encounters with former president Ulysses S. Grant and future president Theodore Roosevelt.

Besides organizing and financing regattas for professional rowers, Pilkington ran The Golden Oar, a saloon on Third Avenue near the Harlem River frequented by bookies, betting-syndicate investors, and oarsmen from the busy Boathouse Row nearby. (This was likely America's first sports-celebrity bar, run more than half a century before establishments opened by such famous athletes as boxer Jack Dempsey, baseball great Mickey Mantle, and basketball star Michael Jordan.) Upstairs at The Golden Oar, Pilkington ran faro games and welcomed bets on rowing, horse racing, bowling matches, and anything else worth a wager. When not staging regattas for professional rowers, Pilkington drew crowds to Oak Point with fireworks, band concerts, and sharpshooting exhibitions by Annie Oakley.[7]

Pilkington was at the pier in March 1884 to greet Ross when he landed after winning the English championship. With notable rowers, boxers, and politicians, he hustled Ross off in a carriage parade to a reception at The Golden Oar. Pilkington advanced a $2,500 prize for a

Ross-Courtney race on Decoration Day (May 30), and expected profits from both a huge crowd and his own agile bookmaking.

But with Courtney trouble loomed. As the race neared, rumors sprouted that he sought to avoid this race unless victory was assured. Deception was in the air. A day before the race, the *Times* reported that both Courtney and Ross each "seemed to be pulling his level best, and each was apparently trying to convince the other that he was taking it easy." Such fakery was common among professional rowers as they tried to shift the odds up or down to their favor (depending on whether they might bet for or against themselves). Reporters hounded Courtney about whether he meant to win.[8]

"If I don't win, it will be because I can't row fast enough, that's all," Courtney declared. The reporters should have asked Courtney about whether he even meant to row. He didn't. On race day Courtney complained that the water was too rough, although it seemed fine to Ross and the judges. The angry crowd, quick to believe rumors that Courtney had tried to bribe Ross, was wary to bet. To protect his investment Pilkington postponed the race to June 7.

As that day dawned bright and calm Courtney appeared at the course and joined Ross for a practice row. At noon Courtney and his manager lounged under trees by the Oak Point Hotel, when up stumbled a drunken spectator.

"You old duffer!" he barked to Courtney. "If you don't row this time we'll knock your head off!"

Minutes later, Courtney stood, announced he was "going to the boulevard to get shaved," and strode off. Courtney never returned. Ross sculled out to the referee, who started the race as a row-over. News spread that Courtney could not be found, and the crowds howled: "Kill him!" "Hang him!" "Kick him across the bay!" "The scoundrel has fluked again!"

In a style apocalyptic, the *Times* reporter caught their angry mood:

Then the pent-up hatred of the long-suffering crowd overflowed, and ran down the shore like the roar of surf in a storm. Individual utterances were lost in the general cry of indignation. Men jammed their hats down over their eyes, clenched their teeth, and cursed. Then they opened wide their mouths in blind fury and screeched anathemas at absent Courtney.

Ross rowed the course, accepted the prize, but then admitted that Courtney *had* proposed a fix: giving Ross the money if he would lose. A reporter tracked Courtney to his room at the Astor House, a luxury hotel on Broadway. There, resting not "on his oars" but on his bed, Courtney said matter-of-factly why he had walked away from the Oak Point race: Pilkington failed to pay him the promised one-third cut from his Decoration Day receipts.[9]

That did it for editors at the *Times*. They denounced Courtney in an editorial titled "A Welcher" that called him a "miserable imposter" whose "appearance anywhere among decent people is an insult." Professional rowers can win in two ways, the *Times* averred: "One is to outrow your opponents. This is the method practiced by Hanlan and other eminent oarsmen. . . . The other method is to . . . avoid defeat by refusing to row with any man who will not previously agree to be beaten. This is Courtney's method."

The *Times* lit into Courtney's "poisoned tea, his concealed wires, his sawed boats, and his opportune attacks of colic" as so many frauds on the betting public. The editorial concluded that if Cornell then permitted Courtney to coach its college crew, "They might as well employ Ward to instruct the students in political economy." Ferdinand Ward formed an investment firm with former President Grant in 1880. Using Grant's fame to conceal Ward's own guile he ran a financial scam that had just collapsed, leaving Grant destitute and sending Ward to Sing Sing.[10]

Within a month the *Times* reported a fresh assault on Courtney's sagging reputation: a boycott by his competitors. On July 10, 1884, ten professional rowers issued a public complaint. Because Courtney "has done so much to disgrace professional sculling, we, the undersigned, in order to protect ourselves and encourage square, manly rowing, hereby pledge ourselves never in any respect to associate or connect ourselves with said Courtney, either by rowing with or against him, at regattas or elsewhere." Signers included Wallace Ross, Fred Plaisted, George Hosmer, Albert Hamm, George Gaisel, George Lee, Henry Peterson, James Ten Eyck, James H. Riley, and even the nefarious John Teemer.[11]

Still miffed, the *Times* continued to hound Courtney, warning in another editorial, "If college boys cannot learn to row without associating with persons like Courtney . . . perhaps they would be quite as well off if they devoted a little more time to classics and mathematics and a little less to rowing." But success beat out scolding, and thanks to Courtney's coaching Cornell crews did so well that he was rehired in 1884, despite his shady career.[12]

A FINAL RACE, A FINAL EXCUSE

Hanlan was off in Australia racing a sixth time for the world sculling championship and did not sign the professional rowers' boycott against Courtney. But two years later, he consented to race him one last time, for a $3,000 purse. The men had not spoken for three years, and finally met again at Rockaway Beach, in August 1886, when a local politician intervened. James M. Oakley had been a New York state assemblyman and state senator representing districts in Queens, and in the lobby of the Seaside House he drew the men together.

"Gentlemen," said Oakley, "it's time you shook hands and became friends."

Courtney complied, his eyes tearing as he grasped Hanlan's hand. "Ned, I feel better. This business was too much like two schoolboys."

"You're right, Charlie," Hanlan agreed. Soon they were chatting.[13]

A week later, fans lined Jamaica Bay and "crowded half a dozen big steamers until their deck lines were almost submerged" to follow the three-mile race. The result was a "foregone conclusion" reported the *Times*, "because Courtney had complained he could not row in rough water" and the course was "somewhat choppy" that day. Hanlan did win easily, at one point so far ahead that "in response to great cheering" he "dropped his oars into one hand and doffed his cap twice. This antic nearly set the crowd wild." After trailing by seven lengths, "Courtney rowed up beside the referee's boat and said for once in his life, 'I have no excuses to make. He can beat me at any time.'"

But, of course, Courtney *did* have an excuse: "Everybody knows that I have been sick for the past 10 days, and that I couldn't pull my best this afternoon."[14]

Reputations (Mostly) Redeemed

Their enduring bitterness and corrupt reputations faded eventually as Courtney and Hanlan became coaches and not competitors. But memories endured, and it took some time for Courtney as a coach to prove he wasn't teaching Cornell's oarsmen any legendary dirty tricks. What he did teach them was a disciplined rowing technique and a fierce commitment to physical training, both on the water in paper shells and in the gym using rowing machines he had designed and built. In 1883, Courtney had been hired to coach a Cornell four of novice rowers. He agreed, worked the boys hard, and on Lake George they beat the country's two best crews, from the University of Pennsylvania and Princeton, by thirty-two seconds.[15]

A decade before, colleges were debating how to encourage and fund athletics. A physical-fitness craze energized the country, but with it came fears of professionalism, gambling, and, in the case of "foot-ball," grave injury. In 1873, Cornell's first president, Andrew Dixon White, had joined with the faculty to forbid students from traveling to Cleveland for a football match against the University of Michigan, refusing, as he put it, "to let forty men go four hundred miles just to agitate a bag of wind." A decade later, Cornell and ten other colleges joined to consider banning professional coaching and barring games and races away from campus. But no agreement resulted.[16]

Putting ethical questions aside, many colleges did hire professional rowers as crew coaches, especially for the intercollegiate regattas held in June and July. As early as 1864 Yale had paid the New York professional sculler William Wood to coach its crews, and in 1879 had enlisted the help of another professional, Mike Davis. Harvard's senior class hired Boston's famous professional sculler George Faulkner to help it train for intramural races, and he also coached the varsity.

Disregarding Courtney's foul reputation, the *Cornell Daily Sun* had been mostly positive about him; in part because he was a local figure from just up the lake, in part because he turned out winning crews. In May 1884, the *Sun* reported, Courtney coached at Cornell for two weeks. In May 1885, Courtney was back at Cornell for nearly two months. But at the intercollegiate regatta at Worcester that summer, a rower complained,

Courtney was to "put on the finishing touches on our crew" but "with no excuse deserted us and was not in town until after the crew departed." Still, Cornell's crew rehired Courtney for the 1886 season.[17]

At the time, competitive sports at Cornell were not funded by the university but by subscriptions from students and faculty. The *Sun* became an avid booster for the crew. Each fall the paper urged students to donate money for equipment and coaching, and in 1886 publicized a fund-raising scheme that included an "exciting and laughable" race on Courtney's rowing machines at a local skating rink.[18]

It is not clear what happened next, but after some incident or dispute between Cornell and Courtney he never finished the 1886 season at the school. Instead, gymnastics instructor W. C. Dole took over coaching the crew. The *Sun* concluded he "did the work and did it as well as could be done by a man who did not himself row. . . ." Dole was no slouch, however. He had just set a world record of four hours and fifty minutes for "continuous swinging of Indian clubs."

Courtney's absence from Cornell in 1886 might have been due to his still-cloudy reputation as a professional oarsman, because that July he and John Teemer had rowed double-sculls in Maryland in a race that was widely reported as a barefaced fix. This the *New York Times* condemned with a story headlined "Farcical Boating Race. Clown Courtney Again Makes an Exhibition of Himself."[19]

By January 1887, the *Sun* reported that an old debt had been paid Courtney for past services, perhaps implying his coaching there had ended. In February the paper predicted, "The crew will undoubtedly have a professional coach in the spring and it won't be the noted Mr. Courtney either." Something unpleasant had happened between Courtney and his boys, and in March it was reported that the new coach would be none other than John Teemer. Editors at the *Sun* didn't seem to know about Teemer's fixed Maryland race and notably sour reputation—or they didn't choose to mention it.[20]

Yet Teemer lasted only that one season, no doubt because in 1887 the *New York Times* attacked him by name when denouncing the whole enterprise of professional rowing. Cornell rehired Courtney in the spring of 1888, and when he was condemned in the popular sports magazine

Outing for his "unenviable reputation" the *Sun* stoutly defended both him and the practice of paying professional rowers as university coaches.

Courtney went on to regain some respect, and won growing admiration both at Cornell and even among other rowing colleges. Just as Harvard had considered hiring John Biglin in 1872, after he coached Amherst College to a surprise victory, the university invited Courtney to visit Cambridge in 1893, ostensibly "to advise on rigging." But after word reached Ithaca that Courtney had been seen on the Charles, training students and coaches, the Cornell Athletic Association secured Courtney's "full and exclusive services" with a lucrative three-year contract. This proved a worthy investment because under Courtney's coaching, from 1873 to 1920, Cornell won 117 races and lost only forty-seven.[21]

While Courtney eventually gained praise for Cornell's many victories, he was still chided for being—like John Biglin—too secretive about his training techniques and too rough on his crews. Courtney was so strict about his rowers' diets that he once expelled five varsity crewmembers for eating strawberry shortcake. Even his friend and biographer Charles Young complained that at Henley, where Courtney brought the first American eight to the regatta in 1895, his methods "were extremely distasteful to the English rowing public." Before the race, Courtney "kept his charges so close in hand that social intercourse with their jolly and hospitable rivals was grimly tabooed." This imparted to the Cornellians "the strenuous and secretive life of professional contestants," in contrast to "the spirit of the carnival" that enlivened the regatta.[22]

The English public's disdain stiffened to "positive resentment" against Courtney and Cornell once racing began. The eight's first heat was against the Leander Boat Club, the prior year's champion. After pulling half a dozen strokes Leander protested the start, and quit rowing. Cornell eased its pace. But from his launch the umpire waved them on, and followed down the course. Cornell rowers said afterward they regretted winning by default, but had to obey the umpire. Cornell was leading in its second heat, against Trinity Hall from Cambridge, when a rower "caught a crab which knocked the oar out of his hand, and the crew went to pieces, thus dashing their hopes with a humiliating failure."[23]

Coach Courtney in a launch, c. 1910–1915 GEORGE BANTHAM BAIN COLLECTION, LIBRARY OF CONGRESS

Through the 1880s and 1890s, rowing historian Peter Mallory highlights, "Courtney became the first full-time professional coach to be officially hired by any American college in any sport, and the public knew his name well from his involvement in those questionable races against Hanlan." At first, professionals were hired as "riggers"—adjusting oarlocks to gain uniform height and pitch, for example—while just coaching on the side. Yale did this for sculler John A. Kennedy from Portland, Maine, in 1898, and named him crew coach in 1901. And in 1904, Harvard hired the Australian professional sculler James Wray away from Boston's Union Boat Club.[24]

Hanlan, too, tried some coaching, but with less success than Courtney gained. In 1897 he became head coach for the University of Toronto Rowing Club, and three years later was hired away by Boston's Union Boat Club. Hanlan then trained Columbia's oarsmen for the Intercollegiate Rowing Association's national championship at Poughkeepsie, in 1900. Under Hanlan's direction Columbia never won the IRA regatta, but with delight did once finish second to the dominant Cornell crew in 1901. In later life, Hanlan took up running his father's hotel on Toronto

Island, and became a city alderman. In 1908, Hanlan contracted pneumonia and died, at age fifty-two.[25]

Courtney coached Cornell until 1920, the year he died from a stroke at age seventy. Beginning in 1883, Courtney's Cornell crews established a formidable record. In IRA regattas Cornell's varsity won fourteen of its twenty-four races, and six times finished second. In its thirty-nine dual or triple races with the country's dominant college crews—from Harvard, Yale, or Princeton—Courtney's men won twenty-nine. Today, Courtney is best remembered for this triumphant era in college rowing, and not for his craven misbehavior as a professional sculler.[26]

Unavoidably, the stigma of professional rowing lingered even after the champions had retired. In 1892, the *New York Times* reported that while Harvard and Yale "have persistently sneered at Cornell and Pennsylvania for employing a professional coach" Yale had in fact sent a man to Ithaca to try to lure Courtney to New Haven. Harvard had tried that too. Courtney refused both offers, although he did agree to return to Cambridge for the fall rowing season in 1902, to advise Harvard's crew. This prompted sportswriter and editor Caspar Whitney to sound off in *Outing* magazine, that he deemed "the professional coach to be the most serious menace to college sports today.... Sport is fast ceasing to be sport ... because of the craze for winning which dominates."[27]

One retired professional rower soon proved Whitney's point. Sculler James Ten Eyck became rowing coach at the US Naval Academy in 1899, and at Syracuse University in 1903—where his crews went on to win ten national championships. But one victory in particular bolstered historian Samuel Crowther Jr. in his contempt for professional rowing's sordid past. Known as "The Sly Fox of the Hudson" for his often secretive coaching, Ten Eyck committed what Crowther called "unfair dealing" before the championships for freshman eights during the 1906 IRA Regatta at Poughkeepsie. "Coach Ten Eyck, a few days before the race, reported that his son [James Ten Eyck Jr.] the stroke, was ill; he kept him out of the boat for several rows and then put him in to win the race. All of which was an unpardonable ruse to obtain bets."[28]

CHAPTER 13

The Ruin of Professional Rowing

THERE CAN BE NO "DREAM TEAM" OF PROFESSIONAL ROWERS COMPETING at the next Olympics, as there often is for pro basketball and hockey players. That's because for more than a century competitive rowing has been chiefly amateur. In their heyday, the professional oarsmen who rowed for a living, the syndicates that sponsored their training and ran

Professional eight-oared crew on the Harlem in 1888. From bow: Fred Plaisted; Albert Hamm from Halifax; Peter H. Conley from Portland, Maine; Jack Largan from London; Wallace Ross from New Brunswick; Jacob Gaudaur from Ontario; George Bubear from Richmond, England; and George Hosmer from Boston. The coxswain is James Pilkington, owner of The Golden Oar saloon near Boathouse Row in Harlem. NEW YORK HISTORICAL SOCIETY

betting pools for their races, and the "sporting men" who drove and dominated the rampant gambling on the sport, all grew so greedy that the whole enterprise was at first suspected by the public. Then scorned. And finally banned by its original civic sponsors.

Growing ever more fretful as the sport degraded, the *New York Times* in 1887 asked: "Are all these professional oarsmen only so many puppets in the hands of speculators, puppets that sometimes move independently for their own profit and the discomfiture of their backers, but generally obey the instructions of the gamblers who manage them and who lay plans for deceiving and fleecing simple-minded outsiders, who believe that they are encouraging honest rivalry and enjoying honest battles of muscle and skill?" The answer was an irate Yes! "The people are fond of humbug and they are willing to pay for it."[1]

And yet, the public had to be charmed before it could be cheated. Professional rowing's corruption was innate, and only grew with the sport's popularity. When rowing's public appeal was destroyed, the next popular sports business to replace it was professional baseball. The convenience and frequency of baseball games far exceeded annual regattas and the occasional match races. Ballgames were played in town, almost every day, and in many cities where professionals rowed the waterways were becoming jammed with commercial shipping and girdled by docks and embankments, making the public's free access to the races ever more difficult. Baseball prospered because team sponsors and promoters could erect wooden fences and bleachers to capture a paying audience. Spectators were much closer to the athletes than when watching often-distant rowers from a riverbank or lakeshore.

Yet scandals also clouded the "national game." Only six years after America's first professional baseball game was played, four players on the Louisville Grays hatched the "1877 Conspiracy" to throw games for payoffs. All were punished with lifetime suspensions, but the business of baseball endured. And, compared with professional rowing, such deceit was rare. Baseball's most memorable scandal to date remains the plot by eight Chicago White Sox players to throw the 1919 World Series. They were banned from professional play for life in what became known as the "Black Sox Scandal."[2]

Significantly, baseball games in the nineteenth century offered a clear contrast to rowing races, where drunken fans and pickpockets roamed. Baseball historian David Nemec notes that "In keeping with the morals of the day, Sunday games were forbidden, liquor wasn't sold at parks, and admission was kept high to keep out the 'common element.' Baseball was a gentleman's game."

Nemec points to one rowdy exception. In 1882, when professional baseball was controlled by the owners of the six teams in the National League, a new American Association (AA) opened for business and rewrote the rules. It played games on Sunday, cut admission prices in half, and promoted not just beer but also whiskey. During its eleven-year history, the AA still had relatively few disruptions in actual play, although some players were known to drink during games. But much more so than drinking at the time, the largest problem was player rowdyism—in all leagues. "By the 1890s umpiring became a rather dangerous profession. Fights on the field between players or players and umpires were frequent enough to require police presence at most Major League parks during games."[3]

One way for rowing to compete with baseball was to become more entertaining. Rowers and their syndicates had to become almost theatrical when staging races for the sport's superstars. In one desperate effort Ned Hanlan, George Hosmer, and George Lee agreed to tour and perform together like a circus act, racing wherever their managers could book them. In July 1883, this trio rowed on Lake Neatahwanta, near Fulton in upstate New York; then at St. Paul for a turn on the Mississippi; then back to New York for races on Seneca Lake, at Watkins and at Geneva. That September, Hanlan teamed with fellow Canadian Jacob "Jake" Gaudaur to race near Saint Louis, on a course laid out where the Missouri and Mississippi Rivers meet. On race day *The Sporting Life* reported,

> *the water was choppy, and they contented themselves with rowing about in their shells, much to the disgust of the onlookers who had hoped to see a grand display of boating skill. The oarsmen simply got into their boats, and paddled around for a few minutes, after which Gaudaur rowed ashore and disappeared, leaving Hanlan alone in his glory. To this moment the crowd are at loss to know what the two men*

were driving at, and the non-success of the affair has so surprised the
owners of the steamboats, who got it up in the anticipation of reaping
a large harvest, that they are not likely to lend their aid to another
such hippodrome.

Hanlan had also planned some "exhibition rowing," but over two days only five hundred people appeared to watch him. During 1883 Hanlan and other professionals staged races or exhibitions at Cincinnati; Pullman, Illinois; and Vallejo and San Francisco, California.[4]

For his part, Hosmer made money during the winter of 1883 in long-distance walking races, the sport known as "pedestrianism," on which spectators bet eagerly. He also coached Princeton University's crew in 1884. And, following the example of New York racing promoter James Pilkington, Hosmer opened a saloon in his hometown of Boston that he also called "The Golden Oar," a venture later managed by another out-of-work professional rower, Fred Plaisted.

Making a late attempt to salvage the rowing business, in 1884 Boston's famous professional rower George Faulkner tried to organize a National Association of Professional Oarsmen, a move that rowing historian Thomas Mendenhall suggested "might have mitigated the corrosive effects the gamblers were having on the sport." But by then it was too late, and Faulkner drew scant response or support for his effort.[5]

Courtney had been scorned for his years of ignoble behavior in a shell, but the ten professional rowers who proclaimed, in 1884, that they would boycott any races with him were themselves no crew of worthies. John Teemer, especially, had by this time rowed against both Courtney and Hanlan in races reporters and fans saw as fixed. Teemer was also denounced for routinely throwing races.[6]

If the public couldn't trust Teemer, neither could his patrons. "He is the most crooked oarsman in the United States, and he will betray his best and closest friend," Teemer's manager decried. "No man can keep him straight." The manager called Teemer an "unprincipled scoundrel" and accused him of "perfidy, sham, cant, and hypocrisy" after being double-crossed and losing $4,000. In a single-sculls race at Annapolis in July 1886, Teemer had privately conspired to let Wallace Ross win, while the manager bet on Teemer. Later it was revealed how Teemer had even given a friend $1,500 to bet on Ross.[7]

Teemer had connived with Courtney for years, and at the Annapolis regatta the two were favored to win in double sculls against Ross and George Lee. With no surprise they purposely lost. They allowed Ross and Lee to lead around the turning stake, but then seemed to move on them. "Whether the two spurts Courtney and Teemer made before the grand stand were intended to rope the unwary into bets is not possible to say," carped the *Times*, "but at the finish, as it had been intimated would be the case," Ross and Lee won by a length. The paper called this Courtney's "customary defeat."[8]

Professional rowing's collapse took corruption by not only the oarsmen but also some race officials. "Looks As Though It Was Fixed" headlined the *New York Times* report about a Hanlan-Ross singles race near Montreal in 1886. The organizers broke with custom and refused to let the press ride the referee's launch. Yet by "considerable bullying" the paper's reporter boarded a police launch. But then, suspiciously, that launch "kept a long distance behind the oarsmen" and near the mid-course turn it veered away, leaving stretches of the race "hidden from view." Hanlan and Ross seemed to know the outcome, however, as "both men slacked down and sawed away leisurely" during their race.[9]

The *New York Times* was not alone when lambasting professional rowing, but more than other papers in major cities—in Boston or Philadelphia or Chicago or San Francisco—it consistently faulted the sport as it shattered. After yet another sketchy season in 1887, an editorial cited a recent race at Pullman—on Lake Calumet, near Chicago—where Jake Gaudaur's patron "freely acknowledged that he had directed his man to come in second" against Hanlan in single-sculls. That race was rowed at sunset, with "the smoke of the tugs and darkness" obscuring most of the course. "And yet," bemoaned the *Times*, "thousands of people will attend such races, risk money upon their favorite, and yell until they are hoarse, although the result has been predetermined by correspondence or by a bargain made in the back room of some saloon."

"Miserable Farce" was the *Times* headline about a sculling match Gaudaur rowed against Teemer in September 1889. Albert Hamm trained Gaudaur for this race, but when seeing that Teemer had a good lead Hamm rowed out onto the course. He rammed Teemer's shell and spiked a hole in it. Teemer claimed a foul, and that night when he chanced on Hamm at a hotel they threw insults and punches.[10]

SPECTACLES AND TRICYCLES

While the public still enjoyed a good sports spectacle, the late nineteenth century also saw a transformation—from athletics as something you watch (and bet on) to something you do. Industrialization had given workers in factories more predictable hours, allowing time for leisure as a part of their weekly calendar. A physical-fitness craze after the Civil War gave new popularity to ballgames ordinary people could play (baseball, badminton, tennis, croquet) and to personal exercise in social settings (gymnastics, swimming, long-distance walking). Cycling became a passion for the expanding middle class, and to profit from the country's physical exuberance new commercial ventures arose. Roller-skating rinks and bowling alleys opened in cities and towns across America. Public parks offered—or at least simulated—nature and open spaces for urban dwellers. Railroads sped passengers to rural spas, to seashores and lakes, and to mountain resorts. Closer to home, streetcar companies ran their idle fleets on weekends to move riders from cities to their newly created amusement parks.[11]

Despite press and public disdain, a few professional oarsmen still remained celebrities in the eyes of their loyal fans. Perhaps, as the sport became self-destructive the public seemed to crave it all the more. In September 1885, the Boston sculler George Hosmer was the star in a dramatic production at the Manchester Opera House in New Hampshire. There he performed in his single by rowing on a flooded stage. Posters promised "Marvelous Aquatic Scenes!" with "3,000 Feet Of Real Water!" Also on the program was an "Electrical Storm and Shower of Rain." Special trains brought attendees from cities across New England for what was billed "The Greatest of Melo-Dramatic Productions." The night's highlight was "A Dark Secret," a play whose final scene had Hosmer rowing at the Henley Royal Regatta. The show ran for years: sometimes with Teemer racing Hosmer on stage, and once, in New York, with Hanlan the star sculler.[12]

Hosmer and others professionals were also featured on tobacco-company trading cards, along with Jake Gaudaur, George Bubear, Edward Trickett, John Teemer, Wallace Ross, William Beach, Albert Hamm, John McKay, Charles Courtney, and Ned Hanlan.

In 1885, the year Hosmer entered show business in Manchester, Courtney chanced a different performance with Ross. Their "novel rowing race" wasn't at Oak Point this time, but "on dry land under cover" at the Manhattan Rink. On Broadway near Central Park, this fashionable roller rink attracted finely dressed skaters who, despite the rowers' competition, still swirled around for a truly dizzying scene. Ever wary, the *New York Times* doubted this stunt would even transpire, unless "Courtney's courage holds out." But it did, and he arrived to confront a grooved circular track set amid the gliding skaters. Along the track rolled a square wooden box on wheels. Racers sat in this box and "rowed" by dropping bladeless oar shafts between wooden pegs. Each stroke lurched the box about six feet.[13]

But with just a single track the men could only race the clock. First to appear, in pink rowing costume, Ross tugged around the track, making a mile (twenty-one laps) in seven minutes thirty seconds. As a comical lure, a bottle labeled "Sour Mash" was dangled on a wire before him. Courtney rowed a half-mile in two minutes thirty seconds. Then, as he had done so often on water, he just quit. A newspaper ran cartoons of the men. One had Ross smiling and waving off that Sour Mash bottle. And a sketch titled "Courtney's Vision of a Saw" revived the theme he would sooner forget: It showed him rowing on the track while a man reached from below, poised to cut his oar with a hand saw.[14]

Audiences could also watch and bet on professional rowers at grander arenas like Madison Square Garden where, at the time, six-day bicycle races were wildly popular. Advertised in October 1888 as "a decided novelty," $10,000 in prize money was offered for a different six-day race. This time, professional rowers would race "roadscullers" that, like shells, had sliding seats and wooden oar-like handles. Contestants included rowing celebrities of the day: John Teemer, Jake Gaudaur, George Bubear, Albert Hamm, James Ten Eyck, Wallace Ross, John McKay, and Fred Plaisted. Also racing was Canada's national sculling champion, William O'Connor. The men were to race these tricycles around a furlong-per-lap

Ad for a Six-Day Roadsculler Race at Madison Square Garden in 1888 PUBLIC
DOMAIN

track by tugging on handles that moved chains and pulleys to power the
wheels. These contraptions sped at about fifteen miles an hour, and, as
they whizzed around a track that was only twenty-one feet wide, they
became both comical and perilous. For the indoor rower, the only advantage over sitting in a shell was that at least he faced forward—a life-saving
necessity once this race began.

As *The Sun* described the opening scene:

*The twelve oarsmen set off upon the first six hours of their sixty amid
the glare of 35 electric arc lights and some hundreds of gas jets, the
blare of 75 musicians, each trying to outblow the other, and the cheers
of something more than 7,500 spectators, among whom were included
some hundreds of women whose bright costumes illuminated the boxes
all around the track, and the battery of whose eyes made even the electric lights dim, and the music and huzzas were terrific for those of the
oarsmen who had susceptible hearts beneath the gay and scanty gauze
shirts which covered their manly forms.*[15]

Just minutes into this spectacle half a dozen machines broke down. Rowers suffered "cuts and abrasions." Teemer crashed his racer, and, *The Sun* reported, "Wallace Ross' machine was on top of him in an instant, and Gaudaur's on top of them both." Suddenly the crowd was enthralled. Now "the possibility of serious injury to some of the racers was at once apparent" there came "a redoubled interest in the contest." New York's coroner rose to leave, then sensed a grim public responsibility, sat down, and said: "I guess I'll stay."

Soon "two men were kept busy in dragging off the damaged steeds while the oarsmen completed their laps on foot." By the race's second day Gaudaur led with 172 miles. Teemer had pulled 165 miles, but then, the *New York Times* revealed, he "awoke with blisters as large as copper pennies and the dry and inflamed skin was cracked at all the joints" making it "a physical impossibility for him to close his hands." More discreetly, the paper noted how O'Connor had been "crippled elsewhere" by his faulty sliding seat, "and moved about with an effort."

Exhausted and irate, the rowers demanded new rules. They negotiated cutting the ten-hour daily regime to eight. They arranged to race in relays, not all at once. This assured the stable of roadscullers could be kept in repair, while also reducing collisions. Crowds from "all classes of society" arrived each night, and cheered the racers for hours. They enjoyed the betting, the drinking, and the feasting—along with "sparkling music" by the Thirteenth Regiment Band led by the famous Frederick Neil Innes. On Sunday's opening night they performed "A Grand Sacred Concert," and tooted popular marches and ditties all week.

"Scores of club men and hundreds of fashionably dressed ladies occupied the boxes," as the rowers rattled round and round the track. Most evenings the Garden's atmosphere swirled with cigar smoke so thick "the colored lights over the band stand twinkled like stars in a mist and the racers made holes in a sort of London fog." But one night "clouds of suffocating smoke" from a food vendor's charcoal stove obscured the track, choking one rower and disabling another.

The sixth day offered new indignities. Two trainers started a fistfight and Teemer punched O'Connor's assistant. In the end, Gaudaur won by racking up 465 miles. Ross pulled a close second with 462, and Plaisted with 455. Poor Teemer, blistered and bruised, "rowed" just 177. As sports historian George Gipe observed, "Perhaps the only thing that was certain as a result of the disastrous event was that sometimes rowing on land can be almost as difficult as walking on water."[16]

Professional scullers Fred Plaisted and James Ten Eyck teamed up to bring rowing to vaudeville. Performing on stages in the United States and in Europe, "With mechanical appliances, the pair would row in competition. Revolving sculls of miniature dimensions would indicate the progress of each competitor." Silly as this may seem today, at least the spectacle kept the era's rowing superstars in the public eye, earned them some cash, and still prompted betting.[17]

Not all pro rowers were so fortunate, and the fate of the Biglins' longtime racing partner Dennis Leary proved especially sad. Leary worked as a fireman, a civil court officer, and then as a patrolman. By 1880, Leary found a new way to use his skills. "He was a good oarsman," the *Herald-Tribune* reported, "and was to row about the Narrows and Coney Island to see whether the captains of tugboats employed by the Street Cleaning Bureau towed the garbage scows out to sea before unloading them." But even for this duty Leary often failed to appear, and the paper noted how "his superior officers did not believe his mind to be well balanced." He died in 1890.[18]

About this time Harry Clay Palmer, a reporter for the Chicago *Tribune* and *Sporting Life*, captured popular sentiments about rowing in a sports history:

The amateur sculler is the pride of aquatics. To him is due the credit for all those bright ideas which have improved and advanced the pastime. There is more genuine spirit and earnestness in the humble amateur than can be found in the whole rank and file of the professional. The public, that critical factor which the average sportsman fears so much, is a staunch believer in the doings of the amateur, and supports in every way his lightest works; whereas, in the case of the professional, crooked deeds and shady methods have severed the ties between him and the masses. That's why the amateur is fostered and the professional is cursed.[19]

BANNED IN BOSTON

Boston had been the first in America to sponsor an annual city regatta, setting an example then followed by Worcester, Springfield, Newburgh, Poughkeepsie, Newark, Detroit, New York, St. Louis, and San Francisco. For decades, these Independence Day affairs on the River Charles were popular and profitable, drawing huge crowds and sparking gamblers to follow the races on shore and at betting parlors nationwide. But as professional rowing foundered from public mistrust, with its ever-bolder deceptions, Boston was also the first American city to ban the sport outright.

Claiming to be the "Cradle of Liberty" (a title it long disputed with Philadelphia), Boston energetically celebrated each and every July Fourth, and from 1854 its City Regatta grew to become the country's biggest rowing event: always attracting the best professionals, while also drawing fleets of eager amateurs. Boston had a determined Committee on the Celebration of the Fourth of July, and its debates, beginning in the early 1890s, reveal growing displeasure with how and why Boston should continue to enrich professional rowers.

In 1892, the July Fourth celebration committee voted to distinguish between "open" and "local" professional races, as a way to assure that at least some of the prize money stayed near home; a "local" rower had to live within fifty miles of Boston. Then, in 1895, the committee decided there would be "no open professional single scull race" at all. The only three events would be for local professional scullers, local professional four-oared working boats, and amateur twelve-oared barges. In 1896, the committee's debate uncorked divisions between different wards and different sports. Should bicycle races replace regattas?[20]

Boston's outright ban on professional rowing came the next year, when a Joint Special Committee on the Fourth of July (including both aldermen and councilmen) debated how to allocate funds for the celebration, and sought to encourage amateur rowers. "An amateur oarsman should not row for money, or for the value of the prizes that he gets," one councilman argued. "He should row for the prize itself . . . [and] $400 is enough to give proper prizes for amateur sports." Moreover, he added, "it is certain that there has not been a professional oarsman of any note in Boston on the 4th of July at the regatta for years."

Finally, on June 22, 1897, the Council voted to fund the City Regatta but "making an amateur affair exclusively. . . ." Regattas for professionals in Canada, England, and Australia lasted a few years more, but with Boston's ban other cities soon discarded the sport. The era of professional rowing was ending.[21]

Halifax had been the first Canadian city to stage an international regatta for professionals, in 1871, and after its last, in 1896, cities across the Dominion followed. Rowing for money as a civic spectacle was gone.[22]

THE PROFESSIONALS DRIFT AWAY

James Pilkington, the dynamic sports promoter who ran The Golden Oar saloon in Harlem when professional rowers made it their headquarters in the 1880s, went on to support amateur athletics, and for more than a decade was president of the National Association of Amateur Oarsmen. In 1916, Pilkington lamented that professional rowing was all but forgotten, while baseball and football prospered as lucrative businesses attracting young athletes. "[A]s the professionals disappear," he told the *New York Times*, "the patterns for the aspiring amateurs are lost, the practical illustration of theoretical oarsmanship is seen no more, and the niceties of sculling execution and boat construction become a lost art." Since "the sport has lost a glamor that won many enthusiasts to take it up, the youngsters at the game have lost their best models. . . ."[23]

The sole contest to survive from professional rowing's heyday was the sculling Championship of the World, first held on the Thames at London in 1831, then on the Tyne where generations of working-class rowers became national sports heroes. This all-England competition finally became international in 1863 when the first non-British challenger, Australian Richard A. W. Green, lost to four-time champ Robert Chambers. Soon challengers from across the Empire overwhelmed England's pro scullers, and from 1876 to 1911 all world singles champs hailed from Canada, Australia, or New Zealand.

Reviewing this history it is clear that world champions have only come from Britain, its dominions, and its former North American colonies. In this expanded realm four Americans challenged for the title: James Hamill from Pittsburgh lost to English champion Harry Kelly on the Tyne in 1866; John A. Kennedy from Portland, Maine, lost to Canadian Ned Hanlan at Point of Pines, near Boston, in 1883; Major L. Goodsell from San Diego lost to Englishman Ted Phelps at Long Beach, California, in 1932; and William G. Miller from Philadelphia lost to Canadian Henry "Bobby" Pearce at Toronto in 1934.[24]

Tobacco companies had celebrated professional rowers on their trading cards since the 1880s, and continued this attention with full-page magazine and newspaper ads. A spread in 1935 for Camel cigarettes showed baseball star Lou Gehrig and pro-golf champion Gene Sarazen along with Bill Miller, the sculler who had earlier been four-time US national amateur champion. In another Camel ad that year, a cartoon strip in the *Philadelphia Inquirer* showed Miller puffing a cigarette, then during a practice row for a regatta diving from his single to save a drowning boy. After barely winning his race, Miller reached up from his shell for another Camel, boasting they are "So Mild—You Can Smoke All You Want!" Not mentioned in this ad were Miller's recent performances; the year before, he lost two contests: the US nationals and the world pro sculling championship, where he became exhausted and trailed Pearce by fifteen lengths.[25]

After sporadic races in the first half of the twentieth century, the world's last professional sculling championship was rowed on the Clarence River in New South Wales, in 1957, when Evans Fischer beat fellow Australian Evans Paddon.[26]

Chapter 14

The Triumph of the Amateurs

Amateur rowing evolved throughout the twentieth century: shaped by changing social trends, enjoyed by more diverse participants, and in some countries even nationalized.

With the decline and disappearance of professional rowing during the closing days of the nineteenth century, those Americans still eager to bet on staged professional sporting events for human competitors found three new ways to lose their money: on baseball, boxing, and cycling. Professional rowing configured money, betting, and corruption as essential elements in American professional sports. After John Morrissey with his racetracks and rowing regattas came James Pilkington to promote matches for professional boxers, wrestlers, bowlers, and rowers. Then baseball team franchises were moneymakers, and their owners became public figures: brewer Jacob Ruppert Jr. bought the New York Yankees in 1915; chewing-gum magnate William Wrigley Jr. bought the Chicago Cubs in 1916.[1]

Once sports fans assumed that rowing races were rigged, they and the "sporting men" who could no longer rely on "an honest fix" all turned to betting on other sports. "It's a boat race!" became slang at thoroughbred tracks for a fix. In professional rowing's place came franchises and monopolies that dominate America's sports scene today—with the owners still prospering and the fans still betting, rooting, and often funding hometown teams with their taxes.

In turn, baseball, boxing, and cycling all endured scandals, but none so severe they were banned. Ballparks rose in cities across the country. Madison Square Garden became a mecca for prizefights. And there, six-day bicycle races survived into the 1960s. And, just like spectators at professional rowing regattas, cycle enthusiasts enjoyed their sport for a similar reason. As low-life chronicler Damon Runyon declared, "There's no place better to get drunk than the Six Day Bike Race."[2]

AMATEUR ROWING

As professional rowing sank in its final days, amateur rowing expanded nationwide at clubs and colleges. No longer the domain of rough and rowdy boatmen, rowing gained social appeal. Boathouses had to have not only storage racks for shells and showers for oarsmen but also bars and ballrooms. Social elites disdained anything "professional" but were eager to glorify and promote "amateur" traditions and values.

In Washington, DC, rowing was so popular early in the twentieth century that amateur champion Eugene M. Foster recalled how "newspapers not only carried an account of rowing events on the sport sheet, but the society column, too."

> *Whenever a man joined one of the clubs he was required to equip himself with three suits, a full dress uniform consisting of a double-breasted coat with brass buttons, a stiff front shirt and a navy cap with a club emblem on it; the whole outfit resembling the full military dress of the midshipmen of today, and was worn on all social occasions.*
>
> *Another suit was his barge outfit, which consisted of a naval blouse uniform and cap, and he was required to wear same whenever ladies were present on barge trips. The other suit was his shell costume which was similar to those in use today only the trunks were a little longer.*

It was "a mighty poor boat club that could not boast of at least a dozen real men of money," he bragged in a 1916 article. "Of course all this was before the days of automobiles and golf, and the millionaires of the day took to the river for sport and recreation."[3]

Rowing clubs in New York City had been both sporting and social centers, with the winners at their regattas and the guests at their parties all hailed in the press. In 1896, thirteen rowing clubs competed at the thirtieth annual Harlem River Regatta. Yet even while boat clubs were maintaining popularity, some of their courses were being destroyed by industrial and civic "improvements." Big-city boathouses disappeared as rail lines and highways lined the riverbanks (on the Harlem in New York City), or as cement works and rendering plants crowded the shore (on the Potomac in Washington, DC). Some few rowers were lucky enough to move to the suburbs. The New York Athletic Club built a boathouse at Travers Island, just over the Bronx-Westchester line in Pelham, New York, where rowing thrives today. But for most, when working-class and middle-class rowers lost their in-town boat clubs, many had to abandon their sport.[4]

In 1937 New York City's Boathouse Row met its doom when Parks Commissioner Robert Moses condemned nine Harlem River clubs to make way for his grand highway development schemes. After Moses evicted the Waverly Boat Club from its pier on the Hudson at 155th Street to build the Henry Hudson Parkway, the *Times* eulogized how this club's "long retreat has marked the retreat of boating itself." In retrospect, reflected the paper, "Commerce was the Nemesis of boating. The city grew, and the rivers remained the same, and local waters were too small for both. Perhaps the motorboat contributed to a dwindling interest in rowing. But it was a manly sport. The Waverly Club, capitulating to eighty years of progress, knew it at its best."[5]

The Harlem River rowing scene did survive, but just barely, and is again expanding. Columbia University crews continued to train and race there, later joined by Fordham University, Manhattan College, and neighborhood rowers at a new Peter J. Sharp Boathouse, built as a city facility with funds raised by entertainer Bette Midler and city foundations. Today rowing centers are flourishing in scores of cities and towns nationwide.[6]

Besides rowing revivals in and around older eastern cities, the sport continues to expand inland. Austin, Texas, sponsored one of the country's last professional regattas in the late nineteenth century, and in the early twenty-first century is a lively rowing center. So are Lake Casitas, California; Aiken, South Carolina; Oklahoma City, Oklahoma; Grand Rapids, Michigan; Indianapolis, Indiana; Oak Ridge, Tennessee, Sarasota, Florida; and West Windsor, New Jersey, among many more.

Historically, numbers for rowing organizations and institutions are elusive and records spotty, difficult to calculate and verify because of the sport's inherently amateur and informal nature. The United States had about 90 amateur rowing clubs in the 1860s and more than 230 by the mid-1870s. At century's end there were more than 400 clubs, but by the 1920s fewer than 280 had survived. Then, since the 1950s rowers and regattas have multiplied steadily, boosted during the 1970s by expanding opportunities for women. In the early twenty-first century, the many kinds of rowing institutions in North America (boat clubs, aquatic centers, schools, colleges, parks) now number more than a thousand. In the United States in 2019 there were more than 106,000 members of US Rowing, the organization that began in 1872 as the National Association of Amateur Oarsmen. In US Rowing, women outnumber men 52 percent to 48 percent. Worldwide, men are 55 percent, women 45 percent.[7]

Professionals on the Thames and the Tyne were the first to make rowing a big-money sport, yet the amateur spirit also took hold in English tradition (and readers' imaginations) with the likes of the 1857 Thomas Hughes novel *Tom Brown's School Days* about athleticism at the Rugby School. In their strict definition of an "amateur," the stewards who ran the Henley Royal Regatta refused any entry by rowers "whoever competed with or against a professional for any prize" or taught or coached the sport. They also excluded anyone ever "employed in or about boats for money or wages; or who is or has been, by trade or employment for wages, a mechanic, artisan, or labourer."[8]

As rowing historian Thomas C. Mendenhall explained the differences, England could keep defining an amateur as "a gentleman whose independent income gave him the leisure to row for pleasure" whereas in America the amateur was seen as "a working man whose job or business would effectively prevent him from training as regularly or extensively as a professional. Somehow the sturdy Calvinist work ethic had to come to terms with a growing national interest in leisure and play." As became clear through decades of social change, being an "amateur" depended on your country and your profession.[9]

Amateurism as a gloried concept gained its staunchest advocate in the 1880s when the French aristocrat Pierre de Coubertin aspired to reform French education and decided to visit England's Rugby School for ideas. Himself an avid sculler, Coubertin inspired a wave of "athletic chivalry" that led him by 1896 to found the modern Olympic Games. Bad weather at Athens that year scuttled all rowing, but since 1900 Olympic competition has erased any lingering attraction to the era of the professionals. An American eight from Philadelphia's Vesper Boat Club won at Paris in 1900 over Belgium and the Netherlands, and again at St. Louis in 1904 over Canada. Great Britain finally triumphed in 1908 and 1912, both years with no US entries. Then came The Great War, and it was only in 1920, at Antwerp, Belgium, that the Olympics resumed. There, John B. Kelly from Vesper (film star Grace Kelly's father) beat Jack Beresford Jr. from London's Thames Rowing Club by one second for the Olympic gold medal in single sculls.

Kelly was a phenomenal athlete who had already won 126 consecutive races, including six US national championships. But he is best known for the race he never rowed. Before entering the 1920 Olympics, Kelly applied to row for the Diamond Sculls at Henley and was irate when the stewards rejected him. Kelly had performed "manual labor" as a bricklayer's apprentice, and their rebuff has become rowing history and legend. For Kelly, the win at Antwerp was sweet revenge because it was over Beresford, who had just won the Diamonds weeks before. Kelly also joined cousin Paul Costello to win a gold medal in double sculls, becoming the only rower in Olympic history to win in both boats the same year. In 1947 Kelly savored a different revenge when his son, John B. "Jack" Kelly Jr., did row at Henley and did win the Diamonds.[10]

Through more than half the twentieth century Americans were cocky about their rowing, and for decades nonchalant about the Olympics. Why not just pick the season's best club or college eight and send it off? This they did, and at Antwerp in 1920 a US Naval Academy crew beat eights from Great Britain and Norway. The Yale eight that defeated Canada and Italy at Paris in the 1924 Olympics included a gangly New Haven native named Benjamin Spock, later revered for his theories and popular book about child rearing. A University of California eight from Berkeley won the 1928 Olympics in Amsterdam over Great Britain and Canada, and four years later, at Long Beach, another Cal boat beat Italy and Canada.

Adolf Hitler watched in disgust as a University of Washington eight edged by Italy and Germany at the 1936 Olympics in Berlin.[11]

After World War II, games resumed with the 1948 Olympics at London, and for the third time an eight from Berkeley took the gold, beating Great Britain and Norway. It all seemed so easy, and was as long as rowing remained a gentleman's sport not too aggressively pursued. At Helsinki in 1952, a US Naval Academy crew beat eights from the Soviet Union and Australia. And at Melbourne in 1956, a spunky Yale eight came from behind after poor showings in early heats to best Canada and Australia for the Olympic gold medal. Then, at Rome in 1960, the rowing world changed forever.[12]

TWO GERMANYS REFORM THE SPORT

Germany, first in the West and then in the East, revolutionized amateur rowing with winning ways that abide today. Karl Adam had been training a rowing club he helped establish at Ratzeburg, in West Germany, in 1953. A competitive boxer, he cast a fresh eye to rowing and its intricate motions. He changed his crew's training, the rowing style for the athletes, and the rigging for the boats. Off the water, Adam had his men do *fartlek* (Swedish for "speedplay," a routine developed in 1937 by Swedish coach Gosta Holmer), mixing continuous and interval training with running and weightlifting. This strenuous regime developed both aerobic and anaerobic stamina, and with it Adam's crews proved they could row high-rated but shorter strokes in bursts that amazed other coaches. For a livelier spring at the catch, Adam used oars with broader tulip-shaped blades that scooped more water than those that were traditionally tapered. All this pushed his eights to win seven European or world titles. Ratzeburg eights won Olympic gold at Rome in 1960 (where a crew from Annapolis finished fifth) and at Mexico City in 1968 over Australia and the Soviet Union.[13]

Ratzeburg's only break in this revolutionary success came at the 1964 Tokyo Olympics, when a Vesper Boat Club eight from Philadelphia pulled a more traditional and longer stroke and still beat Adam's crew and an eight from Czechoslovakia. Adam and Vesper's coach, Allen P. Rosenberg, taught different rowing styles, prompting debates and experiments for years to come.[14]

But these debates about rowing styles were scuttled in the 1970s by triumphs in East Germany (the German Democratic Republic [GDR]). There, amateur rowers were nationalized. Leaders had made competitive sports a crusade, and their state-run efforts forever raised international rowing standards. Rowers there became state employees. From 1966, the first year the GDR competed under its own flag, to 1990, after the Berlin Wall had fallen and Germany reunited, East German rowers won 153 gold, 74 silver, and 42 bronze medals at international regattas. Their Olympic wins totaled 33 gold, 7 silver, and 8 bronze medals for a total of 48. (US rowers in that period won 17 medals.) The GDR men's eight finished behind New Zealand and the United States in its first Olympic bid, at Munich in 1972, and then won gold medals at Montreal in 1976 and at Moscow in 1980.[15]

The GDR's "stupendous achievement," wrote rowing historian Christopher Dodd, recruited young rowers to attend special training schools and employed hundreds of full-time professional coaches. Sustaining this network were a Research Institute for Physical Culture and Sport in Leipzig; a medical facility in Kreischa near Dresden; and an Institute for the Development of Sport Equipment in Berlin. At Leipzig, seventy scientists spent fifteen years studying human nervous, respiratory, muscular, and hormonal systems to understand just how athletes perform with different training regimes, diets, and competitive styles. Research on drugs to boost athletic performance (termed "Supporting Means") thrived at Kreischa, its studies and records classified as state secrets. But intensive studies revealed that steroids were of little use to rowers for building the endurance needed to survive the punishing ordeal of a race. More important was their rigorous training—including miles and miles on the water—and at that, too, the East Germans excelled. "They didn't invent anything new; they went back to basics," said a coach whose crews raced the GDR. Watching these closely drilled crews, many observers have simply called them "awesome."[16]

The boats also came under meticulous study. To improve rowing equipment, every force to and from the oars and shells had to be analyzed. GDR technicians learned that the rowing basin for the 1976 Montreal Olympics was much shallower than at other courses, which allowed the compression wave a shell creates to bounce back up from the bottom. They designed a new hull to compensate, and won their first gold for eights.[17]

The amateur ideal quickly fell to new international standards that required early recruiting, intensive training, and constant competition. Also essential was the financial support to create national teams that could sustain athletes for years of training, while also maintaining and improving the delicate and costly equipment. National training centers now operate in many countries, usually on a year-round schedule. US national teams have been funded since 1966 by a National Rowing Foundation, which today helps recruit rowers to centers at Princeton, New Jersey; Chula Vista, California; and Oklahoma City, Oklahoma. Participants who qualify receive stipends and expenses to help them compete abroad. In a sense, they have become like the professionals of old who were paid to train for months and race all season with support from patrons and syndicates. But, also like those professionals, their numbers are few and they are a distinctive elite.

WOMEN ROWERS

In their zeal to create "socialist sports personalities" and gain global stature, the East Germans were more inclusive than Western counterparts when it came to enlisting women rowers. As a result, they won four of the six gold medals at the first World Championships for Women in 1974, and four of six in 1976 when women first rowed in the Olympics.[18]

But forces beyond centralized state programs underlie how profoundly women have joined and enhanced the sport of rowing over the last half-century. Early on, there were a few women in the United States who set out to row, despite scant encouragement from their male counterparts. Among the pioneers was New York's Berkeley Ladies' Athletic Club, which included dressing rooms at its Manhattan clubhouse in 1890, and allowed women to row from its boathouse in the Bronx.

But it took four young women living in San Diego, California, to establish America's first women's rowing club in 1892. They named it the ZLAC Rowing Club after their first-name initials—Zulette Lamb, who joined with Lena, Agnes, and Caroline Polhamus, three daughters of the

The ZLAC Rowing Club launches a new barge at San Diego in 1895 ZLAC ROWING CLUB

harbormaster. Five years later, women in Philadelphia created The Bicycle, Barge & Canoe Club on the Schuylkill by the lighthouse at the north end of Boathouse Row, and in 1905 named their enterprise the Sedgeley Club, after a nearby mansion. In 1900, the Oakland Women's Rowing Club first raced on San Francisco Bay, soon joined on Lake Merritt by two municipal boathouses used by women's crews.[19]

Beyond these modest gains, for American women the rowing world opened up radically after 1972, when the US Congress passed education amendments to the Civil Rights Act of 1964. In a new "Title IX" it became national law that no person "shall, on the basis of sex, be excluded from participation in, be denied the benefits of, or be subjected to discrimination under any education program or activity receiving federal financial assistance...." Title IX would do more than all the Eastern European bloc's socialist sports edicts and secret programs to draw women into both recreational and competitive rowing because it required schools and colleges to spend as much for women's sports programs as they did for men's.

This "title wave"—as commentators called it—came at a time when many all-male colleges were just beginning to admit women undergraduates. And US women's crews flourished: In the Olympics US women's

Wellesley College crew, 1889 WELLESLEY COLLEGE ARCHIVE

eights won a bronze medal in 1976, a silver in 2004, and gold medals in 1984, 2008, 2012, and 2016. US women's eights were the first to win at three consecutive Olympics, and won all their Olympic and international races for a decade.[20]

Even though rowing has become vastly more accessible for American women since the 1970s, a few had taken up the sport nearly a century before Title IX. When Wellesley and Smith Colleges instituted rowing programs to improve their students' finesse and physique, participation was mandatory. Rowing at Wellesley began in 1875 with what is the country's oldest surviving organized women's program. Eights with sliding seats were introduced in 1892 to advance "scientific oarsmanship" aimed at developing physical fitness, and two years later the college hired a full-time rowing coach. In 1896, a Wellesley crew dared men from the Massachusetts Institute of Technology to a race, but the challenge was rebuffed, and competitive rowing was not organized for intercollegiate races until 1970.[21]

Smith College began intercollegiate rowing in 1971, although its traditions date to the 1890s. By 1916, rowing was part of the curriculum, with drills on the Mill River in wide-hulled fours to develop the students' posture and poise. At first races were discouraged, although in 1933 some Smith students made bold to challenge a men's four at Yale. They planned a journey to New Haven until the college administration decreed, "there will be no intercollegiate competition."[22]

In England, meanwhile, Newnham College, Cambridge, organized a "boating society" for women in 1876. Women at Oxford's Somerville College were first allowed to row on the Cherwell, a tributary of the Isis (Thames) in 1884, but only when no men's crews were about. The London-based Hammersmith Sculling Club, founded in 1896, offered rowing on the Thames for both women and men. Women from Oxford organized a university boat club in 1926, and first raced Cambridge for a rowing "exhibition" in 1927. On this historic occasion "large and hostile crowds gathered on the towpath" to heckle the crews, the *New York Times* reported. At Cambridge crews from Newnham College joined with Girton College rowers in 1941 to officially begin a university boat club that raced Oxford. But enmity by male rowers on the River Cam endured, and as late as 1962 the crew captain from Selwyn College wrote the Cambridge University Women's Boat Club to protest: "I personally do not approve of women rowing at all. It is a ghastly sight, an anatomical impossibility (if you are rowing properly, that is) and physiologically dangerous." Since then times have changed, and today Oxford and Cambridge women row the same course in London on the same day as the men's Boat Race.[23]

In upstate New York, professional sculler Charles Courtney began teaching women to row in the 1870s at a seminary in Union Springs, his hometown; and when coaching Cornell he organized a women's crew in 1897. In 1904, the University of Washington began a women's rowing program, which ran intermittently until becoming permanent in 1969. A National Women's Rowing Association began in 1962, vied with the National Association of Amateur Oarsmen (NAAO) for acknowledgment and respect, and, in 1982 joined NAAO's successor, the United States Rowing Association (US Rowing).

Regrettably, these transitions weren't always easy. Women were first admitted as Princeton undergraduates in 1969, but well into the 1970s the university boathouse had no locker rooms for them. Women were not allowed to enjoy the social rooms upstairs in the boathouse whenever men were present, and at first they had to row discarded shells using beat-up oars. Title IX funding improved their lot, but only gradually.

At Yale it took some celebrated nudity to gain women the equality they long deserved. Four years after beginning its women's crew program in 1972, Yale's boathouse on the Housatonic River at Derby still had no separate locker room or showers. After practice the women had to wait for the men to shower, then endure a half-hour bus ride back to campus to use facilities in the gym. Their complaints eventually gained them a trailer with four showers in the boathouse parking lot—but it had no hot water. After a cold-weather practice in March 1976, the women's patience was finished, and they met to take action. First they drafted a statement that began: "These are the bodies Yale is exploiting. On a day like today the ice freezes on this skin. Then we sit for half an hour as the ice melts and soaks through to meet the sweat that has soaked us from the inside."

To bolster their point nineteen crewmembers met at the gym, where they wrote "Title IX" on their backs and chests in Yale-blue paint, donned their sweatsuits, and walked to the office of the athletic department's director of women's activities. The crew had tipped off the campus paper, and was joined by a reporter and photographer as they all crowded into the director's office. Calmly, the women stripped naked, and senior Chris Ernst read their three-hundred-word statement. News spread fast beyond New Haven: The *Yale Daily News* reporter was also a stringer for the *New York Times*, which ran his story on its second section's front page, headlined "Yale Women Strip to Protest a Lack of Crew's Showers." The Associated Press moved the story nationwide, and this bad publicity prompted alumni donations to the cause. A few weeks later, hot water was connected to the trailer showers. But nearly a year passed before more hot showers were installed in a new women's locker room at the boathouse.

The incident was later exalted in the 1999 documentary film *A Hero for Daisy*, which by then could show Ernst and C. B. Sands winning the 1986 World Championship in lightweight doubles. Ernst had also been a member of "The Red Rose Crew," a determined group of women from diverse backgrounds who enlisted legendary Harvard coach Harry Parker to teach and train them for serious competition. Their eight won a silver medal at the 1975 World Rowing Championships, finishing just 1.6 seconds behind mighty East Germany.[24]

In the United States, women's rowing programs have proliferated and expanded at colleges and universities because, since 1997 the sport has been governed by the National Collegiate Athletic Association (NCAA), whereas men's rowing has traditionally been ruled by the Intercollegiate Rowing Association (IRA) or regional groups. With its broader involvement in many college sports the NCAA provides women rowers both financial support and publicity. In the United States, 205 colleges sponsored varsity-rowing crews during 2019, with fifty-seven men's teams and an impressive 148 women's teams competing. Among all varsity rowers women outnumbered men by more than two-to-one, with 7,200 participants compared with 2,340 men. In NCAA Division I schools 5,600 women are now rowing, more than those playing both basketball and softball. Among high school rowers, too, women now predominate with twice the number of athletes as men.[25]

The late twentieth century also brought a significant increase in rowing by seniors. "Masters" is the age category for rowers twenty-seven years and older, and for this group club and community rowing opportunities has expanded notably. There are now masters' regattas for men and women at Henley, and masters' races at leading regattas in North America and beyond. In 2017 at Bled, Slovenia, a record forty-seven hundred raced in the World Rowing Masters Regatta.

Masters racing has become especially popular because age handicaps make crews of all ages closely competitive. For example, an eight-oared shell with rowers averaging twenty-seven years old has no handicap, but seconds-off the race time increase significantly with age. An eight with a fifty-year-old crew can deduct 10.6 seconds from its time. At age sixty the handicap is 21.8 seconds, and averages in the seventies range from 37 to 54.1 seconds. These adjustments let masters finish within seconds of crews that are much younger.

Rowing in Popular Culture

Because of their continuing and distinguished rowing programs, the crews from Philadelphia's Boathouse Row, the Ivy League, and New England prep schools have dominated media coverage of the sport. But rowing's image as an elite sport was upset in 1980 in a facetious take on upper-crust American society, *The Official Preppy Handbook*. At issue was the Princess Elizabeth Challenge Cup, a race at the Henley Royal Regatta begun in 1946 for public—by which they meant private—schools in the United Kingdom. Predictably the Cup was won by the likes of Winchester (founded 1382), Eton (1440), St. Paul's (1509), Bedford (1552), and Shrewsbury (1552). That is, until 1964. When the race was opened to crews from overseas that year it was won by Washington-Lee (now called Liberty), a public (public) high school in Arlington, Virginia. From then until the *Handbook* was published it made the point that the country's best schoolboy crews did not come from such Establishment landmarks as St. Paul's in New Hampshire or Kent in Connecticut, but from Holy Spirit, a Catholic diocesan high school in New Jersey. By 1980 Holy Spirit had tied Washington-Lee with two victories each. St. Paul's, Kent, and Tabor Academy in Massachusetts had each won the Cup once—but so had another Virginia public high school, JEB Stuart (now called Justice).[26]

Still, in popular culture rowing remains marked as an elite sport, and one not always admired. Thomas Hughes penned a sequel to his schooldays novel in 1861, *Tom Brown at Oxford*, which featured the hero's adventures as a college oarsman. Juvenile literature also celebrated rowing and water sports in the popular Oliver Optic series with *The Boat Club* in the 1850s, written by William Taylor Adams. Mark Sibley Severance's 1878 novel *Hammersmith: His Harvard Days* featured rowing on Worcester's Lake Quinsigamond. In 1867, *Beadle's Dime Handbook of Yachting and Rowing* by Henry Chadwick presented basic knowledge, encouragement, and rowing lore to a generation of youngsters. Beginning in 1896, Gilbert Patten, writing under the name Burt L. Standish, published more than two hundred titles in the Frank Merriwell series, many set in boathouses and on the river. Merriwell was an idealized lad meant to personify youthful decorum.

Other writers who described rowing for young readers included Ralph D. Paine in *The Stroke Oar* in 1908, and Leslie W. Quirk in *The Freshman Eight* in 1913. Through the 1930s, rowers were featured on the covers of magazines for young readers, including the *American Boy, Boy's Life, Boy's Magazine, Top-Notch Magazine,* and the *Youth's Companion.* Older readers saw rowing covers on *Harper's Weekly, Liberty,* the *Outlook, People's Magazine, Physical Culture, Police Gazette,* the *Popular Magazine, Scribner's Magazine, Senator, Sportsman, Sport Story, Strength,* and *Thrilling Sports.*[27]

Zuleika Dobson; or, An Oxford Love Story by English satirist Max Beerbohm introduced readers in 1911 to an enchantress and the captivating spell she cast over the university's May Week boat races. P. G. Wodehouse's 1946 novel *Joy in the Morning* has the idle-rich and waggish Bertie Wooster put down a rower he knows with blasé disdain, saying his "entire formative years, therefore, as you might say, had been spent in dipping an oar into the water, giving it a shove and hauling it out again. Only a pretty dumb brick would fritter away his golden youth doing that sort of thing."[28]

In other literary realms, American poet Walt Whitman admired physical grace in "I Sing the Body Electric" by praising "The Bending forward and backward of the rowers. . . . " In the heat of a race, those bending forward and backward who at the moment find the sport diabolical might appreciate Nietzsche's perspective: "When one rows it is not the rowing which moves the ship: rowing is only a magical ceremony by means of which one compels a demon to move the ship."[29]

Mass-circulation magazines were America's most popular print medium through the early twentieth century, and publications such as the *Saturday Evening Post, Collier's,* and *Leslie's Weekly* decorated their covers with gallant rowing images—mostly showing idealized and muscular young men pensively holding an oar, joyously hoisting a shell, or boldly straining in mid-race. But exhausted rowers and exasperated coxswains were also on public view: *Life* and the *Literary Digest* showed rowers in cover photographs, the *New Yorker* in several mostly whimsical sketches. Full-page magazine ads also featured rowers to help sell cigarettes, pipe tobacco, cocoa, beer, ale, stout, ginger ale, whiskey, automobiles, tires, motor oil, long-distance telephone service, breakfast cereal, chewing gum, men's suits and underwear, radios, electric razors, knitting yarn, candy bars, motor launches, cameras, watches, and Cracker Jack. Management consultants out to stress discipline and coordination dressed their ads with eight-oared crews, and rowers have even been shown to sell paper products, medical insurance, computer software, and female contraceptives.[30]

From 1895 to 1949 the Intercollegiate Rowing Association regatta on the Hudson at Poughkeepsie drew national press and public attention, especially as crews from Washington, California, Wisconsin, and the Mid-Atlantic and New England states all raced there, making it a truly national contest. More limited, but no less intense, was the annual race on the Thames at New London between crews from Harvard and Yale, a regatta that continues as America's oldest intercollegiate sports competition.

Popular films often portrayed rowers as bold and heroic. *The Young Rajah* in 1922 starred matinee idol Rudolph Valentino as a Harvard student and winning oarsman. By contrast, comic genius Buster Keaton is a hysterically inept (yet winning) coxswain in *College*, his 1927 film about campus life and romance. Stereotypically, in MGM's 1938 film *A Yank at Oxford* Robert Taylor is the cocky American who makes social gaffes galore but goes on to stroke the varsity eight to victory in the Boat Race. *Let's Go Collegiate* is a silly 1941 romantic comedy with coxswain and stroke as lead characters. Before their big race the stroke needs seasick pills but instead gulps mothballs—giving him astounding power to win. *Oxford Blues* was a 1984 remake of *A Yank at Oxford*, and in 1986 Canadian and world champion Ned Hanlan was celebrated in *The Boy in Blue*, a melodramatic film starring Nicolas Cage as a sculler dominated by gamblers. In 1996 the story of the 1987 "mutiny" at the Boat Race by Americans in the Oxford eight is told in the British film *True Blue*—released in the United States as *Miracle at Oxford*.

In this century the 2010 film *The Social Network* about the origins of Facebook included rowing scenes at Harvard with the Winklevoss twins, Tyler and Cameron, training on the Charles and racing a pair at Henley. In 2016 a PBS *American Experience* program, "The Boys of '36," documented the University of Washington eight that beat Germany and Italy at the 1936 Berlin Olympics. Two anticipated films are *The Boys in the Boat* and *The Red Rose Crew*, adapting them to the screen. *Swing* is an

Rudolph Valentino is a Harvard rower in *The Young Rajah* in 1922 PARAMOUNT PICTURES

Buster Keaton is an inept but ultimately winning coxswain in *College* in 1927 UNITED ARTISTS

upcoming film about Columbia University rowers and their encounters with a demanding coach.

AMATEUR OR PROFESSIONAL?

Competitive rowing has revived a once-essential feature from the commercial days of the nineteenth century: corporate sponsorship. Rich patrons and syndicates paid for prize money and training then, often honored by seeing their names on trophies and racing shells. Businessmen like Asa Soule had his Hop Bitters company sponsor two of the celebrated Courtney-Hanlan races. Today US Rowing credits more than twenty-four sponsors for its programs. Fittingly, it was Ladbroke's, the betting and gambling company, that became the first corporate sponsor for the Oxford-Cambridge Boat Race, beginning in 1976. Just as fitting, its second sponsor was Beefeater Gin.[31]

Tensions between social and economic classes have always shaped perceptions of rowing, especially as a sport seemingly most enjoyed by a wealthy elite. But how elite was, and is, rowing? In 2012, Australian-born social activist Trenton Oldfield (himself a private boarding school graduate) chose to protest British elitism at the Oxford-Cambridge Boat Race on the Thames in London. Donning a wetsuit, he swam toward the approaching eights. Referees halted the race for half an hour, then restarted it—amid complaints about the unfairness of it all. Oldfield was arrested, jailed for two months, and deported, but his feat sparked vigorous debate about rowing and elitism, especially in Britain and Australia. "Elitism leads to tyranny," Oldfield had shouted, condemning the amorphous Oxbridge world as England's main source of social injustice.[32]

For truer effect, Oldfield might have taken his swim a few miles up the Thames at Windsor, where Eton College, the boys' boarding school founded by King Henry VI in 1440, enshrines the epitome of class, privilege, and elite rowing. Twenty prime ministers have attended, along with aristocrats and sons of the royal family; and Eton routinely packs off more graduates to Oxford and Cambridge than does any other school. In fact, Eton is credited as the source of amateur rowing in England, ever since its students first challenged older rival Winchester

College (founded in 1382) to a boat race in 1818. Their competition has continued since 1829. And except for its brutal and comical "Wall Game," in which a ball is wrestled and kicked and nudged along a muddy furrow for an hour, rowing is Eton's hallmark sport. The college Boat Club has more members and more shells than any other club on Earth.[33]

Eton is noted also for its annual Procession of Boats, dating from 1793, that features rowers in fancy dress and flower-trimmed hats who stand upright with their oars in shells as they drift by the college. And Eton's 1863 "Boating Song" typifies the sport's easy pleasures:

> Jolly boating weather,
> And a hay harvest breeze,
> Blade on the feather,
> Shade off the trees,
> Swing swing together,
> With your bodies between your knees,
> Swing swing together,
> With your bodies between your knees.

The best-known Old Etonian rower in recent times is Sir Matthew Pinsent, a four-time Olympic medal winner. A direct descendant of Edward I and William the Conqueror, Pinsent's most notable achievements were in the pair-oared shell, where partnership is essential. But Pinsent's partner was hardly aristocratic. Stephen Redgrave attended a comprehensive (public) school. He won seventeen sculling and sweeps victories at Henley, four world championships in the pair with Pinsent, and five gold medals at the Olympics (with Pinsent, twice in a pair and once in a quad). For this he also attained knighthood, not inherited but earned, becoming Sir Stephen Redgrave in 2001.[34]

Yet the fact that such different backgrounds remain essential to the Pinsent-Redgrave success story confirms how class always matters in England, and especially in rowing. The first competitive rowers were working-class watermen, not elite gentlemen who no doubt found the whole idea rather toilsome. But by the nineteenth century, class divisions had helped define the sport. The Amateur Rowing Association was founded in 1882 and promptly excluded from its rolls anyone who had raced for money, worked to train athletes, belonged to a club that admitted "mechanics or professionals," or was himself a "mechanic or artisan." In protest, middle- and working-class men formed the National Amateur Rowing Association in 1890. The two associations coexisted uneasily until 1947 when British rowers needed to join FISA (the world rowing association) in order to compete at the upcoming Olympics. That year the Amateur Rowing Association dropped its ban on manual laborers, and the two associations finally merged in 1956, now called British Rowing.[35]

Like England's first notable rowers, Australia's were also hardly elite gentlemen but tough and sturdy waterfront workers. Rowing historian Robin Poke notes that Edward "Ned" Trickett, the first Australian to win the World Sculling Championship, in 1876, was a quarryman; a later victor, Bill Beach, was a blacksmith. Some Australian private schools are known for rowing, but are outnumbered by proletarian rowing clubs.[36]

When helping to create the modern Olympics, de Coubertin saw a divide in rowing that came to be defined by class. "Particularly for working class men, de Coubertin seemed to value sport and physical activity for its prosaic qualities," sports historian Douglas Brown has noted. "In other words, ensuring that sport and occasions for physical activity were available to urban working class men was a means of keeping the unpredictable in check." Brown noted that such a "prosaic view of sport did not extend to all of de Coubertin's theories. For elite athletes and men of means, some activities were held out as potential sources of human creativity and ingenuity. Rowing, for example, was the modern sport par excellence because of the poetic potential that lay in its refined mechanics and demanding techniques."[37]

Yet, over the years "elite" has gained a new meaning in the rowing community, and today denotes the very best athletes: those racing for national and international championships and at the Olympics. And an "Elite" category at regattas today includes rowers who are simply the world's best.

For sheer scale and excitement, amateurs of all levels have triumphed on the River Charles, where once the professionals dominated the wildly popular City Regatta. Since 1965, amateur rowers have competed in the Head of the Charles Regatta (HOCR). Begun in England, a head-of-the-river race is held on narrow waterways where no more than two crews might safely row abreast. Instead, shells start off at quick intervals, every ten or fifteen seconds. They are really racing the clock. To minimize collisions, the fastest boats from the past year start first. Passing—or being passed—adds to the excitement for rowers and spectators, but may not affect the overall standings. Unlike the broad courses where six or more crews race abreast (at the Olympics or on the Schuylkill, the Potomac, the Hudson, Lake Cayuga, Lake Merritt in Oakland, Mission Bay in San Diego) "head" races are free-for-alls, with screaming fans in easy shouting range from the passing shells. In 1997 Boston's HOCR drew so many rowers it became a two-day affair, and is now the largest in the world. Each October, more than eleven thousand athletes in more than nineteen hundred shells race in sixty-one events, drawing a quarter-million spectators. This regatta recreates sensations from the past—the riverbanks jammed with spectators cheering so loudly rowers could barely hear their coxswain.

Some years the spectators themselves were a problem, as when at the nineteenth-century professional races the main contest became how much you could drink. "By the mid-1980s ... the venue had become a beer-soaked bacchanal for collegians from local schools who couldn't tell port from starboard and didn't care," the regatta's official history recounted. Chug-a-lugging students saw the regatta as an off-season version of spring break. Some years the regatta was best remembered for "rampant rowdiness" in an "aquatic Woodstock" sparked by "open fires, tents, and overnight camping" along with nonstop boozing.

Change finally came when nearly three hundred police officers moved in: most on foot, some on horseback, and a few aboard boats and helicopters. "The scene on Race Day 1987 resembled the beginning of Prohibition," the regatta history noted, "with officers summarily disposing of illicit bottles and cans." In years since, spectators have appeared on the banks of the Charles—again anticipating a regatta and not a riot.[38]

In an ironic twist on professional rowing's grim history, the Head of the Charles Regatta attracted not only rowdy fans but also cash prizes—albeit briefly, and so far with scant effect. From 1999 to 2001, to help attract the world's best scullers, the Charles Schwab Corporation offered a $30,000 "Dash for Cash" at the conclusion of the three-mile HOCR races. The money was open to the three fastest scullers in the weekend's races, for a 350-meter sprint. With separate races for men and women, first prize was $7,500, second $5,000, and third $2,500. But these cash prizes did nothing to revive the glory (or greed) of professional rowing, and after three years Schwab dropped the whole idea.

Since then, the regatta has continued to thrive, attracting competitors in ever-growing numbers—world champions and novices alike. For, in the end, it isn't money that drives this sport today. It's the aching excitement shared during a race, and the pleasure gained out on the water during a relaxing row just for fun. Today pro rowing is all but forgotten, while to the growing armada of amateurs "there is nothing—absolutely nothing—half so much worth doing as simply messing about in boats."[39]

Appendix

The Rowing Legacy of Thomas Eakins

We know the Biglin brothers, at least by their rugged appearance, thanks to the attention and artistry of Thomas Eakins. In the spring of 1872, the young painter riveted his attention to the Biglins as they arrived in Philadelphia for their historic championship pair-oared race. This encounter would inspire a series of vivid images that charm and captivate us to this day. The Eakins rowing pictures, now on view at nine galleries across the United States, are admired in countless posters on boathouse walls. They came to define athleticism and masculinity in nineteenth-century America. And they remain our most tangible link to the lost world of professional rowing.[1]

In 1871, the same year the Biglins had first begun training in a pair-oared shell, Eakins had just finished and shown his own first rowing picture. Like the Biglins' challenge, Eakins' artistry, too, was bold, and quite odd. On a broad three-by-four-foot canvas he depicted no race in this first rowing picture. Instead, *The Champion Single Sculls* or *Max Schmitt in a Single Scull* reveals the shadowy Schuylkill River valley late one fall afternoon, its hills spotted with soaring trees and spanned by bridges. Other craft dot the calm water, but at the center of the stream a single sculler glides our way—not even rowing, but at ease. He is Eakins's high school classmate Max Schmitt, and this painting was the artist's gift to his longtime friend, then a lawyer and competitive amateur rower in Philadelphia.[2]

Eakins had first displayed this imposing oil at the city's Union League Club in April 1871. Eakins, wrote the *Evening Bulletin*'s art critic, "who has lately returned from Europe" has a picture "which, though peculiar, has more than ordinary interest. The artist, in dealing so boldly and broadly with the commonplace in nature, is working upon well-supported theories, and, despite somewhat scattered effect, gives promise of a conspicuous future." Rowing was the commonplace, and Eakins would make it not only conspicuous but also special.[3]

Eakins in Paris and Philadelphia

Thomas Cowperthwait Eakins was born in Philadelphia in 1844, son of a writing master who penned and prepared public documents. He grew up in a large brick row house a few blocks east of Fairmount Park. From there Eakins, his parents, and his three younger sisters all enjoyed rowing from nearby Boathouse Row. From the Pennsylvania Barge Club Eakins liked to scull along with Schmitt, who first won the Schuylkill Navy's amateur singles championship in 1866.[4]

Having studied drafting in high school, Eakins was skilled at both close observation and precision drawing. He tried freestyle drawing classes at the Pennsylvania Academy of the Fine Arts. Then, to better understand the human body, he sat in on the anatomy lectures at Jefferson Medical College taught by the renowned surgeon Samuel D. Gross.

Eakins's father paid a subscription for him to avoid serving in the Civil War, encouraged his artistic aspirations, and offered him the chance to study at one of the world's finest schools, the Ecole des Beaux-Arts. In 1866, Thomas Eakins sailed for Paris where, with luck, he joined the atelier of Jean-Léon Gérôme, a legendary teacher and artist. Besides learning Gérôme's precise and delicate painting style, Eakins embraced positivist theories derived by Hippolyte Taine, a French critic, historian, and sociologist who saw the scientific method as a potent force in both art and aesthetics.[5]

En route to Paris in October 1866, Eakins wrote his mother about a dream, in which "I had been rowing with Max and I was drinking some cool beer at Popp's at Fairmount...." He later wrote to ask, "Have you been out on the river? It must be very beautiful now with the red and yellow leaves of the trees." While studying in Paris Eakins gazed at the Seine, realized how he missed the Schuylkill, and in letters home asked about Max's gains as a sculler.[6]

During his three years in Paris, Eakins learned an academic regimen that used meticulous sketches and perspectives in a disciplined process for constructing a painting. This was most unlike the new spontaneous style, "Impressionism," that other young painters were trying in and around the French capital. But Eakins moderated Gérôme's precision after moving on to Spain, where, in Madrid's Museo del Prado, he first saw vibrant paintings by Goya, Titian, and Velasquez. Their potent colors and forms created an art he said "stands out like nature itself" that gave him the "courage" to expand his own evolving style.[7]

Landing home in Philadelphia, on July 4, 1870, Eakins was eager to rediscover American subjects and themes. Forsaking any Continental airs he soon found what he was craving back on the Schuylkill. "For the next three years," wrote art historian Helen A. Cooper, "the theme of rowers and rowing would hold Eakins in a kind of imaginative possession. It was an intensity of focus that he would never repeat with any other subject."[8]

When he began that first rowing picture of Schmitt, Eakins had few examples to follow—or, in his often-contrary manner, examples to reject. He was free to create a genre that introduced the ease and the effort of rowing to the artistic salon. Eakins rarely left his hometown, and likely never saw one of America's first oil paintings of the sport, *Scull Race, Boston Bay*, which George D. Hopkins completed in 1856 and kept in Massachusetts. But Eakins would have known the popular 1867 Currier & Ives lithograph showing the championship-sculling match at Newburgh between James Hamill and George Brown.[9]

In 1869 *Harper's* illustrated its coverage of the celebrated Harvard-Oxford race by showing the riverscape thronged with spectators. In this era, rowing provided spectacle, and artists commonly portrayed regattas as crowded affairs in open landscapes. By contrast, Eakins strove for an art that was more immediate, personal, and intensely focused on the rowers themselves.

To celebrate Schmitt's third Schuylkill Navy championship, Eakins painted not the bustling scene on race day but the near-empty river course, a calm and silvery surface sweeping through hilly Fairmount Park. In this subtle locale it was the rowers alone who captivated the twenty-seven-year old artist, not their ardent and boisterous fans. Rowers were Eakins's friends and also his paragons, for they personified both athletic and aesthetic ideals. He admired the muscular poise and skill rowers need to power and steer their delicate racing shells for miles of searing competition. He also saw the oarsmen's virile physiques as a glorious, almost abstract, perfection. Rowing revealed for him an American egalitarian spirit—blending intellect, precision, and stamina to attain a new and democratic heroism.[10]

For this first rowing picture, Eakins placed Schmitt in the center foreground. He sits in his Elliott-built cedar single "Josie," named for his sister. Schmitt is relaxed, just after pulling a stroke. He grips both oars with one hand, and turns to stare forward at us while his shell skims across the mirroring water. By contrast, another sculler in the middle distance pulls away from our view: shoulders taut and gaze intense. This is Eakins himself, hard at work while his friend Max drifts at ease. He signed this canvas "EAKINS 1871" on his shell's wash-box, the wooden strake above the deck that surrounds the rower's cockpit to deflect splashes. This is the first of several oils in which Eakins included himself as a participant, depicting here a masculine ideal and in others his astute intensity.[11]

With Eakins rowing energetically past Schmitt *The Champion Single Sculls* is subtly his self-portrait. As art historian Elizabeth Johns has observed, a

single rower alone propelled himself and steered. Like good men in all endeavors, he "rowed within himself," not allowing himself to be swayed by transitory fears of losing or even of falling behind, but demanding of himself loyalty to the measured discipline that he had perfected in his training. Eakins himself, metaphorically, was to be a single sculler all his life.[12]

Eakins captured the rowers and their shells in exacting detail, but exceeded straightforward depiction by ringing them in their own sumptuous reflections. Eakins also revealed delicately exquisite ripples on the Schuylkill's shiny surface, achieved before touching brush to canvas by how he calculated each crest and trough in measured perspective sketches and drawings. These perspectives are artistic in their own way, applying trigonometry and descriptive geometry to transform three-dimensional action to a two-dimensional canvas. Art historians consider Eakins's ten surviving perspective drawings for his rowing pictures as special artifacts, keys to the tension and magnitude he revealed in the finished paintings. Amy Werbel has described how Eakins gave horizontal and vertical planes notable depth by constructing a foreshortening grid.[13]

"Each wave being curved has an infinity of planes which could not all be examined separately," Eakins wrote in a drawing manual prepared for his art students. Instead, he devised perspective drawings with simplified level and tangent planes that allowed him to capture waves and light in almost photographic detail. "There is so much beauty in reflections that it is generally well worth while to try to get them right." This sedulous preparation made both his preliminary works and all his finished canvases vitally artistic.

EAKINS PORTRAYS THE BIGLINS

In the spring of 1872, Eakins paid rapt attention to the Biglins, creating a famous series that expanded his artistic concepts and techniques while he captured their images as robust athletes. The first Biglin oil painting grew from elaborate perspective calculations that revealed the brothers as they practiced on the Schuylkill for their pair-oared race in May 1872. The second and third oils captured the brothers at key moments during the race itself.[14]

Eakins befriended the Biglins when they arrived in Philadelphia to begin training for their championship race, and met them at the Vesper Boat Club where they stored and launched their shells. Philadelphians speculated about this race for months, and Eakins chatted about it with rowers along Boathouse Row.

Eakins studied the Biglins intensely as they practiced, calculating just how to capture both their brisk movements and the river valley's overall light and shadow. Scholars of art and of gender have speculated about how Eakins might have been depicting (or projecting) his own masculinity into these paintings. In other later paintings, his focus on naked men led some historians and critics to highlight a homoerotic interest. That interest does not appear in these early rowing pictures as the Biglins and all other oarsmen Eakins sketched and painted wore their usual rowing garb. In fact, he even added shirts to rowers who raced bare-chested.[15]

Painting the Biglins' pair race posed artistic problems galore, and Eakins was eager to solve them. But first he turned his creative ingenuity to a pre-race, straight-on view by crafting perspective drawings for *The Pair-Oared Shell* or *The Biglin Brothers Practicing*.[16]

To render the Biglins in their intense practice session, Eakins first devised a matrix with a viewpoint just under the old Columbia Railroad Bridge. Here he put the brothers in mid-stroke, erect and energetic in their posture yet calm and confident, centered at a fulcrum of shadow and light. "A boat is the hardest thing I know of to put into perspective," Eakins told his student Charles Bregler. "It is so much like the human figure, there is something alive about it. It requires a heap of thinking and calculating to build a boat." For his Biglin images, Eakins recalled, "I made a little boat out of a cigar box and rag figures, with the red and white shirts, blue ribbons around the head, and I put them out into the sunlight on the roof and painted them, and tried to get the true tones."[17]

First, Eakins calculated a perspective grid with relative positions for the shell, its red metal outriggers, the oars, and above it all a looming bridge pier. A second perspective drawing captured reflections on the water, a surface of patterns set off in light and shade. The finished oil has the brothers' heads at its center, their pates wrapped in dark blue silk bandanas. As they scowl astern at us their shoulders swing back. Arms taut, they draw the oars through the water to finish a stroke. The dusky and massive bridge fills half the canvas, its stone blocks highlighted in sunlight, its reflection rippling toward us and around the slender shell. Here Eakins captures and constructs dark and light, force and finesse.

Curator Darrel Sewell has noted that to achieve this stunning image, Eakins "broke the water's surface into tilted planes containing fragments of color from the boat, the pier, and the clothing of the rowers, and made notations on the drawing as to where a reflection might fall. . . ." What gives this painting its power is an angular interplay of radiance and shadow, all arrayed across the glimmering water. The art critic for the *New York Times* detected a quality of surprise when first seeing *The Pair-Oared Shell* in 1879 at the National Academy of Design: "If it were possible to conceive that an artist who paints like Mr. Eakins had a poetic impression, we would like to think that in this composition he had tried to express the peculiar charm that every one has experienced when row-ing out of the sunlight into the shadow of a great bridge."[18]

For his two oil paintings of the race itself, Eakins highlighted the brothers' stern features and stolid bearing. In *The Biglin Brothers Racing*, he sets us right by the rowers as they ease into the second mile of their five-mile race, so intimately close that we see them in detail but glimpse only parts of their shell. Barney watches John's oar, stroke-for-stroke, as a bow rower must in a pair. This picture is compressed, capturing a scene of rippling reflections as the Biglins clear the bow of the other shell. Both men seem relaxed, gliding on their seats toward the stern, just beginning to square up their blades for the next mighty catch.

Here Eakins inserts many realistic details, such as the leather ridge that keeps the oar from slipping outward through the oarlock. He has spectators tracking the race aboard launches and cheering from ashore. Two steamboats packed with fans chug along the course and rowers in a four try to keep up. One gent gallops on horseback to keep pace with the speeding shells. Eakins also captures the Schuylkill valley's contours, shadowed and hilly around the sparkling water. Observers who have admired this Eakins riverscape often assume from the setting that the Biglins hail from Philadelphia, although this was the only race they ever rowed there.[19]

For *The Biglin Brothers Turning the Stake* Eakins reveals physical ten-sions with an engaging narrative. At first glance the Biglins seem still, as if resting or even posing for the artist. You wonder: Are they even racing? Then Eakins draws us in with details that create a special moment. Pro-fessional races were seldom rowed straight away, but instead had at least one turn; this, so spectators could view more of the contest: coming and going, start and finish. Here, in shadows from the Girard Avenue Bridge, the rowers had to turn at mid-course. These moves held special allure for rowing fans because it was often at the stake where accidents and fouls occurred. In fact, fouls had already become so common that this course and others installed a stake for each crew.[20]

The picture's story unfolds as we see the red-capped Pittsburgh crew in the distance, just nearing its red-flagged stake. Dominating the fore-ground are the Biglins, already clearing their blue-flagged stake and set to drive back upstream to the finish. Eakins depicts the brothers at their most demanding moment in the race when, to pivot around the stake quickly, they row against each other. Barney in the bow pulls the shell around while John seems to hold water or even back his blade a bit, stirring a slight splash. As he did in his first rowing canvas celebrating Max Schmitt, Eakins painted himself into this scene. He is the single sculler waving at us from beyond the red-flagged stake.[21]

Later in his career, Eakins used photographs to project outlines and images on the canvases he painted. But before the camera he had help by making meticulous calculations to create perspective and depth. Art historian Christina Currie has discovered that in a lecture Eakins gave on vanishing points he explained how by using colored inks he could organize a complicated subject as a drawing before producing it in oils. Next, Eakins transferred the forms from paper to canvas by making pinpricks that define the shapes he would then paint.[22]

John Biglin was a champion single-sculler, and while in Philadelphia he agreed to row on the Delaware River with Eakins in attentive pursuit. This excursion resulted in several images famous today, rendered in watercolors and oil. Eakins first tried watercolors as a child, and only returned to the medium as an adult when he painted his father in 1870. In 1873, he employed watercolors again to create stunning views of John Biglin sculling. Art historian Marc Simpson noted that Eakins differed from other American artists of his time (Winslow Homer especially) by preparing studies in oils *before* painting them in watercolors. Helen Cooper suggested Eakins liked the easier control and the chance to paint over his strokes with oils, and could study and plan effects and techniques later achieved with the quicker, less-controllable watercolors.[23]

Eakins again made skillful perspective drawings before reaching for a brush. His perspective studies of John Biglin sculling—in pencil, ink, and wash—include grids with John's head the focal point.

Eakins also created an oil of *John Biglin in a Single Scull*. In it Biglin seems framed by planes of color. The top third of this canvas is a gray-blue sky with daubed trees along the distant New Jersey shore; the bottom third has scrambled hues, reflecting in the water suggestive elements of the rower's arms, shirt, and red silk bandana. The center third of this

Perspective sketch for *John Biglin in a Single Scull* by Thomas Eakins (c. 1873)
MUSEUM OF FINE ARTS, BOSTON, GIFT OF CORNELIUS V. WHITNEY

vibrant oil highlights Biglin, with bulging forearms and his typically somber stare. He embodies bold potential—knees rising and back flexing as he slides toward the stern, coiling to spring at the next hard stroke.

Once confident he could capture in oils Biglin's power and grace, Eakins tried four watercolors. The two that survive are both titled *John Biglin in a Single Scull.* (One is at the Metropolitan Museum, the other at the Yale University Art Gallery.) They seem light and graceful, yet both are still controlled, framed by swirling clouds above and rippling reflections below. The bow of another shell pokes into view beside Biglin's, and along the broad river's eastern shore we spot an eight-oared shell, a schooner, two sloops, and a ferry.

When Eakins sent a John Biglin watercolor to Gérôme in Paris his teacher replied cordially. But he wrote back that he disliked the subject's pose. Too static, he said. Gérôme identified a common problem with most rowing pictures. "There is in every prolonged movement, such as rowing, an infinity of rapid phases, and an infinity of points from the moment when the rower, after having leaned forward, pulls his upper body back as far as it will go." Painters "of our sort" (meaning realists) pick the beginning or end—the catch or the finish—of a stroke, but "you have taken an intermediate point, that is the reason for the immobility in the work."

One reason this image and most rowing paintings and photos appear static is that the motion in a stroke is fluid and continuous, with the apparently still pose really but a moment captured from the recurring sequence. This problem aside, Gérôme found much to admire in his pupil's watercolor: "What pleases me especially, and this in thinking of your future is the mixture of well founded construction and honesty which dominate in this work."[24]

In May 1874, Eakins sent his master a corrected version of the John Biglin watercolor (since lost), which drew a keen reply: "Your watercolor is entirely good, and I am very pleased to have in the New World a pupil such as you who does me honor." Another watercolor version of Biglin in a single, *The Sculler*, Eakins sold in February 1874 for $80 (its location is unknown). This was his first sale.[25]

The last rowers Eakins painted on water were the amateurs he knew around Boathouse Row. He rendered them all in oils, but with a quicker and looser style than used for the Biglins. Instead of portraying celebrities, Eakins next chose as subjects his family friends Henry and "Billy" Schreiber, whom he pictured rowing a pair, rather inelegantly. Their wrists sag on the oar. Their shoulders contort. In *The Schreiber Brothers* or *The Oarsmen* Eakins captures a languor and unsteadiness as they slouch through a stroke, their faces beset by troubled glances.

Eakins feared that the work might seem too dark, with a rowboat he had placed behind the pair barely visible in shadows cast by a stone bridge. Concerned about this picture's display in an 1874 exhibit at the National Academy of Design in New York, and eager to lighten its appearance, Eakins wrote his friend Earl Shinn—also a student of Gérôme. "If you are in the neighborhood and want an excuse to go in [the Academy], you can rub a little linseed oil with your finger on any part of the shadows that are soaked in or on the whole of the picture except the light of the red handkerchiefs & the sky."[26]

After this work Eakins freely brushed in oil a *Sketch of Max Schmitt in a Single Scull* that is blurry and blandly colored. Then he set a four-oared shell in mid-river with *Oarsmen on the Schuylkill* showing a Pennsylvania Barge Club four with Schmitt recognizable in the third seat. Eakins called this a "figure picture" and writer and critic John Updike concluded, more than a century later when all the rowing pictures were exhibited together, that it "does not quite dispel an aura of boredom with the subject of sculling," even "though Eakins returns, with four individualized men, to the same sunlit blue-gray river which supported Max Schmitt in his single scull." Eakins did so reluctantly, it seems, and in haste.[27]

Despite its unfinished appearance, Eakins still defended *Oarsmen on the Schuylkill* when the National Academy of Design rejected it for display. "It is a much better figure picture than any one in N.Y. can paint," he complained to Shinn. "I conclude that those who judged it were incapable of judging or jealous of my work, or that there was no judgment at all on merit, the works being hung up in the order received or by lottery."[28]

Eakins painted his last rowing subjects in 1874. And about *The Schreiber Brothers* or *The Oarsmen* he said, "The picture don't please me altogether. I had it too long about I guess. The drawing of the boats & the figures the construction of the thing & the peculiar swing of the figures rowing pair oared, the twist of the starboard oarsman to one the one side & the port to the other on account of the long sweeps are all better expressed than I see any New Yorkers doing—but anyhow I am tired of it. I hope it will sell and I'll never see it again."[29]

Despite misgivings about rowing as a subject, Eakins exhibited his Biglin pictures in New York four more times after 1874.[30] He may well have "tired" of painting rowers, yet he still held them in mind. The next project, which became one of his most famous and original paintings, was *The Gross Clinic*, a dramatic oil portrait of the surgeon—bloody scalpel glistening in hand—at the center of a crowded operating theater. X-rays of a preparatory sketch for this work reveal that Eakins had first used the paper to plan yet another painting of rowers, but had then turned to surgery instead.[31]

Decades later rowing appeared in Eakins's art one last time, quite obliquely. He had exhibited *The Pair-Oared Shell* in 1879, which reportedly "gave . . . a shock to the artistic conventionalities of Philadelphia. . . ." He went on to portray baseball players and prizefighters. And then, when working on his last sports painting, *Wrestlers*, in 1899, Eakins depicted in the foreground two men entangled in awkward grips on a canvas mat. But there in the background (in both a sketch and the finished oil) Eakins used nearly a fifth of the frame to include a young man rowing. He was not on his beloved Schuylkill, or on any water at all. This time he rowed on a machine, its tension maintained by pulleys and weights.[32]

Eakins might have quit painting rowers in the mid-1870s because he disliked the rising evidence that professionals were corrupting their sport, making them less admirable subjects. But the only professionals he had painted were the Biglins and their rivals in Philadelphia, who, to date, had not been shamed by any scandals. Among the amateurs he painted, his pal Max Schmitt had stopped rowing competitively, so the sport itself had lost a friendly local connection. Updike's suggestion about Eakins's "boredom" with the subject is shared by Helen Cooper, who noted that "between 1871 and 1874 he produced 24 extant rowing pictures—oils, watercolors, oil sketches, and drawings. He had examined the subject in painstaking visual and scientific detail. What more was he to explore? Portray another heroic rower? To what end? Rowing as a subject was an intense preoccupation for a few years—sort of like a love affair—and then it was over. He was on to other things."[33]

And yet, while Eakins was at it he gave us the most tangible evidence we still have—and can still discover—from that lost world of professional rowing. With pen and brush he personified the grim work of being a champion, and also the ease and pleasures of being an amateur.

Acknowledgments

Three special people helped launch and sustain my research for this book. *Smithsonian* magazine editor Bruce Hathaway commissioned me to write about the 1996 exhibit *Thomas Eakins: The Rowing Pictures*, leading me on a joyful search for the Biglins and their colleagues. Helen A. Cooper at the Yale University Art Gallery, who organized the exhibit and catalogue, answered my many queries about Eakins. Then Bernard (Bern) Biglin, John Biglin's great-grandson, spotted my name in Helen's catalogue and tracked me down. Bern has shared his family records and photos, searched archives and online sites, and even decided to take up sculling.

David Kelly, a sports specialist at the Library of Congress, led me to countless helpful sources. And my earliest and most productive ally throughout this quest has been rowing historian and collector Thomas E. Weil Jr.

The other rowing history buffs who aided me reliably were Bill Miller, Goran Buckhorn, Peter Mallory, Christopher Dodd, Daniel J. Boyne, Hart and Gillian Perry, Bill Pickelhaupt, and Edward A. English. Fellow rowers who contributed included Mark Mattison, Bill Richards, James Sciales, David Kappes, Philip Greipp, Katharine McCormick, Andy Anderson, Barry Strauss, Xavier Macia, Karen Klinger, and Sarah Risser. Essential perspectives came from sports historians Robert Edelman, David Nemec, Daniel Okrent, and Adam Hornbuckle. Thanks as well to Brett Johnson at US Rowing and Hilary Gehman at Cornell .

Once launched on this delightful search, I gratefully enlisted help from many archivists, curators, and librarians. These skilled folks included Wayne Wilson at the LA84 Foundation Library; Maygene Daniels, Ann Halpern, and Josephine Rogers at the National Gallery of Art; Heather McNabb at the McCord Museum; and Jane E. Allen, E. Ann Wilcox, and Sarah Sullivan at the Independence Seaport Museum. I'm also thankful to Edward O'Reilly and Dale Neighbors at the New York Historical Society, Dan Miller at The Antique Boat Museum, Kristen Swett at the

City of Boston Archives, Jon Schmitz at the Chautauqua Institution, Zoe Nousiainen at the Saratoga Springs Public Library, Holly Hallaman at the Saratoga Springs Historical Society, Roberta Y. Arminio and Jean Sutherland at the Ossining Historical Society, Fire Department of New York historian Donald van Holt, Scout Noffke at Dartmouth's Rauner Special Collections Library, and Isabel Navarro at the Saint James Cathedral Basilica in Brooklyn. Essential help came from the staffs at the New York City Municipal Archives, the Museum of the City of New York, the Brooklyn Historical Society, the Ossining Historical Society, the Nyack Historical Society, the Nyack Public Library History Room, the Dutchess County Historical Society, the New York Public Library, the Philadelphia Free Library, the Boston Public Library, the Harvard University Archives, and the G. W. Blunt Library at the Mystic Seaport Museum. The Biglin genealogy was meticulously traced for the Biglin Family Ancestry Page by Susan Sanchez and Margie Reynolds, with additional details from Ed Johnson.

I appreciate all the encouragement and helpful questions during my wandering research from Priscilla McMillan, Joel Rogers, William Doherty, Steve Altman, Paul and Ceil Hendrickson, Jean Richards, Tony and Mary Alice Wolf, Geoff and Terry Lewis, Drew Fetherston, Amanda Harris, Christopher and Alison Parker, Daniel Semick, Joan and Ralph Widner, Bill McKenzie, Arnold J. Mandell, Helen Weiss, Raymond A. Schroth, John Yakaitis, John T. Williams, Katherine Flynn, Amin Kamran-Rad, and Hal and Lis Wackman.

At the Potomac Boat Club, I had special help from Alfred Bigelow, Jim Edmonds, Floyd Galler, Chuck Levy, Don Spero, and Elizabeth Webber. Helpful questions and comments abounded from fellow PBC rowers Kate Dowling, Ken Dreyfuss, Camilla Durfee, Don Gantz, Betsy Garside, Caryl Greenfield, Andy Hewitt, Dave Jaffe, Tony Johnson, John Lavery, Stan Marcuss, Jack McGirl, Larry Mosher, Ralph Oser, Bob Parke, Bruce Parker, Paul Pearlstein, Allen Rosenberg, Chuck Selden, Bob Spousta, Elmira Togliatti, Ron Uscinski, Chandler van Orman, and Jack Wells.

At the San Diego Rowing Club, the fellow rowers who gave useful advice included Lisa Roth, Brian Armstrong, David Ward, Sean Durkin,

Chris Feuge, David Frost, Francis X. Hartmann, Rob and Kim Hibler, Ralph Johnson, Scott and Kathy Kemper, Stuart Neffler, Dan O'Neill, Ed Parrish, Glenn Schweighardt, Sonya Sullivan, Dodd Wragg, and Chris Callahan.

At the ZLAC Rowing Club, Meredith Alcock and Karen Bachofer were especially helpful.

Coaches I've interviewed include a mighty roster: G. Ernest Arlett (Northeastern University), Ted Bonnano (Fordham), Hartmut Busch-bacher (US Olympic women), Charlie Butt Jr. (Potomac Boat Club), Charley Butt III (Harvard), Steve Gladstone (Brown, University of California at Berkeley, and Yale), Tony Johnson (Yale and Georgetown), Ted Nash (University of Pennsylvania), Harry Parker (Harvard), Hart Perry (Dartmouth and the Kent School), Allen Perry Rosenberg (Vesper Boat Club, US Olympic men, Potomac Boat Club), Harrison "Stork" Sanford (Cornell), and Mike Spracklen (US Olympic men).

Meredith Dias and Joshua L. Rosenberg skillfully and most patiently edited the manuscript. And I'm also grateful to Thelonious Sphere Monk, whose solo piano—so sprightly and so loose—created the perfect atmosphere for my editing.

Special thanks are due to my agent, John Thornton, and my editor at Lyons Press, Rick Rinehart. And above all, I'm deeply grateful to my wife, JoAnne, who has kept me on course through a sometimes choppy adventure. We're a pair!

Although aided and sustained by all these generous people, I alone am responsible for this book's errors and omissions.

NOTES

Introduction

1   *All-Day City Item* (Philadelphia), May 20 and 21, 1872.

2   *The Press* (Philadelphia), May 21, 1872, 6, quoted in Allen and Allen, "Flashing Oars," note 154; *New York Clipper*, June 1, 1872, 68.

3   *Aquatic Monthly and Nautical Review* [hereafter *Aquatic Monthly*], June 1872, 56–58; Lanouette, *Smithsonian*, July 1996, 89–99.

4   Timothy Jack Ward, *New York Times*, June 20, 1996, C3. "Baseball's First Professional Game," May 4, 1871, in Gipe, *Great American Sports Book*, 8.

5   Johns, *Thomas Eakins*, 24–30; Helen A. Cooper et al., *Thomas Eakins*, 32.

6   *Daily News* (Saint John, New Brunswick), July 19, 1879; *New York Times*, July 29, 1887.

7   Halberstam, *Amateurs*, 25 and 28; Brown, *Boys in the Boat*; Boyne, *The Red Rose Crew*.

8   Engelhardt, *American Rowing Almanac* 1873, 78ff and 84–85; *Aquatic Monthly*, July 1872, 125–29; Mendenhall, *Short History*, 20.

Chapter 1

1   *Wilkes Spirit of the Times* [hereafter *Spirit of the Times*], August 16, 1862, 372; Jackson, *Encyclopedia*, 582 and 599. The song "No Irish Need Apply" was popularized by the famed singer and impresario Tony Pastor.

2   *New York Times*, November 13, 1881.

3   *Spirit of the Times*, August 16, 1862, 372; Washington, DC, *Evening Star* (from the *New York Herald*), April 23, 1886, 6.

4   Johnson, *History of Rowing*, 61; Peverelly, *Pastimes*, 268 and 323; D. T. Valentine, *Manual of the Corporation of the City of New York for 1858*, 102.

5   Peverelly, *Pastimes*, 268 and 291; Peverelly, *Aquatic Monthly*, October 1872, 370–71; Johnson, *History of Rowing*, 61; *Springfield Daily Republican*, July 16, 1873; Adelman, *Sporting Time*, 194; *Aquatic Monthly*, October 1872, 370–71; *New York Times*, April 23, 1886, 8.

6   *Proceedings of the Board of Councilmen of the City of New York*, vol. CVII, 208; Johnson, *History of Rowing*, 50.

7   Norsen, *Ward Brothers*, 56–62.

8   Norsen, 63.

9   Peverelly, *Pastimes*, 265–68; *New York Times*, September 7, 1860; Peverelly, *Pastimes*, 288, 291–94, 306–7; *Annual Illustrated Catalogue*, 228; McElroy and McBride, *Life Sketches*, 153–55.

10   Woodham-Smith, *Great Hunger*, 19.

11 Burrows and Wallace, *Gotham*, 1003–8; and Kevin Kenny, "Race, Violence, and Anti-Irish Sentiment in the Nineteenth Century," in Lee and Casey, *Irish American*, 367.

12 Wilcox, "Irish Americans in Sports: The Nineteenth Century," in Lee and Casey, *Irish American*, 446.

13 Peverelly, *Pastimes*, 259–60.

14 McCarthy, "Irish Americans in Sports: The Twentieth Century," in Lee and Casey, *Irish American*, 451.

15 Henry Adams mentioned Benjamin Crowninshield in *The Education of Henry Adams*; Smith, *Sports and Freedom*, 26–27.

16 "Songs of the Harvard versus Fort Hill Boy Rowing Match of 1858," *The Harvard Monthly* July 1858, (Vol, 4), 101.

17 Crimson became the official color by a student vote in 1875, replacing magenta. Crowninshield, *Private Journal*, 143–45; History of Harvard University website, http://www.harvard.edu/history, Harvard University Archives; "Second Beacon Regatta," *The Harvard Monthly* July 1858 (vol. 4), 262–63. See also Mendenhall, *Boat Race*, 11, 15–19, and 31.

18 Mendenhall, *Boat Race*, 20 and 30–31; Whiton, "The First Harvard-Yale Regatta (1852)," *The Outlook*, 286.

19 Whiton, 9 and 289; *New York Herald*, August 10, 1852, 2; *Boston Daily Evening Transcript*, August 5, 1852, 1; Mendenhall, *Boat Race*, 18–21.

20 Peverelly, *Pastimes*, 259, 266, 270 for mixed-boat races; 264 for crews in the Second Beacon Regatta, June 19, 1858; "Second Beacon Regatta," *The Harvard Monthly* July 1858 (vol. 4), 262–63; Wilcox, "Irish Americans in Sports: The Nineteenth Century," in Lee and Casey, *Irish American*, 451.

21 "Songs of the Harvard versus Fort Hill Boy Rowing Match of 1858," *The Harvard Monthly* July 1858 (vol. 4), 267. For more on Irish athletes, see Ralph C. Wilcox, "The Shamrock and the Eagle: Irish-Americans and Sport in the Nineteenth Century," in Eisen and Wiggins, *Ethnicity and Sport*, 55–74. See also "A Few Memories of William Reed Huntington by His Sister Mary Huntington Cooke."

22 Crowninshield, *Private Journal*, 151.

23 Smith, *Sports and Freedom*, 36.

Chapter 2

1 Strauss, *Rowing Against the Current*, 99–106.

2 John R. Hale to Thomas E. Weil Jr., September 22, 2015.

3 Hale, *Lords of the Sea*, 24, 27, 41 and 304; Lutz Weber, *Rekonstruktionsversuch der Agyptischen*, cited in Hans Georg Brecklinghaus, *The Human Beings Are Awoken*.

4 Latham and Matthews, *Diary of Samuel Pepys*, II, 101, entry for May 18, 1661.

5 Hitchcock article on "Rowing" in *The Universal Cyclopaedia*, 199; Dodd, *World Rowing*, 411 and 99–100; Cook, "Sports Papers: Rowing" in Rickards and Twyman, *Encyclopedia of Ephemera*, 307–8. My thanks to Christopher Dodd and Thomas E. Weil Jr. for use of their coordinated chronologies to compose this brief summary.

6 Hitchcock, *The Universal Cyclopaedia*, 199; Dodd, *Water Boiling*, 19.

7 Dodd, *World Rowing*, 72.

8   Holliman, *American Sports*, 155–56; Laumann and Wharton, *Rowing*, 109.

9   Johnson, *History of Rowing*, 47; Kelley, *American Rowing*, 19.

10   Weil, "A Time Line of Rowing History," Friends of Rowing History website, www
.rowinghistory.net/Time%20Line/TL%20-1849images.htm; Dodd, *World Rowing*, 101.

11   Peverelly, *Pastimes*; *Spirit of the Times* "Rowing Retrospect," 1871; Kelley, *American
Rowing*, 21; Johnson, *History of Rowing*, 53; *Manual of the Corporation of the City of New
York*, 459; Holliman, *American Sports*, 10 and 155–58; Goldstein, *Playing for Keeps*, 12.

12   Gordon Carruth and Associates, *Encyclopedia of American Facts and Dates*, 203;
Adelman, *Sporting Time*, 101; Betts, *America's Sporting Heritage*, 102. For problems
with "hippodroming" see Cross, *Social History of Leisure Since 1600*, 153. "Hippodrome"
was defined by *The Century Dictionary*, vol. 4, 1895, as "To conduct races, equestrian,
pedestrian, or aquatic, or other contests, in which the result is prearranged by collusion
between the managers and the contestants, in order to make gain through betting." My
thanks to Michael Quinion of "World Wide Words" for this citation.

13   Peverelly, *Pastimes*, 304–6. Crews from New York competed at Charleston in
November 1851 in a two-day regatta for purses of $500, $300, and $200. There they
raced competitors from Charleston, Wadmalaw Island, Edisto Island, St. Andrews, and
Beaufort, South Carolina; North Carolina; and Savannah and Darien, Georgia. My
thanks to sports historian Melvin L. Adelman for this lead and citation. See Adelman,
Sporting Time, 191–92; *Spirit of the Times*, September 17, 1836; see also Kelley, *American
Rowing*, 17–21.

14   Sometimes the organization was known as the Castle Garden Amateur Boat Club
Association. In addition to Wave and Gull, member clubs included Aerial, Pearl, and
Gazelle. Soon other clubs joined: Eagle, Swan, Saint Andrew, Medora, Jersey, Atlantic,
Undine, Pilot, and Wakona. Their records are at the New York Historical Society.

15   Adelman, *Sporting Time*, 191 and 197; *New York Herald*, July 19 and 26, 1837; Weil,
"A Time Line"; Norsen, *Ward Brothers*, 18; Engelhardt, *American Rowing Almanac*, 29;
New York Times, August 13, 1856.

16   Recorded races were first rowed in Baltimore in 1825; in Philadelphia in 1833; on
the Hudson at Poughkeepsie and Newburgh in 1834; at Fort Lee, New Jersey, in 1837;
and in Boston by 1842.

17   Competitive rowing's popularity began to expand steadily through the 1840s and
1850s, gaining for the best oarsmen the public's increasing attention and respect. The
first race in New Haven was in 1844, and around New York City notable races went off
at Hoboken in 1845, at Jersey City in 1850, and at Newark in 1858.

18   *New York Times*, July 13, 1858. The lunatic asylum's ornate octagonal dome remains a
landmark on Roosevelt Island.

19   Pickelhaupt, *Club Rowing*, 39 and 51 and *Rowing Clubs of California*, 14–15; Bill
Pickelhaupt correspondence with the author, June 9, 2015; *New York Clipper Annual*
1893, 16–25; Peverelly, *Pastimes*, 258–69; Laumann and Wharton, *Rowing*, 111; Weil,
Preliminary Survey.

20   *New Haven Palladium*, reprinted in *New York Times*, July 7, 1859.

21   *New York Times*, June 21, 1855, 4; Peverelly, *Pastimes*, 259–77.

22   Adelman, *Sporting Time*, 193; *New York Times*, July 6, 1859.

Chapter 3

1 John was born in the parish of Street in County Westmeath, near Dublin, on May 21, 1816; Ellen, who also went by Eleanor, was born in the parish of Granard in County Longford, in central Ireland, on April 9, 1816. 1840 census; New York City surveys; city directories. My thanks to Margie Reynolds and Susan Sanchez for the use of their Biglin family genealogy, and to Ed Johnson (a Biglin descendant) for his family records. Johnson to O'Brien, National Gallery of Art Curatorial Archives for "The Biglin Brothers Racing" by Thomas Eakins; Isabel Novarro to the author from St. James office, August 26, 2013; Certificate of Marriage for John Beglin [sic], copy dated August 22, 2013; Kroessler, New York Year By Year, 82–83. See Burrows and Wallace, Gotham, 480.

2 Rode, New York City Directory, 73 listed "Biglan, John, laborer, 404 Av. 3"; Manhattan New York State Census, 1855, E.D. 4, Ward 21, New York City; New York Herald, July 19, 1891, 18; See also United States Federal Census, 1860, for John Biglin, Ward 21, District 5; and US Census for Pennsylvania, 1850. John and Eleanor Biglin's responses to various census-takers were inconsistent about both the ages and birthplaces of many family members. The Biglins lived at 404 and then at 414 Third Avenue.

3 New York State Census, 1855. E.D. 4, Ward 21, New York City; Jackson, Encyclopedia, 599. See also Lee and Casey, Irish American, 371–72.

4 Jackson, Encyclopedia, 268 and 744. For more on Mitchell, Vance & Company, see Edwards, New York's Great Industries, 96–97. See United States Federal Census, 1860, for John Biglin, New York City, Ward 21, District 5, Image 58.

5 In Barney's day, the Eighteenth Assembly District was bounded by the East River, East 42nd Street, Lexington Avenue, East 23rd Street, Third Avenue, and East 26th Street thence back to the East River. New York Herald, July 19, 1891, 18. Father McGlynn advocated social reforms, and fostered the economic theories of Henry George.

6 New York Herald, July 19, 1891, 18.

7 Costello, Our Firemen, 586–88; Annual Report of the Chief Engineer of the Fire Department of the City of New York, Document No. 14, New York, Edmund Jones & Co., 1863, 36. The Knickerbocker Engine Company No. 12 moved seven times between 1780 and 1865. Alexander Joy Cartwright Jr. was a member of the engine company when it was at William and Duane Streets, and in 1845 helped found the Knickerbocker Base Ball Club that first played on the Elysian Fields in Hoboken, New Jersey. My thanks to FDNY historian Donald Van Holt for this tally. The annual salary figure comes from Lt. M. J. Yanega, et al., Centennial Issue, Fire Department 1865–1965, a commemorative booklet by the Fire Department of the City of New York, New York, FDNY, 1965, 17.

8 New York Times, July 3 and July 6, 1860. My thanks to Thomas E. Weil Jr. and Bill Pickelhaupt for the July 6th citation. Peverelly, Pastimes, 300–301; Johnson, History of Rowing, 58 and 61.

9 "I Want to Be a Soldier," Library of Congress accession No: SCO BD0471, published in Philadelphia by A. W. Auner, 1861. Original Tune: "I Want to Be an Angel."

10 Map of Franklin and Quay, New York Public Library; Matthew Dripps, Map of the City of Brooklyn, New York, M. Dripps, 1869, Map Div. 87-470, no. 8. (1869); Annual Illustrated Catalogue, 253; Brooklyn Eagle, July 18, 1932.

11 Peverelly, *Pastimes*, 307–8.

12 *New York Times*, July 14, 1863; Jackson, *Encyclopedia*, 343–44.

13 Peverelly, *Pastimes*, 275–78, 292–93, 296, 297, and 308–9; *Brooklyn Eagle*, October 6, 1863, 3.

14 Peverelly, *Pastimes*, 309–10.

15 My thanks to Bernard (Bern) Biglin and Drew Fetherston for useful details about the many qualities of Spanish cedar. "Death of Capt. Charles B. Elliott," *New York Times*, January 21, 1896.

16 Kernan, *Reminiscences of the Old Fire Laddies*, 775–78; *New York Times*, January 21, 1896; "C.B. Elliott Steering Devices" were patented March 10, 1874, US Patent No. 148,434. My thanks to rowing historian Bill Miller for his compilation of rowing-equipment patents for the "Friends of Rowing History" website rowinghistory.net. Durick, *Gentlemen's Race*.

17 Engelhardt, *American Rowing Almanac*, 33; Johnson, *History of Rowing*, 70; James, *Modern Oarsman*, 51; Peverelly, *Pastimes*, 310–11.

18 *New York Times*, July 19, 1865; *Harper's Weekly*, August 5, 1865; *New York Herald*, July 19, 1865, 5; *Poughkeepsie Eagle*, July 19, 1865, in *New York Herald*, July 20, 1865, 8.

19 *New York Herald*, July 19, 1865, 5.

20 Adelman, *Sporting Time*, 194; *New York Times*, July 19 and September 12, 1865; *New York Herald*, July 19, 1865, 5, July 20, 1865, 8, and July 21, 1865, 8; *Spirit of the Times*, July 22, 1865, 328, and July 29, 1865, 337, 344, and 349; *New York Herald*, July 19, 20, and 21, 1865; *New York Clipper*, July 29, 1865, 122–23; and Peverelly, *Pastimes*, 311–12; *Poughkeepsie Eagle*, July 19, 1865; *New York Times* reprint from *Poughkeepsie Eagle*, July 20, 1865 report published July 21, 1865; August 21 letter by Charles Gausmann to *New York Times*, published August 22, 1865.

21 *New York Times*, September 12, 1865.

22 *The Republican* (Sing Sing), September 28, 1865. *New York Times*, September 26, 1865. The town of Sing Sing was renamed Ossining in 1901.

23 Ed Johnson to Marsha Reynolds, April 24, 2013; FDNY register; *New York Times*, December 27, 1866. *New York Clipper*, 1864–1867. My thanks to Bernard Biglin for this reference. John Biglin's career as a fireman was exemplary but for one formal complaint that led to the company's driver being fired and a colleague losing two days' pay.

24 *Annual Illustrated Catalogue*, 228 and 270; Johnson, *History of Rowing*, 71–72; Peverelly, *Pastimes*, 284; *New York Times*, July 29, 1866; Peverelly, *Pastimes*, 282–83; Engelhardt, *American Rowing Almanac*, 1873, 35; Peverelly, *Aquatic Monthly*, October 1872, 371; Peverelly, *Pastimes*, 287; *Aquatic Monthly*, November 1874, 299; Johnson, *History of Rowing*, 73; James, *Modern Oarsman*, 51.

25 Engelhardt, *American Rowing Almanac* 1873, 39; *New York Times*, April 23, 1886, 8; McElroy and McBride, *Life Sketches*, 153–54.

26 *New York Times*, September 10, 1867.

27 *New York Times*, September 7, 1867; Crowther and Ruhl, *Rowing and Track Athletics*, 156–57.

28 Crowther and Ruhl, 156–57; *New York Times*, September 10, 1867.

29 *Aquatic Monthly*, March 1876, 933–34.

30 *New York Times*, September 8, 1868.
31 John Thorn, "Introduction to Peverelly's 'National Game'" and "New York Base Ball Club (a.k.a. Washington BBC, Gotham BBC)" in Morris et al., *Base Ball Founders*, 46–49. Baseball historians once thought their game was first played at the Elysian Fields by members of the Knickerbocker Club, in 1845, although evidence suggests that even earlier Manhattan and Brooklyn may have been the scene of New York's first games. In 1869 the Cincinnati Red Stockings became America's first professional baseball team, and the country's first game between professional squads was played two years later, between the Cleveland Forest Cities and the Fort Wayne Kekiongas at Fort Wayne, Indiana. *New York Times*, September 8, 1868; *Aquatic Monthly*, October 1872, 371 and November 1874, 299; James, *Modern Oarsman*, 52. See also Goldstein, *Playing for Keeps*, 12–13.
32 Mendenhall, *Short History*, 7; Lovett, *Old Boston Boys*, 51–52.
33 Engelhardt, *American Rowing Almanac*, 371.
34 Newspaper clip about an interview with Barney Biglin is from the personal collection of John A. Biglin's great grandson, Bernard (Bern) Biglin. No paper title, date, or page number is visible.

Chapter 4
1 Peverelly, *Pastimes*, 115–333. Peverelly was an avid oarsman and early member of the Atalanta Boat Club in New York City. Peverelly, *Pastimes*, 164; *New York Times*, May 3, 1888.
2 Peverelly, *Pastimes*, 116–17.
3 Mendenhall, *Short History*, 13–20.
4 Fred Plaisted died in 1943. *Turf, Field and Farm*, March 31, 1876, 203; *Aquatic Monthly*, April 1876, 970 and 1008; *Turf, Field and Farm*, April 7, 1876, 212.
5 The Elysian Fields race was won by John McKiel. *Aquatic Monthly*, October 1872, 371, and November 1874, 299; James, *Modern Oarsman*, 1878, 52; Plaisted quote from rowing historian Bill Pickelhaupt; Bill Pickelhaupt to the author, March 19, 2014 citing the *New York Clipper*.
6 Mendenhall, *Short History*, 19.
7 Dodd, *World Rowing*, 76–77; *Aquatic Monthly*, January 1873, 605–6; Mendenhall, *Short History*, 10.
8 Mendenhall, *Boat Race*, 74–75; Dodd, *World Rowing*, 76–77; *New York Times*, July 11, 1874.
9 C. B. Elliott, Steering Devices, U.S. Patent No. 148, 434, patented March 10, 1874.
10 Ken Kupery, 2011, "A Short History of Paper Boats. . . . and more"; "Elisha Waters, More Than Just an Ink Maker"; Ed and Lucy Faulkner, *Bottles and Extras*, Summer 2006, 35–37; Federation of Historical Bottle Collectors magazine; "Troy's paper boats" in *All Over Albany*, alloveralbany.com.
11 Charles Vinton Waters to the *New York Times*, published July 10, 1927 in "Sports of the Times" by John Kieran.

12 Letter from "Mark Twain." [From the special correspondent of the Alta], San Francisco, *Alta California* vol. XX, no. 6817, 1 (November 15, 1868, "International Boat Race. Hartford, October 22, 1868."

13 For more on the Paris Crew see Flood, *Saint John: A Sporting Tradition*, 33–39 and *Brooklyn Eagle*, October 22, 1868, 3.

Chapter 5

1 *Cambridge Scrap-Book*, ninth plate; Thomas E. Weil Jr. correspondence with the author, September 2015.

2 *Judy*, vol. 6 (October 27 to April 20, 1869-70), cover; *Punch*, June 2, 1866, 237. My thanks to Thomas E Weil Jr. and Goran Buckhorn for these sources.

3 *Spirit of the Times*, June 13, 1868, 288 and 289.

4 Details from the *Pittsburgh Weekly Post*, July 23, 1870.

5 The value of the watch was cited in the day's press accounts. The $2,000 prize was mentioned in a *New York Times* "Yachting and Boating" column on September 14, 1870.

6 "The Girls' Boat-Race. Novel and Exciting Scene at Glenwood, Near Pittsburg. . . . ," *New York Times*, July 20, 1870, relaying a July 18 dispatch from the *Pittsburgh Commercial*.

7 *The Days' Doings*, August 20, 1870.

8 "Novel Aquatic Spectacle. Rowing Contest Between Young Women on the East River—Description of the Female Athletes—Scenes and Incidents," *New York Times*, September 7, 1870, 1 and September 14, 1870, 8.

9 *New York Times*, September 14, 1870.

10 *New York Times*, September 26, 1871, 2.

11 *Godey's Lady's Book*, vol. LXXIII (1866)—2, 13; *Frank Leslie's Illustrated Newspaper*, October 14, 1871, 69, depicts "Regatta of Empire City Rowing Club at Harlem—The Ladies' Double-Scull Race" in a wood engraving. Image appears in Cooper, *Thomas Eakins*, 26; *The Days' Doings*, October 28, 1871, 212–13. See also *New York Times*, September 26, 1871, 2, which reported two races by women at the Empire City regatta on September 25, 1871.

12 *Harper's*, August 30, 1873, 768; *Harper's New Monthly*, 1874.

13 Thomas E. Weil Jr. to the author, May 2, 2013; *Atkinson's Saturday Evening Post*, November 2, 1833; *Waltham Sentinel*, nos. 38, 2, 39, 2, and 43, 1; *Spirit of the Times*, June 13, 1868, 288–89; *The Days' Doings*, October 28, 1871, 212; see also Ellen Williams, "How I, Rare Books Cataloger, Became the World's Expert on The Days' Doings," http://pennrare.wordpress.com/author/willellen/ and Mendenhall, *Short History*, 40.

14 *Montreal Daily Witness*, October 16, 1879, 4; *Forest and Stream*, May 5, 1878, 10. See, for example, the color lithographs "The Champion in Danger . . ." and "The Champion in Luck. . . ." Published by Currier & Ives, 115 Nassau St. N.Y., Copyright 1882, by Currier & Ives, New York.

15 Richard MacFarlane to Edward English, April 15, 2014.

16 *New York Times*, August 31, 1877; *Turf, Field and Farm*, September 26, 1879, 13, 29.

17 Look, *Courtney*, 70; *Aquatic Monthly*, July 1876, 39; *Turf, Field and Farm*, July 6, 1877, 25, 1; *Turf, Field and Farm*, October 25, 1878, 17 and 27; the *Binghamton Times* description of Johnson appeared in the *Ithaca Journal*, July 14, 1877.

18 *New York World*, August 31, 1877, 3 and 8; *New York Herald*, August 31, 1877.
19 *Turf, Field and Farm*, October 4, 1878, 27, and January 2, 1880, 30; *New York Times*, October 18, 1877; *Forest and Stream*, June 6, 1878, 10, 1; *New York Times*, August 16 and December 11, 1878.
20 *Jamestown Daily Journal* (New York), October 6, 1879; *Montreal Daily Witness*, October 16, 1879, 4; *Brentano's Monthly*, October 1, 1879, 2.
21 *New York Times*, February 2, 1880; *Brentano's Monthly*, June 1, 1880; 3.
22 Flood, *Saint John: A Sporting Tradition*, 50; *Brentano's Monthly*, August 1880, 506.
23 *Turf, Field and Farm*, July 7, 1882, 35 and December 22, 1882, 35; *New York Clipper Annual* 1893, 18. Over the years, a few minority athletes have excelled at rowing. Notably, in 1996, African-American sculler Aquil Abdullah won the US National Championship, and finished third in the US Olympic Trials. He won several international races, including in 2000 the Diamond Challenge Cup at the Henley Royal Regatta. See, Abdullah, *Perfect Balance*.

Chapter 6
1 Hunter, *Rowing in Canada*, 16; *New York Times*, August 8, 1871; *Morning Chronicle* (Quebec), August 23, 1871.
2 Whitehead, *James Renforth*, 121–30; *Daily Acadian Recorder*, August 23, 24, 25, 1871, 2. See also Mac Trueman, "The Great Race of 1871," *Telegraph-Journal*, Saint John, New Brunswick, August 11, 1984.
3 Cooper, *Thomas Eakins*, 37; Notman Photographic Archives, McCord Museum of Canadian History, Montreal, Negative No. 68911-1.
4 Hunter, *Rowing in Canada*, 17.
5 *Morning Chronicle* (Quebec), September 2, 1871 from the *Montreal Gazette*, September 1, 1871; *Annual Illustrated Catalogue*, 314; *Yarmouth Herald* [no date] from the *Halifax Chronicle*; the *Daily British Colonist*, September 6, 1871, 1; *Daily Saratogan*, September 8, 1871, 2, 7/8.
6 *Daily Acadian Recorder*, August 30, 1871, 1/4; Woodgate, *Boating*, 105. The *Daily Acadian Recorder* has the only contemporary description that I have found of the Biglins using sliding seats. A mention of distinctive "sliding motion" by English and American crews appears in an unmarked newspaper clip about "The Aquatic Carnival," pasted in the minute book of the Royal Nova Scotia Yacht Squadron between the minutes of July 10 and July 31, 1871 (MG 20 vol. 796, no. 1) at the Nova Scotia Archive in Halifax. My thanks to reference archivist Philip L. Hartling for this citation.
7 Hotaling, *They're Off*, 93.
8 *Daily Saratogan*, September 18, 1871, 2; *New York Times*, September 10, 1871, 1/4.
9 *New York Times*, September 12, 1871, 8/2; Hotaling, *They're Off*, 93; *The World* (New York), September 12, 1871, 9; Reports by the *Turf, Field and Farm* and *Newcastle Daily Chronicle* in *Annual Illustrated Catalogue*, 318–19.
10 *Annual Illustrated Catalogue*, 319–20 reporting *Spirit of the Times*; *Daily Saratogan*, September 12, 1871, 2; *Turf, Field and Farm*, September 15, 1871, 170/3; Engelhardt, *American Rowing Almanac* 1873, 71.

11 *Turf, Field and Farm*, September 29, 1871, 199; James, *Modern Oarsman*, 53; cited in *Springfield Daily Republican*, July 16, 1873, 5; *New York Times*, September 27, 1871, 8; *New York Times*, September 28, 1871, 8.

Chapter 7
1 *Newcastle Chronicle* article of December 28, 1871, and Barney Biglin's December 9, 1871 letter are available through Cumberland & Westmorland Newspaper Transcriptions in the British Newspaper Archive, www.cultrans.com.
2 The Biglins' opponents, Coulter and Cavitt, boated from the Quaker City Barge Club. *The Press*, May 21, 1872, 6.
3 Peverelly, *Aquatic Monthly*, June 1872, 56; *The Press*, May 21, 1872, 6; Allen and Allen, "Flashing Oars" note 154.
4 *Spirit of the Times*, May 25, 1872, 228. Several articles analyze Eakins's masculinity as expressed in rowing and painting. See, for example, Berger, "Negotiating Victorian Manhood" and "Painting Victorian Manhood." Cooper, *Thomas Eakins*, 102–23. Other works are excerpted in Fort, *Manly Pursuits*, and in Adams, *Eakins Revealed*, 193ff.
5 *All-Day City Item*, May 21, 1872, 4/2; *The Press*, May 21, 1872, 6; *New York Times*, May 21, 1872, 1.
6 *The Press*, May 21, 1872, 6.
7 *The Press*, May 21, 1872; *All-Day City Item*, May 21, 1872, 4.

Chapter 8
1 Lanouette, *The National Observer*, May 18, 1970, 12.
2 Weil, "Why Rowing Is Unique Among Team Sports," rowinghistory.net.
3 Smith, *Sports and Freedom*, 35–37; Mendenhall, *Boat Race*, 60 and 169; Wood, *Manual of Physical Exercises*; Reviewed in *Harper's New Monthly Magazine*, vol. 35, no. 207 (August 1867), 401. Wood's *Manual* was republished in the *Aquatic Monthly* in January 1874, 50–63; Blaikie, *How to Get Strong and How to Stay So*. Another popular book by Blaikie was *Sound Bodies for Our Boys and Girls*.
4 Mendenhall, *Boat Race*, 73; Adelman, *Sporting Time*, 198; Smith, *Sports and Freedom*, 38–41.
5 Mendenhall, *Boat Race*, 71–76; *New York Times*, August 28, 1869, 1; "The University Rowing Match," *Harper's New Monthly Magazine*, vol. XL, no. 235 (December 1869), 49–67.
6 Rowing was fast becoming a fully developed collegiate sport, with crews competing in 1873 from Cornell, Princeton, Columbia College, St. John's College (Annapolis), the Massachusetts Agricultural College (now the University of Massachusetts, Amherst), Amherst College, the US Military Academy, Ohio Wesleyan, Griswold College (Iowa), and Lafayette College. For more on rowing's popularity see Miller, "Wild & Crazy Professionals," Friends of Rowing History website, rowinghistory.net; *Springfield Republican*, July 12, 1871, 8; Mendenhall, *Short History*, 77.
7 Mendenhall, *Short History*, 77; Engelhardt, *American Rowing Almanac*, 142; *The Republican* (Springfield, Massachusetts), July 12, 1871, 8.

8 *New York Times*, July 19, 1872, 3 and July 11, 1873, 1. See also "The College Regatta," *New York Times*, June 13, 1874.
9 Engelhardt, *American Rowing Almanac*, 51, 62, 73. Celebration card and watch from Bernard (Bern) Biglin, John's great grandson. Peverelly, *Aquatic Monthly*, November 1872, 484, December 1872, 522–23, and May 1873, 947.
10 *Springfield Daily Republican*, July 25, 1872, 1/3; *New York Times*, July 11 and 22, 1871 and July 5, 1872, 5; *Aquatic Monthly*, October 1872, 368–73.
11 *Spirit of the Times*, July 20, 1872, 363; *Amherst Student*, newspaper clip, n.d., "The Inter-Collegiate Regatta," Amherst College Library, Rowing files; *Boston Journal*, July 1872, "The College Regatta"; *Springfield Daily Republican*, July 25, 1872, 1/3.
12 *New York World*, July 25, 1872; also quoted in *Harper's Weekly*, August 10, 1872, 621.
13 Boston Daily Evening Transcript, July 25, 1872, 4; *Aquatic Monthly*, August 1872, 229; *Springfield Daily Republican*, July 25, 1872.
14 *New York World*, July 25, 1872; *Amherst Student*, 1872, 118.
15 *Springfield Daily Republican*, July 25, 1872; *Aquatic Monthly*, August 1872, 228.
16 Boston Post, July 25, 1872; *Springfield Daily Republican*, July 25, 1872.
17 *Brooklyn Eagle*, July 25, 1872, 2.
18 *New York Clipper*, reprinted in the *Auburn Daily Bulletin* (New York), August 8, 1872.
19 *Aquatic Monthly*, March 1873, 783 and May 1873, 949; *New York Times*, July 12, 1873, 1; Bartlett and Gifford, *Dartmouth Athletics*, 186–87; Fred A. Thayer to Asa D. Smith [Dartmouth president], December 14, 1872 and February 26, 1873, Dartmouth College Special Collections, DP Box 7; *Daily Graphic*, October 26, 1874; *New York Times*, July 15, 1873, 1.
20 *New York Tribune*, June 27, 1873; *Springfield Daily Republican*, July 16, 1873, 5/2; Colin A. Norberg, "The History of Rowing at Dartmouth College," History 102 report, Dartmouth College Special Collections, D.C. Hist., D 8. N67.1958, 2–3.
21 *New York Tribune*, dispatch of July 10, 1873.
22 *Brooklyn Eagle*, July 16, 1873, 2, quoting a *New York Tribune* correspondent; *New York Times*, July 17, 1873.
23 *New York Times*, July 18, 1873, 1.
24 *New York Times*, July 16, 1873, 1.
25 *New York Times*, July 18, 1873.
26 *Aquatic Monthly*, August 1873, 213–14; *New York Times*, June 25, 1874.
27 *New York Times*, July 17, 1873, 4 and July 3, 1874.
28 In early 1873 the Rowing Association of American Colleges voted to ban professional rowers as coaches in the 1874 regatta. See Smith, *Sports and Freedom*, 149; *Aquatic Monthly*, August 1874, 71; William Blaikie obituary in the *Boston Evening Herald*, December 7, 1904.
29 *The Sun* (Baltimore), June 11, 1874, 1; *Aquatic Monthly*, August 1874, 99–102; *New York Times*, July 4, 1874; *Aquatic Monthly*, August 1874, 103–4, March 1875, 136; November 1875, 667; McElroy and McBride, *Life Sketches*, 155.

Chapter 9

1 For details about Eakins's portrayal of the Biglin brothers, see Cooper, *Thomas Eakins*, 24–78. For details of the NAAO convention, see Peverelly, *Aquatic Monthly*, July 1872, 156; September 1872, 233–35 and 274–75; and March 1873, 783–91.

2 *Aquatic Monthly*, September 1872, 235.

3 *Aquatic Monthly*, September 1872, 274–75.

4 Laumann and Wharton, *Rowing*, 123.

5 Gorn and Goldstein, *Brief History*, 227–28.

6 Engelhardt, *American Rowing Almanac*, 78; *Documents of the Assembly of the State of New York*, vol. 4, 678.

7 Fire Department of New York history website at www.nyc.gov/html/fdny/html/history/fire service.shtml; *New York Times*, July 4, 1874, 8; Judge Charles B. Elliott's boat-building shop was at the corner of Quay & Franklin Streets on the East River in Greenpoint, L.I. (Brooklyn). See Elliott's advertisement in Watson, *Rowing and Athletic Annual for 1874*; *Spirit of the Times*, August 31,1872, 42; Jeffrey Kroessler, *New York Year By Year*, 111.

8 *Aquatic Monthly*, October 1872, 368–73; *Spirit of the Times*, August 31, 1872, 42.

9 For Ward's races, see *Philadelphia Times Almanac 1887*, 62; *The Columbian Cyclopedia* lists Ellis Ward as racing on April 1, 1 mile in 5 minutes 1 second, in 1872.

10 *Aquatic Monthly*, October 1872, 368–70; *Rockland County Journal*, September 14, 1872, 1, and September 21, 1872, 4; Berman, "Julian O. Davidson and the Nyack Rowing Association."

11 *Aquatic Monthly*, September 1872, 311–12.

12 *New York Clipper*, September 7, 1872, 20. *Brooklyn Eagle*, May 20, 1878, 4.

13 "The Biglin-Ward Race," *New York Times*, September 20, 1872, 8.

14 The Biglin-Ward meeting at Nyack that September 1872 was but one of more than 150 regattas and match races rowed in the United States in 1872.

15 *Aquatic Monthly*, October 1872, 368–73; Johns, *Thomas Eakins*, 43.

16 *Aquatic Monthly*, March 1873, 783 and May 1873, 949; *New York Times*, July 12, 1873, 1 and July 15, 1873, 1; Bartlett and Gifford, *Dartmouth Athletics*, 186–87; Fred A. Thayer to Asa D. Smith [Dartmouth president], December 14, 1872 and February 26, 1873, Dartmouth College Special Collections, DP Box 7; *Daily Graphic*, October 26, 1874.

17 *Harper's Weekly*, August 10, 1872, 622/1: Map of the Connecticut River at Springfield, 1872.

18 *Springfield Daily Republican*, July 15, 1873, 5/3 and July 16, 1873, 5/4.

19 *New York Tribune*, July 16, 1873, 1; *Springfield Daily Republican*, July 16, 1873, 5/2; *New York Times*, July 22, 1871.

20 *Springfield Daily Republican*, July 16, 1873, 5/3.

21 *New York Times*, July 16, 1873, 1/4.

22 *New York Times*, August 8, 1873, 8; *Morning Freeman* (Saint John, New Brunswick), September 18, 1873; *Daily Acadian Recorder*, September 20, 1873, 3; *The Novascotian*, September 22, 1873, 6; *Aquatic Monthly*, October 1873, 317. Biglin quote is from *Canadian Illustrated News*, October 11, 1873, 232. A double-truck (two-page spread) in the

Canadian Illustrated News (pages 232–33) included vignettes that showed scenes from the regatta. In one, New York "sporting men" are being taunted after the race by a man waving his top hat and shouting, "How are you Biglins." Also shown are a "Refreshments" tent with its staggering patrons, and reporters dashing to the telegraph office with their dispatches.

23 *Morning Chronicle*, September 24, 1873, 3 and September 25, 1873, 2; *New York Times*, September 25, 1873; *Daily Acadian Recorder*, September 24, 1873, 4 and September 25, 1873, 4; *The Novascotian*, September 29, 1873, 5; *New York Times*, October 12, 1873, 1.

24 *The Sun* (Baltimore), June 11, 1874, 1; *Aquatic Monthly*, August 1874, 99–102; *New York Times*, July 4, 1874; *Aquatic Monthly*, August 1874, 103–4, March 1875, 136, November 1875, 667.

25 *New York Times*, August 7, 1874; *Aquatic Monthly*, September 1874, 178, November 1874, 297–300, and March 1875, 139; *Omaha Daily Bee*, October 10, 1874, 1/5; *New York Times*, October 10, 1874, 5; Watson, *Rowing and Athletic Annual for 1874*, 16 and 30.

26 *Brooklyn Eagle*, May 28, 1875, 2.

27 Potter, "The Red Wing—Stillwater Boat Race," 63–64.

28 "Ellis Ward's Little Game . . . ," *New York Times*, July 23, 1875, 5; C.A. Rasmussen, *History of the City of Red Wing*, 112–13; Potter, "The Red Wing—Stillwater Boat Race," 62–65; Norsen, *Ward Brothers*, 62. The most likely encounter between the Jubilee Singers and Ellis Ward may have occurred in July 1872 when the singers spent seventeen days in Boston and Ward rowed in the city's celebrated July Fourth Regatta—winning in the double-sculls race. See Louis D. Silveri, "The Singing Tours of the Fisk Jubilee Singers: 1871–1874" in Keck and Martin, *Feel the Spirit*, 105–16. My thanks to rowing historian Sarah Risser for additional details in this story. See Sarah Risser, "Out-Foxed in Red Wing" on the *Hear the Boat Sing* rowing blog, March 30, 2018.

29 "Sports and Swindlers," *Brooklyn Eagle*, August 11, 1875, 2; *New York Times*, August 10, 1875.

30 "Rowing. A Specimen of Professional Fraud," *Brooklyn Eagle*, August 20, 1875, 4.

31 *Aquatic Monthly*, February 1876, 842–843 and March 1876, 951; *Turf, Field and Farm*, March 10 and 31, 1876, 131 and 203; *Brooklyn Eagle*, October 16, 1876, 4.

32 *Aquatic Monthly*, April 1876, 970 and 1008; *Turf, Field and Farm*, April 7, 1876, 212.

33 *New York Times*, May 19, 1876, 2; *Turf, Field and Farm*, May 26, 1876, 338.

34 *Turf, Field and Farm*, July 14, 1876, 18. See also *Aquatic Monthly*, July 1876, 39–40. This accident was later described as "breaking an outrigger when they had the race well in hand." *Turf, Field and Farm*, December 29, 1876, 403. See also *New York Times*, July 5, 1876, 10.

35 *Aquatic Monthly*, July 1876, 52–53. At Providence the four included John Biglin, captain; Fred Plaisted; William Maxwell; and Thomas Elliott, stroke.

36 *New York Times*, July 17, 1876, 2/4; August 2, 1876, 2; August 30, 1876, 2/2; and September 4, 1876, 2.

37   Price and McLeod, *Oarsman's Pocket Guide*, 44–46, 49–50, and 53, including excerpts from *New York Herald*'s "extended and most graphic account"; *New York Times*, September 6 and 7, 1876; *Turf, Field and Farm*, September 8, 1876, 155.

38   *Spirit of the Times*, cited in Cosentino, *The Canadians: Ned Hanlan*, 39. My thanks to rowing historian Peter Mallory for this example.

39   *Brooklyn Eagle*, October 16, 1876, 4.

40   *Turf, Field and Farm*, September 29, 1876, 203; *Brooklyn Eagle*, October 10, 1876, 4; *Aquatic Monthly*, October 1876, 210; *Turf, Field and Farm*, October 13, 1876, 234–35; "Argonaut," *Rowing Almanack and Oarsman's Companion 1877*, 127.

41   *New York Times*, June 26, July 5, and July 5, 1877.

42   *New York Times*, August 26, 1877; *New York World*, August 31, 1877, 3 or 8 [type unclear]; *New York Herald*, August 31, 1877; *New York Times*, September 2, 1877.

43   *New York Times*, February 2 May 31, 1878; "The United States Weighers," *Boston Morning Journal*, July 6, 1878. My thanks to Barry Strauss for this clip. *New York Times*, July 5, 1878.

44   *New York Times*, July 12, 1879, 5; July 15, 1879, 1.

45   *Washington Post*, March 11, 1880, 1.

46   *New York Times*, July 11, 1879 and September 21 and 22, 1880.

47   Garfield and Arthur faced Democrats Winfield S. Hancock, a Gettysburg-battle hero from Pennsylvania, and US Rep. William H. English from Indiana.

48   Harriet Davis-Kram, "Gashouse District," in Jackson, *Encyclopedia*, 414. The district's odor was not the now-familiar mercaptan added to make odorless natural gas easily detectable, but, rather, the aroma of sulfur from the coal then used to manufacture gas.

49   *Brooklyn Eagle*, April 17, 1877, 4; *New York Times*, September 28, 1902, 26; Low, "Tammany Hall" in Norman and Roberts, *World's Work and Play*, 380; Myers, *Tammany Hall*, 299; *Dallas Morning News*, September 28, 1902, 5. Golway, *Machine Made*, Chapter Ten.

50   von Drehle, *Triangle*, 27; Welch, *King of the Bowery*, 71 and note 45; Weiss, *Charles Francis Murphy*, 19 and 103, at 19 quoting the *Literary Digest* LXXXI, 38–44; *New York Times*, September 28, 1902 and April 26, 1924; *The World's Work*, vol. VI (May 1903 to October 1903); *A History of Our Time*, 3910. Accounts differ about whether the Sylvan Club four won one race or two of three heats.

51   *Brooklyn Daily Eagle*, August 1, 1881, 3; *New York Times*, December 18, 1881, 9; *New York Herald*, April 23, 1886, 9. "Sinn fein" is Gaelic for "we ourselves," and at this early date the New York club had more to do with socializing than with advancing Irish nationalism. The *Herald* spelled the club name "Shin Fane." My thanks to Terry Golway for advice about early Sinn Fein activities in New York City.

52   Susan Sanchez Biglin family tree, Ancestry: http://trees.ancestry.com/tree/52422575. Catherine is not buried with the many Biglins at Calvary Cemetery in Queens, but at St. Raymond's Cemetery in the Bronx.

53   *Sporting Life*, September 24, 1883, 8; U.C. City Directories, 1821–1989 (Beta) Record for John Biglin; *New York Times*, July 13, 1884; *Brooklyn Eagle*, April 21, 1886, 4.

Appropriately, John Biglin's last address, 614 Second Avenue, today houses a sports club and exercise center.

54   George Pocock quote from Yale and Georgetown coach Anthony Johnson to the author, June 17, 2013; *New York Herald*, April 21, 1886, 8; *New York Times*, April 23, 1886, 8; Washington, DC, *Evening Star*, April 23, 1886, 6; *Turf, Field and Farm*, April 30, 1886, 354; *New York Herald*, April 23, 1886, 8; Calvary and Allied Cemeteries June 1996 family record. My thanks to Bernard (Bern) Biglin for this source.

Chapter 10

1   *Spirit of the Times*, July 13, 1872, 347; Engelhardt, *American Rowing Almanac* 1873, 90.

2   *New York Times*, September 29, 1888. Jackson, *Encyclopedia*, 928; Mollie Keller, entries for "U.S. Custom House" and "U.S. Customs Service" in Jackson, *Encyclopedia*, 1215–16; Prince and Keller, 158; Leish, *American Heritage Pictorial History of the Presidents*, 537; Kroessler, *New York Year by Year*, 8. According to Keller (at Jackson 1215), "Apart from Moses Grinnell, whose embarrassing honesty cost him the collectorship in 1870, all collectors and many subordinates between 1829 and 1877 used their positions to enrich themselves." Details about Arthur's income are from Justus Doenecke, "Chester A. Arthur: Life Before the Presidency," The Miller Center, University of Virginia.

3   Reeves, *Gentleman Boss*, 72; McElroy and McBride, *Life Sketches*, 153.

4   *New York Tribune*, July 19, 1891, 18.

5   *New York Herald*, July 19, 1891, 18. Brother John was also hailed for his rescues, and one especially when, in 1877, he and Barney attended a regatta on the Schuylkill. Seeing a rower capsize, John Biglin sped out from the shore in a single to help the sculler back into his shell.

6   Moynihan, 475. Ferdinand C. Weyrich ran an oyster saloon at 250 Bleecker Street (by Leroy Street) beginning in 1856, to which Barney Biglin and Chester A. Arthur often repaired. *The Sun* (New York), February 7, 1906, 12; Lee and Casey, *Irish American*, 318; Golway, *Machine Made*, 9–71.

7   *Aquatic Monthly*, December 1872, 549.

8   The seat had previously been held by the Democratic reformer Samuel J. Tilden, who resigned from the Assembly and went on to become New York's governor in 1875 and the Democratic Party's nominee for president in 1876. "Sports on the Water" in *Spirit of the Times*, May 11, 1872, 199; *Aquatic Monthly*, December 1872, 549; McElroy and McBride, *Life Sketches*, 154; *New York Times*, January 15, 1873, 1; *Aquatic Monthly*, August 1873, 168; *Springfield Daily Republican*, July 16, 1873, 5/2. The Biglin children were Helen (1863–1915), William (1864–1884), Mary (1866–1901), Ida (1868–1869), Alice (1871–1953), Pauline (1874–1963), Josephine (1875–1952), and Florence (1876–1907). Ancestry, Sanchez family tree for the Biglins.

9   *New York Tribune*, December 31, 1884, 5, image 5. Chronicling America, Library of Congress. For Polly Biglin's ancestry see 1880 US Census, New York, Roll T9_889, Family History Film 1254889, page 643B, Enumeration District 475, Federal Census website image 0859.

10   *New York Times*, January 15, 1873, 1.

11 *New York Times*, October 21, 1873; *The Nation*, November 13, 1873, no. 437, 317–18.

12 *Hartford Daily Courant*, September 16, 1874; *Aquatic Monthly*, December 1874, 379. McElroy and McBride, *Life Sketches*, 154.

13 William Gardner Choate later served on the US District Court for the Southern District of New York, and with his wife, Mary Atwater Choate, in 1896 founded what became Choate Rosemary Hall, a preparatory school in Wallingford, Connecticut.

14 *New York Times*, November 4, 1874; Ellis, *Epic of New York City*, 347–48. *New York Times*, December 12, 1874, 3.

15 Donald Young, "Rutherford Birchard Hayes," in Leish, *American Heritage Pictorial History of Presidents*, vol. 1, 495–96.

16 *New York Times*, August 24, 1875, 2; Goulding, *New York City Directory for 1876-'77*, 108; *New York City Directory 1876* (Beta) Record for John Biglin, Image 115; *Documents of the Assembly of the State of New York*, vol. 4, 678.

17 *New York Times*, November 3, 1878.

18 *Proceedings of the Board of Aldermen of the City of New York*, 54, 356; *New York Times*, November 4, 1878, 1/3 and November 7, 1878, 2/1; *New York Times*, April 14, 1891. Part of the steam-system work also went to William E. Prall, an inventor with patents for various steam-powered devices.

19 *New York Times*, November 4, 1878, 1 and 3; November 7, 1878, 2/1.

20 *Wisconsin State Journal*, February 12, 1878, 2; Dodd, *Henley*, 66; *New York Times*, July 18, 1878, 4.

21 *Proceedings of the Board of Aldermen of the City of New York*, 242; Robert S. Hunter, *Rowing in Canada*, 11; *New York Times*, August 13, 1878.

22 These included Joseph Biglin, "Barney's" Brother, Appraiser's Department; John Biglin, also "Barney's" Brother, assistant weigher, Custom-House; Daniel Johnson, Brother-in-law of "Barney", Weigher's Department; James Johnson, Brother-in-law of "Barney", Custom-House; John W. Cregan, "Barney's" water collector, Post Office. George Smith, a policeman, was described as holding the door to the anteroom and admitting to the Republican Hall meeting only Barney's "heelers." Nine more men owing their jobs to Biglin were listed as "Protégé" or "Sugar Sampler." *New York Times*, November 21, 1878, 4/7. In February 1878, John A. Biglin had been discharged as a weigher's foreman, at $1,200 a year, along with twelve others by "the enforcement of the order of the Secretary of the Treasury, reorganizing the Weighers' Department of the Custom-house. . . ." *New York Times*, February 2, 1878. In November, John was still at the Custom House, albeit with a new title.

23 *New York Times*, November 30, 1879, 7/4, and October 7, 1880.

24 Leish, *American Heritage Pictorial History of Presidents*, 530.

25 *Washington Post*, April 8, 1908, 6.

26 *New York Public Library Desk Reference*, 1989, 678; Rischin, *Promised City*, 19–24; Higham, *Strangers in the Land*, 15–19; Handlin, *The Uprooted*, 28–33; Jackson, *Encyclopedia*, 583.

27 *New York Times*, August 3, 1884.

28 *Washington Post*, June 1, 1884, 1.

29 *New York Times*, March 20, 1884.

30 *Brooklyn Eagle*, June 28, 1885, 10.

31 *New York Times*, September 25, 1884; Pringle, *Theodore Roosevelt*, 112–15; Morris, *Rise of Theodore Roosevelt*, Chapter 14.

32 *New York Tribune*, December 31, 1884, 5, image 5. Chronicling America, Library of Congress.

33 *Brooklyn Eagle*, February 27, May 5, and August 16, 1883, 4; Alexander, *Political History of the State of New York*, vol. 3, 319.

34 *New York Times*, June 4, 1882 and January 2, 1885, 5; *Evening Telegram*, February 26, 1885, 4; *Providence Journal*, reprinted in *Washington Post*, August 14, 1888, 14; *New York Star* reprinted in *Washington Post*, September 4, 1889; *New York Times*, October 5, 1889 and October 10, 1889, 5; *New York Times*, November 1, 1889.

35 *New York Times*, April 12, 1890; *New York Times*, May 16, 1890 and May 5, 1891; *New York Times*, May 10, 1891, 9.

36 *Brooklyn Eagle*, March 10, 1892, 6; "Biglin Charges Too Much," New York Times, January 26, 1893.

37 *New York Times*, September 23, 1900, 24, June 21, 1902, and May 24, 1924; *Brooklyn Eagle*, June 23, 1902; *New York Times*, December 19, 1907, 16 and July 2, 1908, 5.

38 Kraut, "Records of the Immigration and Naturalization Service."

39 *New York Times*, May 12, 1924. My thanks to Bernard (Bern) Biglin for sharing his Calvary Cemetery and family records and photographs.

Chapter 11

1 Look, *Courtney*, 10; Kelley, *American Rowing*, 214.

2 Young, *Courtney*, 12; Look, *Courtney*, 17–19.

3 Young, *Courtney*, 15; Look, *Courtney*, 29–30, 33.

4 "C. E. Courtney Dies from Shock in Boat" *New York Times*, July 18, 1920; Young, *Courtney*, 16–18; Look, *Courtney*, 33.

5 Young, *Courtney*, 21.

6 For information about regatta hotels see *Daily Saratogan*, September 11, 1871, 2. Morrissey was elected to the House of Representatives in 1866 with Tammany Hall's backing, but then denounced political corruption and testified against William M. "Boss" Tweed at the trial that sent him to prison.

7 Young, *Courtney*, 22; Britten, *Chronicles of Saratoga*, 158–61; *American Leaders*, 241; Young, *Courtney*, 21–23; Look, *Courtney*, 36–37; *Daily Saratogan*, September 5, 1871, 2.

8 Look, *Courtney*, 37–39.

9 Look, *Courtney*, 38; Young, *Courtney*, 22–23.

10 *New York Times*, August 16, 1878 and June 10, 1884.

11 Young, *Courtney*, 26.

12 "The Poisoned Oarsman," *New York Times*, July 16, 1877. Crowd description appeared in the *New York Times*, July 15, 1877. My thanks to Stewart Stokes for this citation. See his thesis, "It Was a Fearful Stroke . . ." 98.

13 "Poisoning an Oarsman, Courtney Drugged by Gamblers," *New York Times*, July 15, 1877.

14 *New York Times*, August 27 and 28, 1877.

15 Look, *Courtney*, 67–69; *New York Times,* June 21 and 29, 1878, July 5, 1878.

16 "The Silver Lake Regatta," *New York Times*, August 16, 1878.

17 *The Canadian Encyclopedia* at www.thecanadianencyclopedia.com/articles/ned-hanlan.

18 Morrow et al., *Concise History*, 32; Look, *Courtney*, 75.

19 Look, *Courtney*, 78–80; *New York Clipper*, October 12, 1878, 229; Glendon and Glendon, *Rowing*, 86.

20 Morrow et al., *Concise History*, 37; Fox, *Edward Hanlan*, 17–19; Hunter, *Rowing in Canada*, 30; *Spirit of the Times*, quoted in the *Brooklyn Eagle*, August 18, 1879, 3.

21 For background on the World Sculling Championship, 1831 to 1957, see www.rowinghistory-aus.info/world-pro-sculling/index.php.

22 *Brooklyn Eagle,* July 11, 1879, 4; Morrow et al., *Concise History*, 37–38; *New York Times,* July 11, 1879; *New York Times,* August 19, 1879; Fox, 19. See also *Daily News* (Saint John, New Brunswick), August 19, 1879, "What Looks Like an Aquatic Burlesque at Barrie."

23 Adams, *Grandfather Stories*, 220.

24 See Hop Bitters trade card in the Joe Gourd Collection at www.peachridgeglass.com/2014/01/the-doyles-soules-hop-bitters-rochester-n-y and the medicine's constituent ingredients in *Prohibiting the manufacture and sale of alcoholic liquors in the District of Columbia*. Hearings before Committee on the District of Columbia, Sixty-fourth Congress, second session, Washington, US Government Printing Office, 1917, 362.

25 Adams, *Grandfather Stories*, 220–21.

26 *New York Times*, "Courtney's Sawed Boats," July 29, 1883.

27 "The Great Boat Race," *Daily Witness* (Montreal), October 16, 1879, 1; Cosentino, *Ned Hanlan*, 1974, 9–10. See also, Look, *Courtney*, Chapter 8. "Who sawed Courtney's boat?" In *Puck* magazine in 1883, for example, it was asked in a column about unsolved mysteries. *Puck*, vol. XIV, no. 355, December 26, 1883, 261. In the 1990s "Who sawed Courtney's boat?" was used as the title of a science-fiction e-zine.

28 *New York Times*, October 18, 1879.

29 *New York Times*, October 18, 1879.

30 Quoted in Cosentino, *Not Bad, Eh?*, 180.

31 Adams, *Grandfather Stories*, 224–26; Cosentino, *Ned Hanlan*, 42–45.

32 "Another Failure," *New York Times*, April 30, 1880, 4; *Frank Leslie's Illustrated Weekly*, May 22, 1880.

33 *Washington Post*, May 18 and 19, 1880.

34 "The Canadian Wins," *Washington Post*, May 20, 1880, 1; Morrow et al., *Concise History*, 38.

35 *New York Times*, May 20, 1880; "Blaikie on Courtney. Riley Tells A Secret About the Boat Race to the Referee," *New York Times*, May 25, 1880.

36 *New York Times*, May 20, 1880.

37 *New York Times*, May 20, 1880; *Washington Post*, May 20, 1880; Morrow et al., *Concise History*, 8; Cosentino, *The Canadians: Ned Hanlan*, 12; "Ned Hanlan and the Golden Age of Sculling," in Berton, *My Country*, 53; Proctor, "Courtney . . ." My thanks to Elizabeth Webber for this citation.

38 *New York Times*, May 20, 1880.

Chapter 12

1 "A Magnetic Oarsman," *New York Times*, May 22, 1880, 4.

2 *Sarina Observer* (Ontario), May 28, 1880, 4.

3 Flood, *Saint John: A Sporting Tradition*, 52; "Courtney Defeats Lee," *New York Times*, September 2, 1882, 5; Cosentino, *The Canadians: Ned Hanlan*, 1978, 47–52 and 54; *New York Times*, July 19, 1883, 1/5.

4 "Epithets Freely Bandied," *New York Times*, July 19, 1883, 1/6.

5 "A Suggestion for Statesmen," *New York Times*, July 19, 1883.

6 Hanlan's reference to Courtney being "hit with a sand bag" is a mystery, as I know of no such incident in his many accident-riddled races. *New York Times*, August 16, 1883; *New York Times*, August 21, 1883.

7 *New York Times*, March 26 and April 8, 1884, February 24, 1887; *Sporting Life* 1886, vol. 6, no. 14, 4; *New-York Daily Tribune*, April 2, 1902.

8 *New York Times*, June 6 and 8, 1884.

9 *New York Times*, June 8, 1884.

10 *New York Times*, June 10, 1884, 4. In 1885, Ward was convicted of larceny and sentenced to ten years in prison.

11 "Oarsman Courtney Boycotted," *New York Times*, July 13, 1884.

12 "Two Coaches," *New York Times*, April 15, 1884, 4; Look, *Courtney*, 112.

13 *New York Times*, August 24, 1886.

14 *New York Times*, September 2, 1886.

15 Look, *Courtney*, 110.

16 Young, *Courtney*, 29; Look, *Courtney*, 111–12; *Cornell Daily Sun*, vol. V, no. 24, October 21, 1884, 2.

17 *Cornell Daily Sun*, vol. III, no. 3, September 26, 1882, 3; vol. IV, no. 94, March 6, 1884; vol. IV, no. 126, May 9, 1884, 1; vol. V, no. 138, May 27, 1885; vol. V, no. 139, May 28, 1885, 1; vol. VI, no. 3, September 22, 1885, 1; vol. VI, no. 5, September 24, 1885, 1; vol. VI, no. 113, April 23, 1886, 3; and vol. VI, no. 115, April 27, 1886, 2.

18 *Cornell Daily Sun*, vol. VI, no. 119, May 3, 1886, 3.

19 *Cornell Daily Sun*, vol. VI, no. 57, January 13, 1886, 1; *New York Times*, July 18, 1886.

20 *Cornell Daily Sun*, vol. VII, no. 66, January 25, 1887, 2; vol. VII, no. 81, February 15, 1887, 3; vol. VII, no. 92, March 3, 1887, 1.

21 Mendenhall, *Boat Race*, 207–8.

22 *Cornell Daily Sun*, vol. VIII, no. 111, April 20, 1888, 4; vol. IX, no. 41, November 21, 1888, 1; Smith, *Sports and Freedom*, 154; Young, *Courtney*, 44.

23 Young, *Courtney*, 42.

24 Mallory, Sport of Rowing, 336; Mendenhall, *Boat Race*, 220–21 and 251.

25 Mendenhall, *Short History*, 77; *Columbia Spectator*, November 2, 1900, 1–2.

26 Young, *Courtney*, 101.

27 *New York Times*, February 28, 1892; Mendenhall, *Boat Race*, 55–56, 241, 246, and 248; Young, *Courtney*, 38–39; Whitney, "The Guiding Hand . . .", *Outing XL* (July 1902), 497.

28   Crowther Jr., "The Ethics of American Rowing," 500. "SYRACUSE'S BAD LUCK. Ten Eyck, Freshman Stroke, Out of the Boat—Cornell Favorite," *New York Times*, June 22, 1906.

Chapter 13

1   *New York Times*, July 29, 1887, 4.

2   See Cook, *Louisville Grays Scandal*. For the "Black Sox Scandal" see *New York Times*, September 29, 1920, 1.

3   David Nemec to the author, September 26 and 27, 2020. See also *The Beer & Whisky League: The Illustrated History of the American Association—Baseball's Renegade Major League*. My thanks to baseball historians David Nemec and Daniel Okrent for their helpful advice contrasting professional rowing and baseball.

4   *New York Times*, July 27 and August 16, 1883; *Sporting Life*, September 24, 1883; *Columbia Spectator*, November 2, 1900, 2.

5   *Sunday Herald* (Boston), January 17, 1886; Mendenhall, *Boat Race*, 188; *New York Times*, August 23, 1900.

6   *New York Times*, July 29, 1887.

7   *New York Times*, July 17 and 19, and August 1, 1886.

8   *New York Times*, July 19, 1886.

9   *New York Times*, July 2, 1886.

10   *New York Times*, July 24 and 29, 1887 and September 14, 1889. My thanks to Bill Miller for the Gaudaur-Hamm information.

11   For background see Cross, *Social History of Leisure Since 1600*.

12   *New London Day*, October 11, 1890, 4. Jackson, *Standard Theatre of Victorian England*, 310; *New York Times*, November 13, 1889; *New York Times*, August 23, 1900 (Hosmer obituary).

13   "The Dark Secret" poster for September 19 at the Manchester Opera House and the Allen and Ginters "World's Champions" chromo-lithograph sports card series, c. 1887, are both from the Thomas E. Weil Jr. collection of rowing art.

14   *New York Times*, June 21, 1885; "Courtney Defeats Ross. He Achieves Success on Maine's New-Fangled Machine. He Rows a Half Mile on Dry Land in Two and a Half Minutes," New York Public Library Print Collection, Miriam and Ira D. Wallach Division of Art, Prints and Photographs. Digital ID: 1218366, Record ID: 546349.

15   *The Sun* (New York), October 7, 1888, 13, and October 9, 1888.

16   *New York Times*, October 10, 11, 13 and 14, 1888; Gipe, *Great American Sports Book*, 272–73; Andy Anderson, "Bad Ideas Never Die," *Rowing News*, February 23, 2003, 25 and 30; Goran Buckhorn, "A 'Roadsculler' Race in 1888" in his rowing history blog *Hear the Boat Sing* at http://www.hear-the-boat-sing.blogspot.com; Gipe in *Sports Illustrated*, March 14, 1977. In August 1887, Ross, Hosmer, and McKay planned to race "rowing tricycles" at the Casino in Cottage City, Martha's Vineyard, Massachusetts; *New York Times*, August 11, 1887.

17   Bill Miller, "Fred Plaisted—Professional Sculler."

18   *New York Herald-Tribune*, March 9, 1880, 8 and March 18, 1880, 8; *New York Times*, October 29, 1890.

19 Palmer, *Athletic Sports*, 611.
20 "Fourth of July Regatta," no paper identified. In Newspaper Clippings (3). Boston City Council, Committee on the Celebration of the Fourth of July, Folder 6, 1892, City of Boston Archives; Boston City Council, Committee on Celebrations, Records, Box 4 (1895-1896), Folder 9, June 20, 1895.
21 Boston City Council Proceedings 1897, 514–18; Committee on July 4th, Committee Records 1897, entry for June 22.
22 Hunter, *Rowing in Canada*, 85; *New York Times*, May 25, 1997 and October 1, 1899.
23 *New York Times*, February 27, 1916.
24 *National Police Gazette*, December 30, 1882, 14; *South Australian Register* (Adelaide), July 13, 1883. Major Goodsell was born in Australia, and from there had won the championship five times. But after becoming a US citizen, he lost his last bid for the title.
25 "Bill Miller Champion Sculler Pulls a Mighty Oar," *Philadelphia Inquirer* Comics Section, May 19, 1935; *New York Times*, September 6, 1934; *Sydney Morning Herald*, September 8, 1934.
26 Cleaver, *History of Rowing*.

Chapter 14
1 See Riess, *American Sporting Experience*, especially Section II, Sport in Antebellum America, and Section III, The Rise of American Sport: 1870–1900.
2 Official Program 75th World Championship 6 Day Bike Race, September 1961, 5 and 22, 8-11 (Collection of the author.); *New York Times*, September 9, 1961; Harold Conrad, "6-Day Bike Race . . ."
3 Eugene M. Foster, *Washington Herald*, February 20, 1916, 12.
4 *New York Times*, April 24, 1985.
5 *New York Times*, April 24, 1937 and May 22, 1939. My thanks to rowing historian Katherine McCormick for these citations.
6 James Sciales to the author, August 20, 2013; interview August 21, 2013. Theodore Bonanno (Fordham crew coach) to the author, August 18 and November 22, 2013.
7 US Rowing statistics, Rowing History Forum estimates, and compilations from Rower's Almanac, 2005 and 2012; William Porter (Yale women's crew coach) to the author, April 22, 2014.
8 Gorn and Goldstein, *Brief History*, 137; Dodd, *Henley*, 86; Boyne, *Kelly*, 115–116. My thanks to UCSD sports historian Robert Edelman for the Gorn/Goldstein citation.
9 Mendenhall, *Boat Race*, 112. Amateur definitions for the (US) National Association of Amateur Oarsmen, the Canadian Association of Amateur Oarsmen, and the English Amateur Rowing Association appeared in the *New York Clipper Annual* 1893, 102.
10 Dodd, *Henley*, 129; Boyne, *Kelly*, 101–5 and 220–23; Anderson, "Elitism and the Legend of Jack Kelly Sr.," *Rowing News*, October 2006, 26–27.
11 See Brown, *Boys in the Boat*.
12 Mendenhall, *Boat Race*, 341–47.
13 Mendenhall, *Short History*, 120–21.
14 For a detailed survey of rowing styles and the Adam-Rosenberg debate see Mallory, *Sport of Rowing*, Chapter 109, 1394–95.

15 Dodd, *World Rowing*, 136.

16 Dodd, *World Rowing*, 136–49; *New York Times*, August 10, 2013, B10; Schnell et al., "Development of Sports Medicine," 340–42; Volkwein-Caplan, *Culture, Sport, and Physical Activity*, 226; Franke and Berendonk, "Hormonal Doping," 1262–79 (1997); Macia, "Continuing Legacy," 46–53; "Sports, Politics, and 'Wild Doping' in the East German Sporting 'Miracle,'" Chapter 8 in Edelman and Young, *Whole World*.

17 Xavier Macia to the author, July 29, 2013.

18 Dodd, *World Rowing*, 136.

19 Dodd, *World Rowing*, 332–34. Riess, *Sport in Industrial America*, 54; King, *Handbook of New York City 1892*, 268 and 530.

20 Dodd, *World Rowing*, 334–35, citing US Olympic rower Jan Louise Palchikoff. Title IX has also boosted women's soccer, leading to US victories at the World Cup in 1991, 1999, 2015, and 2019. At the Olympics US women won silver in 2000 and gold in 1996, 2004, 2008, 2012, and 2016.

21 *Boston Evening Transcript*, June 20, 1905; "Hey-Days & Holidays" from Wellesley College *Legenda*, 1908.

22 *New York Times*, May 2, 1894; Karen Klinger to the author, July 29, 2013.

23 Dodd, *World Rowing*, 338–39; Kingsbury and Williams, *Cambridge*; Ashling O'Connor, "In Rowing, Women Catch Up With the Men," *New York Times*, March 26, 2014. See also "75 Years of Women's Rowing at Cambridge, Parts 1 and 2, at heartheboatsing.com by Goran Buckhorn.

24 *New York Times*, March 4, 1976; Wulf, "Title Waves. . ."; Boyne, *Red Rose Crew*, 189.

25 NCAA statistics. "Women's rowing became an NCAA sport in 1997, which essentially created rowing programs at many universities that, prior to 1997, either weren't varsity status or didn't have a program at all," says Cornell coach Hilary Gehman. "Once it became an NCAA sport, they added rowing and put a lot of money into it and that created so much opportunity."

26 Birnbach, *Preppy Handbook*, 101. Henley Royal Regatta records, "Results of Final Races 1946–2003." US Henley Winners, Friends of Rowing History website, rowinghistory.net . Other US schools to win the Princess Elizabeth Cup once are Tabor Academy in Marion, Massachusetts; St. Ignatius College Preparatory in San Francisco; Belmont Hill School in Belmont, Massachusetts; and St. Joseph's Preparatory School in Philadelphia.

27 My thanks to Thomas E. Weil Jr. for this inventory of magazines from his collection.

28 Optic, *Boat Club*; Betts, *America's Sporting Heritage*, 232–40; Goran R. Buckhorn, "Rowing Women as Belles des Bateaux, or To Say Nothing of the Cat," Note 6, rowinghistory.net; see also Halladay, *Rowing in England*.

29 Walt Whitman, "I Sing the Body Electric" (1855), Section 2; Frederick Nietzsche, *Human, All Too Human*, Cambridge, Cambridge University Press, 1996, 63.

30 My thanks to Thomas E. Weil Jr. for examples of magazine illustrations and advertisements. For more information see rowinghistory.net. See, for example, ads for Jaguar XJ-SC, the software company EDA CAD T.E.A.M., Aetna health insurance plans, Wisconsin Tissue, Lotus SmartSuite software, Olivetti Systems, and CXC Cervical Cap Ltd. My thanks to James Sciales for sharing his rowing-in-advertising collection.

31 My thanks to Tim Koch and Goran Buckhorn for this information, posted January 20, 2016 on Buckhorn's rowing blog heartheboatsing.com.
32 *The Guardian*, June 23, 2013.
33 Eton College rowing website at etoncollege.com (Rowing).
34 *The Guardian*, December 7, 2011; *London Gazette*, August 24, 2001; Stephen Redgrave to the author, August 15, 2013.
35 Dodd, *World Rowing*, 236; Anderson, "Elitism," 27.
36 Nauright and Parrish, *Sports Around the World*; Robin Poke, "Different Strokes for Different Folks—Rowing's Not Elitist," *Sydney Morning Herald*, April 13, 2012, at smh .au.
37 Brown, "Pierre de Coubertin's . . .", 41–48.
38 Powers, *Head of the Charles*, 83; *Rowing*, October 2014, 36.
39 Frederick V. Schoch (Executive Director, Head of the Charles Regatta) to the author, July 29 and August 9, 2013, April 14, 2014; *Harvard Crimson*, October 23, 2000; Grahame, *Wind in the Willows*, Chapter 1.

Appendix
1 See for example the painting "Outrigger pair by St. Mary's Church, Putney" published January 25, 1851 by Messrs. Fores at their Sporting and Finest Print Repository and Frame Manufactory, 41 Piccadilly, London. My thanks to Mystic Seaport historian Goran Buckhorn for this image and citation.
2 Locations of the art works mentioned in this chapter:
    By George D. Hopkins.
    Scull Race, Boston Bay, 1858 (oil), Peabody Essex Museum, Salem, Massachusetts.
    By Thomas Eakins.
    The Champion Single Sculls or Max Schmitt in a Single Scull, 1871 (oil), Metropolitan Museum of Art, New York.
    The Biglin Brothers Turning the Stake, 1873 (oil), Cleveland Museum of Art.
    The Artist and His Father Hunting Reed Birds, 1874 (oil), Art Institute of Chicago.
    The Gross Clinic, 1875 (oil), Philadelphia Museum of Art.
    The Agnew Clinic, 1889 (oil), University of Pennsylvania, on loan to the Philadelphia Museum of Art.
    Swimming, 1884-1885 (oil), Amon Carter Museum of Art, Fort Worth, TX.
    The Biglin Brothers Racing, 1872 (oil), National Gallery of Art, Washington, DC.
    Perspective Drawings for The Pair-Oared Shell, 1872 (pencil, ink, and wash), Philadelphia Museum of Art.
    Perspective Drawings for The Pair-Oared Shell, 1872 (pencil, ink, and watercolor), Philadelphia Museum of Art.
    The Pair-Oared Shell, 1972, Philadelphia Museum of Art.
    Perspective Studies for John Biglin in a Single Scull, (pencil, ink, and wash) c.1873, Museum of Fine Arts, Boston.
    John Biglin in a Single Scull, 1873 (watercolor), Yale University Art Gallery.
    John Biglin in a Single Scull, c.1873 (watercolor), Metropolitan Museum of Art, New York.

John Biglin in a Single Scull, 1874 (oil), Yale University Art Gallery.

The Schreiber Brothers or *The Oarsmen*, 1874, Yale University Art Gallery.

Sketch of Max Schmitt in a Single Scull, c.1874 (oil), Philadelphia Museum of Art.

Oarsmen on the Schuylkill, c. 1874 (oil), private collection.

Wrestlers, 1899 (oil), Los Angeles County Museum of Art.

3 "The Fine Arts: The Third Art Reception at the Union League. III," *Philadelphia Evening Bulletin*, April 28, 1871.

4 Sewell, *Thomas Eakins*, 2001, 390 note 4; Johns, *Thomas Eakins*, 24 note 11, 36–37.

5 For background on Eakins's artistic training, see Cooper, *Thomas Eakins*, 12–22.

6 Johns, *Thomas Eakins*, 8–9; Sewell, *Thomas Eakins*, 2001, 1–4 and 390 note 4; Homer, *Paris Letters*, 20 and 28.

7 Thomas Eakins to Benjamin Eakins, December 2, 1869, Pennsylvania Academy of Fine Arts.

8 Cooper, *Thomas Eakins*, 18 and 22.

9 Fort, *Manly Pursuits*, 214, quoting Johns, *Thomas Eakins*, 34.

10 Johns, *Thomas Eakins*, 24–30; Cooper, *Thomas Eakins*, 32.

11 Fort, *Manly Pursuits*, 179. For perspectives on Eakins's masculine identity see Berger, *MAN MADE*, especially 11–21 and 40–46.

12 Johns, *Thomas Eakins*, 42–43.

13 Werbel, "Perspective in Thomas Eakins' Rowing Pictures," in Cooper, *Thomas Eakins*, 79–89; Johns, *Thomas Eakins*, 38.

14 Eakins, *Drawing Manual*, 82 and 84; Sewell, *Thomas Eakins*, 2001, 28; 390 notes 15 and 16.

15 For more about Eakins's portrayal of nudes see Berger, *Man Made*, 141, note 1. Several articles analyze Eakins's masculinity as expressed in rowing and painting. See, for example, Berger, "Negotiating Victorian Manhood"; Cooper, *Thomas Eakins*, 102–23. Other works are excerpted in Fort and in Adams, *Eakins Revealed*, 193ff.

16 Thomas Eakins to Benjamin Eakins, March 6, 1868; Siegl, *Philadelphia*, 393–94; Siegl, *Thomas Eakins Collection*, 54–56. Cited in Cooper, *Thomas Eakins*, 126.

17 Bregler, "Thomas Eakins as a Teacher," vol. 17, 378–86. See also *The Arts*, vol. 18, 27–42.

18 Sewell, *Thomas Eakins: Artist of Philadelphia*, 17–18, cited in Cooper, *Thomas Eakins*, 40; Sewell, *Thomas Eakins*, 2001, 28, 390 note 15 and 16; *New York Times*, April 20, 1879, 10. The National Academy of Design is now the National Academy Museum and School.

19 Cooper, *Thomas Eakins*, 44–54.

20 Although known as a realist, Eakins also varied a few details in this painting to suit his purposes. The Coulter/Cavitt crew rowed bare-chested and bareheaded that day, but to signify their course when approaching the red-flagged stake Eakins gave them white shirts and red bandanas. And the two crews rounded stake boats anchored in the stream, not the slender sticks shown here. Finally, the race was postponed by rain and wind, but Eakins chose to paint a bright sky.

21 Rowers and coaches analyzing the picture disagree about just what John Biglin is doing with his oar. For a range of opinions, see Cooper, *Thomas Eakins*, 127, note 48.

22 Christina Currie, "Thomas Eakins Under the Microscope," in Cooper, *Thomas Eakins*, 92; Werbel, "Perspective in Thomas Eakins' Rowing Pictures," in Cooper, *Thomas Eakins*, 89. The critic Mariana Griswold van Rensselaer saw this painting a few years after Eakins completed it, and declared: "There is, perhaps, no artist in the country who can rival him for originality of conception, artistic use, no one who imprints a sign-manual of individuality so strongly on everything he touches. . . ." She said *The Biglin Brothers Turning the Stake* "is very strong in drawing. . . . [and the canvas is] pitched in a low and somewhat unusual key, which is yet perfectly justifiable and which justifies itself, indeed, for we comprehend at once that a sunlight effect is intended." She also praised how Eakins dabbed blue for the turning-stake flag and the Biglins' head-scarves, a touch she found "deep and brilliant, and most uncompromising." Mariana Griswold van Rensselaer, "The Philadelphia Exhibition—II," *American Architect and Building News* 8 (December 25, 1880), 303–4; Fort, *Manly Pursuits*, 67.

23 Marc Simpson, "The 1870s," in Sewell, *Thomas Eakins*, 2001, 29; Cooper, *Thomas Eakins*, 59. Goodrich, Foreword to Hoopes, *Eakins Watercolors*, 6–7. In 1880, Eakins permitted *Scribner's* magazine to illustrate a short story using a wood engraving of *The Biglin Brothers Turning the Stake* by Alice Barber (Stephens), but titled the picture *On the Harlem*. Braddock, *Thomas Eakins*, 98–99.

24 Gérôme to Eakins, May 10, 1873; Goodrich, *Eakins*, 164, note 55. See Fort, *Manly Pursuits*, 154.

25 Gérôme to Eakins, September 18, 1874. Translated in Goodrich 1982, vol. I, 116; Simpson, 29. See also Cooper, 58; Sewell, 2001, 29; 391 note 29; Goodrich, *Thomas Eakins*, 71–73. *The Sculler* is lost, the date of its sale reported in Sewell, *Thomas Eakins*, 2001, xxviii.

26 Cooper, *Thomas Eakins*, 70. Helen Cooper to the author, February 3, 2016.

27 Thomas Eakins to Earl Shinn, March 26, 1875. Helen Cooper to the author, citing a second, undated, letter to Shinn. John Updike, "The Ache in Eakins," 10.

28 Eakins to Earl Shinn, March 26, 1875; in Goodrich, *Thomas Eakins*, 1982, vol. I, 121; Unpublished Eakins letter to Shinn, cited by Cooper; Stebbins et al., *New World*, 268.

29 Eakins to Earl Shinn, March 26, 1875; Undated letter by Eakins to Shinn, cited by Cooper in a note to the author February 3, 2016; Cooper, *Thomas Eakins*, 66–67 and 128 notes 60–62.

30 Eakins exhibited *John Biglin in a Single Scull* at the American Society of Painters in Water Color in 1874; *The Pair-Oared Shell* at the Lotos Club in 1877 and at the National Academy of Design in 1879; *The Biglin Brothers Turning the Stake* at the Metropolitan Museum of Art in 1882; and the oil *John Biglin in a Single Scull* at the American Art Association in 1883. Cooper, *Thomas Eakins*, 136–38; Seymour Adelman to John Walker, November 2, 1967, in the National Gallery of Art Curatorial Archives for *The Biglin Brothers Racing*.

31 Werbel, *Thomas Eakins*, 35–36. The critical quotes are from "Art at the Academy," *Philadelphia Press* (November 25, 1880), 5, and from Edward Strahan, 114–115. Notes about *The Gross Clinic* are from Sewell, *Thomas Eakins*, 1982, 16. *The Nation* quote is from Sewell, *Thomas Eakins*, 2001, 390 note 17.

32 *Philadelphia Evening Telegraph*, April 6, 1881 is quoted in Siegl, *Philadelphia*, "Catalogue entries 336a, b and 337" in Philadelphia Museum of Art, 1976, 391–94. Eakins's oil sketch and oil painting of Wrestlers (both 1899) are at the Los Angeles County Museum of Art. Both works were featured in the exhibition "Manly Pursuits: The Sporting Images of Thomas Eakins" (July 25 to October 17, 2010).

33 Helen A. Cooper to the author, July 28, 2016.

BIBLIOGRAPHY

Abdullah, Aquil, with Chris Ingraham. *Perfect Balance*. Washington, DC: Signature Book Printing for Potomac Sculling Publishing, 2001.

Adams, Henry. *Eakins Revealed: The Secret Life of an American Artist*. New York: Oxford University Press, 2005.

Adams, Samuel Hopkins. *Grandfather Stories*. New York: Random House, 1955.

Adelman, Melvin L. *A Sporting Time: New York City and the Rise of Modern Athletics, 1820–1870*. Urbana and Chicago: University of Illinois Press, 1990.

A History of Our Time. New York: Doubleday, Page & Company, 1903.

Alderson, Frederick. *Bicycling: A History*. New York: Praeger, 1972.

Alexander, De Alva Stanwood. *A Political History of the State of New York*, vol. 3. New York: Henry Holt & Co., 1906.

Algeo, Matthew. *Pedestrianism: When Watching People Walk Was America's Favorite Spectator Sport*. Chicago: Chicago Review Press, 2014.

Allen, Jane E., and Roger B. Allen, eds. "Flashing Oars: Rowing on the Schuylkill." September 20–December 30, 1985. The Philadelphia Maritime Museum (now Independence Seaport Museum), Philadelphia.

Allen, Oliver E. *The Tiger: The Rise and Fall of Tammany Hall*. Reading, MA: Addison-Wesley, 1993.

American Leaders 1789–1987. Washington, DC: Congressional Quarterly Inc., 1987.

Anderson, Andy. "Bad Ideas Never Die: The Road Sculler." *Rowing News*, February 23, 2003, 25, 30.

———. "Elitism and the Legend of Jack Kelly Sr." *Rowing News*, October 2006, 26–27.

Anbinder, Tyler. *City of Dreams: The 400-Year Epic History of Immigrant New York*. Boston: Houghton Mifflin Harcourt, 2016.

The Annual Illustrated Catalogue and Oarsman's Manual for 1871. Troy, NY: Waters, Balch & Co.

"Argonaut," ed. Amateur Rowing Association of Great Britain. *The Rowing Almanack and Oarsman's Companion 1877*. London and New York: Virtue & Co., 1877.

Asinof, Eliot. *Eight Men Out: The Black Sox and the 1919 World Series*. New York: Holt, Rinehart and Winston, 1963.

Bancroft, W. A., et al. "The Crisis in Rowing." *Harvard Graduates' Magazine* 3 (September 1894), 30–36.

Bartlett, John Henry, and John Pearl Gifford. *Dartmouth Athletics: A Complete History of All Kinds of Sports at the College*. Concord, NH: Republican Press Association, 1893.

Bayor, Ronald H., and Timothy J. Meagher, eds. *The New York Irish*. Baltimore: Johns Hopkins University Press, 1996.

Berger, Martin A. "Negotiating Victorian Manhood: Thomas Eakins and the Rowing Works." *Masculinities* vol. 2, no. 3, Fall 1994, 1–17. (Published by the Men's Studies Association, Guilford Publications, 72 Spring Street, New York City 10012.)
———. *Man Made: Thomas Eakins and the Construction of Gilded Age Manhood.* Berkeley, Los Angeles, and London: University of California Press, 2000.
Berman, Lynn S. "Julian O. Davidson and the Nyack Rowing Association." In *South of the Mountains.* Nyack: The Historical Society of Rockland County, vol. 30, no. 4 (October–December 1986), 3–13.
Berton, Pierre. *My Country: The Remarkable Past.* Toronto: McClelland and Stewart Ltd., 1977.
Betts, John Rickards. *America's Sporting Heritage 1850–1950.* Reading, MA: Addison-Wesley Publishing Company, 1974.
Birnbach, Lisa, ed. *The Official Preppy Handbook.* New York: Workman Publishing, 1980.
Blaikie, William. *How to Get Strong and How to Stay So.* New York: Harper & Brothers, 1879.
———. *Sound Bodies for Our Boys and Girls.* New York: Harper & Brothers, 1884.
Blodgett, Geoffrey T. *The Gentle Reformers.* Cambridge, MA: Harvard University Press, 1966.
Boyne, Daniel J. *Essential Sculling.* Guilford, CT: Lyons Press, 2000.
———. *The Red Rose Crew: A True Story of Women, Winning, and the Water.* Guilford, CT: Lyons Press, 2000).
———. *Kelly: A Father, a Son, an American Quest.* Guilford, CT: Lyons Press, 2012.
Braddock, Alan C. *Thomas Eakins and the Cultures of Modernity.* Berkeley: University of California Press, 2009.
Bradley, U. T. *The Dad Vail Story.* Winter Park, FL: Rollins Press, Inc., 1961.
Bregler, Charles. "Thomas Eakins as a Teacher." *The Arts,* vol. 17, no. 6 (March 1931), 378–86; vol. 18, no. 1 (October 1931), 28–42.
Britten, Evelyn Barrett. *Chronicles of Saratoga.* Saratoga Springs, NY: Privately published, 1959.
Brown, Daniel James. *The Boys in the Boat: Nine Americans and Their Epic Quest for Gold at the 1936 Berlin Olympics.* New York: Viking, 2013.
Brown, Douglas. "Pierre de Coubertin's Poetic and Prosaic Theory of Every Day Sport." In Kevin B. Wamsley, Robert K. Barney, and Scott G. Martyn, eds. *The Global Nexus Engaged: Past, Present, Future Interdisciplinary Olympic Studies.* Sixth International Symposium for Olympic Research, October 2002. London, Ontario: University of Western Ontario, 41–48.
Buckhorn, Goran R. *A Yank at Cambridge: B.H. Howell: The Forgotten Champion.* Mystic, CT: HTBS Publication, 2015.
Burrows, Edwin, and Mike Wallace. *Gotham: A History of New York City to 1898.* New York: Oxford University Press, 1999.
A Cambridge Scrap-Book. Cambridge and London: Macmillan & Co., 1859.
Carlson, Jack. *Rowing Blazers.* New York: Vendome Press, 2014.
Carruth, Gorton, and Associates. *The Encyclopedia of American Facts and Dates.* New York: Thomas Y. Crowell Company, 1962.

Carter, Alice A. *The Essential Thomas Eakins.* New York: Harry N. Abrams, Inc., 2001.

Cashman, Sean Dennis. *America in the Gilded Age: From the Death of Lincoln to the Rise of Theodore Roosevelt.* New York: New York University Press, 1993.

Churbuck, D. C. *The Book of Rowing.* Woodstock, NY: Overlook Press, 1988.

Ciment, James, ed. *Encyclopedia of American Immigration.* Armonk, NY: M.E. Sharpe, 2001.

Cleaver, Hylton. *A History of Rowing.* London: Herbert Jenkins Limited, 1957.

The Columbian Cyclopedia. Buffalo: Garretson, Cox & Co., 1897.

Committee on the District of Columbia, Sixty-Fourth Congress, Second Session. *Hearings on Prohibiting the Manufacture and Sale of Alcoholic Liquors in the District of Columbia.* Washington, DC: US Government Printing Office, 1917.

Conrad, Harold. "6-Day Bike Race, Back After 22 Years . . ." *Variety,* August 23, 1961, 2.

Cook, William A. *The Louisville Grays Scandal of 1877: The Taint of Gambling at the Dawn of the National League.* Jefferson, NC: McFarland & Company, Inc., 2005.

Cooke, Mary Huntington. "A Few Memories of William Reed Huntington By His Sister Mary Huntington Cooke." Privately published at The Riverside Press, Cambridge, MA, 1910.

Cooper, Helen A., with Martin A. Berger, Christina Currie, and Amy B. Werbel. *Thomas Eakins: The Rowing Pictures.* New Haven and London: Yale University Art Gallery / Yale University Press, 1996.

Cosentino, Frank. "Ned Hanlan—Canada's Premier Oarsman: A Case Study in 19th Century Professionalism," *Canadian Journal of History of Sport and Physical Education* vol. V, no. 2 (December 1974).

———. *The Canadians: Ned Hanlan.* Don Mills, Ontario: Fitzhenry & Whiteside, Ltd., 1978.

———. *Not Bad, Eh? Great Moments in Canadian Sports History.* Burnstown, Ontario: General Store Publishing House, 1990.

Costello, Augustine E. *Our Firemen.* New York: Augustine E. Costello, 1887.

Courtney, Charles E. "Teaching College Men the Art of Rowing." *Illustrated Sporting News* 5 (April 29, 1905), 2.

Cox, Richard William. *Sport in Britain: A Bibliography of Historical Publications, 1800–1988.* Manchester, England: Manchester University Press, 1991.

Cross, Gary. *A Social History of Leisure Since 1600.* State College, PA: Venture Publishing, Inc., 1990.

Crowninshield, Benjamin W. *A Private Journal 1856–1858.* Cambridge, MA: Riverside Press, 1941.

Crowther, Samuel Jr., "The Ethics of American Rowing," *The Outing Magazine,* vol. L, no. 4 (July 1907), 499–502.

Crowther, S., and A. Ruhl. *Rowing and Track Athletics.* American Sportsman's Library. Caspar Whitney, ed. New York: Macmillan Company, 1905.

Davis, Whitney. "Erotic Revision in Thomas Eakins' Narratives of Male Nudity." *Art History: Journal of the Association of Art Historians* 17 (September 1994), 301–41.

Dillon, Peter. *The Tyne Oarsmen: Harry Clasper, Robert Chambers, James Renforth.* Newcastle: Keepdate Publishing Ltd., 1993.

Documents of the Assembly of the State of New York. Albany, NY: E. Croswell, 1873, vol. 4.

Dodd, Christopher. *Henley Royal Regatta.* London: Stanley Paul, 1989.

———. *The Story of World Rowing.* London: Stanley Paul, 1992.

———. *Water Boiling Aft: London Rowing Club, The First 150 Years, 1856–2006.* London: London Rowing Club, 2006.

———. *Unto the Tideway Born: 500 Years of Thames Watermen and Lightermen.* London: Company of Watermen and Lightermen, 2015.

Dodd, Christopher, ed., and Jane Bowen. "The Sliding Seat." Henley-on-Thames: River and Rowing Museum, January 1995, rrm.co.uk.

Doenecke, Justus. "Chester A. Arthur: Life Before the Presidency," The Miller Center, University of Virginia at http://millercenter.org/president/biography/arthur-life-before-the-presidency.

Dolan, Jay P. *The American Catholic Experience: A History from Colonial Times to the Present.* Garden City, NY: Doubleday, 1985.

———. *The Irish Americans: A History.* New York: Bloomsbury Press, 2008.

Durick, William G. "The Gentlemen's Race: An Examination of the 1869 Harvard-Oxford Boat Race." *Journal of Sports History,* vol. 15, no. 1 (Spring 1988), 41–63.

Eakins, Thomas. *A Drawing Manual by Thomas Eakins.* New Haven and London: Yale University Press, 2005.

Edelman, Robert, ed. *History of Modern Sport (HEU 127),* course anthology for University of California, San Diego. University Readers, Inc., Fall 2006.

Edelman, Robert, and Christopher Young, eds., *The Whole World Is Watching: Sport in the Cold War.* Stanford: Stanford University Press, 2020.

Edwards, Richard. *New York's Great Industries* (1884). North Stratford, NH: Ayer Company Publishing, Inc., 1973 reprint.

Eisen, George, and David K. Wiggins, eds. *Ethnicity and Sport in North American History and Culture.* Westport, CT: Greenwood Press, 1994.

Ellis, Edward R. *The Epic of New York City: A Narrative History.* New York: Carroll & Graf Publishers, 2004, 347–48.

Engelhardt, Fred J., ed. *The American Rowing Almanac and Oarsman's Companion 1873.* New York: Engelhardt and Bruce, At the Office of *Turf, Field and Farm,* 37 Park Row, 1873.

———. *The American Rowing Almanac and Oarsman's Companion 1874.* New York: F.J. Engelhardt, 1874.

Farmer, J. David. *Rowing/Olympics.* Santa Barbara, CA: University Art Museum, 1984.

Faulkner, Ed and Lucy. *Bottles and Extras,* Summer 2006, 35–37.

Felter, William. *Historic Green Point.* New York: Green Point Savings Bank, 1918.

Fidler, D. "First Big Upset." North American Society for Sport History. Third annual convention, Boston, 1975.

Flood, Brian. *Saint John: A Sporting Tradition 1785–1985.* Altona, Manitoba: Neptune Publishing Company Ltd., D. W. Friesen & Sons, Ltd., 1985.

Ford, Malcolm W. "The New York Athletic Club." *The Outing Magazine,* vol. 33, no. 3 (December 1898), 248–60.

Fort, Ilene Susan, ed. *Manly Pursuits: Writings on the Sporting Images of Thomas Eakins.* Los Angeles: Los Angeles County Museum of Art, 2011.

Fortmeyer, Fred R., ed. *Minutes of the Forty-First Annual Meeting, National Association of Amateur Oarsmen.* Washington, DC: W.F. Roberts Co., 1913.

Foster, Kathleen, and Cheryl Leibold, eds. *Writing About Eakins: The Manuscripts in Charles Bregler's Thomas Eakins Collection.* Philadelphia: Pennsylvania Academy of Fine Arts, 1989.

Fox, Richard Kyle. *Edward Hanlan, America's Champion Oarsman, with History and Portrait.* New York: Police Gazette Office, 1880; Kessinger Publishing, Whitefish, MT, 1978 facsimile edition.

Franke, Werner W., and Brigitte Berendonk. "Hormonal Doping and Androgenization of Athletes: A Secret Program of the German Democratic Republic Government." *Clinical Chemistry* 43:7, 1262–79, 1997.

French, Bryant Morey. *Mark Twain and the Gilded Age: The Book That Named an Era.* Dallas: Southern Methodist University Press, 1965.

Garran, Daniella K. *A History of Collegiate Rowing in America.* Atglen, PA: Schiffer Publishing Ltd., 2012.

Gems, Gerald. *Sports in American History: From Colonization to Globalization.* Champaign: University of Illinois Press, 2008.

Gilder, Ginny. *Course Correction: A Story of Rowing and Resilience in the Wake of Title IX.* Boston: Beacon Press, 2015.

Gipe, George. "The Roadsculler Made Rowing on Land as Hard as Walking on Water." *Sports Illustrated*, March 14, 1977.

———. *The Great American Sports Book: A Casual but Voluminous Look at American Spectator Sports from the Civil War to the Present Time.* Garden City, NY: Doubleday Dolphin, 1978.

Glendon, Richard A., and Richard J. Glendon. *Rowing.* Philadelphia: J.B. Lippincott Co., 1923.

Goldstein, Warren. *Playing for Keeps: A History of Early Baseball.* Ithaca, NY, and London: Cornell University Press, 1989.

Golway, Terry. *Machine Made: Tammany Hall and the Creation of Modern American Politics.* New York and London: Liveright Publishing Corporation, 2014.

Goodrich, Lloyd. *Thomas Eakins*, 2 vols. Cambridge, MA: Harvard University Press, 1982.

———. Foreword to Hoopes, Donelson F. *Eakins Watercolors.* New York: Watson-Guptill, 1971.

———. *Thomas Eakins. Retrospective Exhibition.* September 22 to November 21, 1970. New York: Whitney Museum of American Art, 1970.

Gookin, Sylvester. "Silver Lake and '78." *The Log of Mystic Seaport.* vol. 29, no. 4 (January 1978), 98–110.

Gordon, Ian. "Thomas Eakins, *The Champion Single Sculls, 1871.*" In *American Social History Project*, The Graduate Center, City University of New York, 2019.

Gordon, Michael A. *The Orange Riots: Irish Political Violence in New York City, 1870 and 1871.* Ithaca, NY: Cornell University Press, 1993.

Gorn, Elliott J. *The Manly Art: Bare-Knuckle Prize Fighting in America*. Ithaca, NY, and London: Cornell University Press, 1986.

Gorn, Elliott, and Warren Goldstein. *A Brief History of American Sports*. New York: Hill and Wang, 1993; Urbana, Springfield, and Chicago: University of Illinois Press, 2013, 2nd Edition.

Goulding, Lawrence G., ed. *Goulding's New York City Directory for 1875-76*. New York: Lawrence G. Goulding, 1875. And *New York City Directory for 1876-77*. New York: Lawrence G. Goulding, 1876.

Grahame, Kenneth. *The Wind in the Willows*. London: Methuen Publishing, 1908, chapter 1.

Halberstam, David. *The Amateurs: The Story of Four Young Men and Their Quest for an Olympic Gold Medal*. New York: William Morrow and Company, Inc., 1985.

Hale, John R. *Lords of the Sea*. New York: Penguin Books, 2009.

Halladay, Eric. *Rowing in England: A Social History, The Amateur Debate*. Manchester, England: Manchester University Press, 1990.

Handlin, Oscar. *The Uprooted: The Epic Story of the Great Migrations That Made the American People*. Boston: Atlantic Monthly Press, Little, Brown and Company, 1973.

The Harvard Monthly. Cambridge, MA. (1885–1917).

Haswell, Charles H. *Reminiscences of New York by an Octogenarian, 1816–1860*. New York: Harper, 1896.

Hatt, Michael. "The Male Body in Another Frame: Thomas Eakins' *The Swimming Hole* as a Homoerotic Image." *Journal of Philosophy and the Visual Arts*, 1993, 9–21.

Haworth, Paul Leland. *The Hayes-Tilden Disputed Presidential Election of 1876*. Cleveland: The Burrows Brothers Company, 1906.

Heiland, Louis, compiler. *The Schuylkill Navy of Philadelphia (1858–1937)*. Philadelphia: Drake Press, 1938.

Henderson, Robert W. *Early American Sport: A Checklist of Books by American and Foreign Authors Published in America Prior to 1860*. Rutherford, NJ: Fairleigh Dickinson, Associated University Presses, 1977.

Hitchcock, Edward Jr. "Rowing" in *The Universal Cyclopaedia*. New York: Appleton and Company, 1900, 199–201.

Hickock, Ralph. *The Encyclopedia of North American Sports History*. New York: Facts on File, 1992.

Higham, John. *Strangers in the Land: Patterns of American Nativism 1860–1925*. New York: Atheneum, 1962.

A History of Our Time. New York: Doubleday, Page & Company, 1903.

Holliman, Jennie. *American Sports (1785–1835)*. Durham, NC: Seeman Press, 1931; Porcupine Press, 1975.

Holt's Shooting Calendar, Fisherman's Reference and Sportsman's Record 1883. London: H. Holt.

Homer, William Innes. *Thomas Eakins: His Life and Art*. New York: Abbeville, 1995.

Homer, William Innes, ed. *The Paris Letters of Thomas Eakins*. Princeton, NJ: Princeton University Press, 2009.

Hotaling, Edward. *They're Off: Horse Racing at Saratoga*. Syracuse, NY: Syracuse University Press, 1995.

Hunter, Robert S. *Rowing in Canada Since 1848*. Hamilton, Ontario: Davis-Lisson Limited, 1933.

Howe, George F. *Chester A. Arthur, A Quarter-Century of Machine Politics*. New York: F. Ungar Publishing Co., 1966.

Huizinga, Johann. *Homo Ludens: A Study of the Play Element in Culture*. Boston: Beacon Press, 1955.

Jackson, Albert Stuart. *The Standard Theatre of Victorian England*. Madison, NJ: Fairleigh Dickinson University Press, 1993.

Jackson, Kenneth T., ed. *The Encyclopedia of New York City*. New Haven and London: Yale University Press, 1995.

James, Ed. *The Modern Oarsman*. New York: Ed. James, New York Clipper Building, 1878.

Johns, Elizabeth. *Thomas Eakins: The Heroism of Modern Life*. Princeton, NJ: Princeton University Press, 1983.

Johnson, Robert B. *A History of Rowing in America*. Milwaukee: Corbitt & Johnson, 1871.

Josephson, Matthew. *The Robber Barons: The Great American Capitalists, 1861–1901*. New York: Harcourt, Brace and Company, 1934.

Keck, George R., and Sherrill V. Martin, eds. *Feel the Spirit: Studies in Nineteenth-Century Afro-American Music*. New York: Greenwood Press, 1988.

Keller, Morton. *The Art and Politics of Thomas Nast*. New York: Oxford University Press, 1968.

Kelley, Robert F. *American Rowing: Its Background and Traditions*. New York: G.P. Putnam's Sons, 1932.

Kelly, John. *The Graves Are Walking: The Great Famine and the Saga of the Irish People*. New York: Picador, 2013.

Kelly, Mary C. *Ireland's Great Famine in Irish-American History: Enshrining a Fateful Memory*. Lanham, MD: Rowman & Littlefield, 2013.

Kernan, J. Frank. *Reminiscences of the Old Fire Laddies and Volunteer Fire Departments of New York and Brooklyn*. New York: M. Crane, 1885.

Kerr, William Henry Corrie. *Edward Hanlan: A Lay of Young Canada (1879)*. Toronto: Belfords, Clarke & Co., Publishers, 1879.

Keys, Barbara J. *Globalizing Sport: National Rivalry and International Community in the 1930s*. Cambridge, MA, and London: Harvard University Press, 2006.

Keyser, Charles S. *Fairmount Park and the International Exhibition at Philadelphia*. Philadelphia: Claxton, Remsen & Haffelfinger, 1875. Map of rowing course at title.

Kiesling, Stephen. *The Shell Game: Reflections on Rowing and the Pursuit of Excellence*. Chicago: Contemporary Books, Inc., 1982.

King, Moses. *King's Handbook of New York City 1892*. Boston: Moses King, 1892; New York: Barnes & Noble, Inc., 2001 reprint.

———. *King's Views of New York 1896–1915 & Brooklyn 1905*. New York: Arno Press, 1980 reprint.

King, Peter. *Art and a Century of Canadian Rowing.* Toronto: Amberley House Limited, 1980.

Kingsbury, Jane, and Carol Williams. *Cambridge University Women's Boat Club 1941–2014: The Struggle Against Inequality.* London: Trireme, 2015.

Kirkpatrick, Sidney D. *The Revenge of Thomas Eakins.* New Haven and London: Yale University Press, 2006.

Kirsch, George B., Othello Harris, and Claire Elaine Nolte, eds. *Encyclopedia of Ethnicity and Sports in the United States.* Westport, CT: Greenwood Press, 2000.

Klein, Maury. *The Life and Legend of Jay Gould.* Baltimore: Johns Hopkins University Press, 1997.

Kraut, Alan M. "Records of the Immigration and Naturalization Service." Series A: Subject Correspondence Files. Part 3: Ellis Island, 1900–1933, July 1995.

Kroessler, Jeffrey A. *New York Year by Year: A Chronology of the Great Metropolis.* New York and London: New York University Press, 2002.

Krout, John A. *Annals of American Sport.* New Haven: Yale University Press, 1929.

Lambert, Craig. *Mind Over Water: Lessons on Life from the Art of Rowing.* Boston and New York: Houghton Mifflin Company, A Mariner Book, 1999.

Lang, F. S. "The Problem of Professional Rowing Coaches." *Illustrated Outdoor News* 6 (May 5, 1906), 2.

Lanouette, William. "A Click, A Swish—The Shell Is Running Nicely." *The National Observer,* May 18, 1970, 12.

———. "Olympic Rowing—You Need Both Grace and Guts." *Smithsonian,* July 1996, 89–99.

Latham, R., and W. Matthews. *The Diary of Samuel Pepys.* London: G. Bell and Sons, 1970, vol. 2, 101. Wager boat races at entry for May 18, 1661.

Laumann, Silken, with Calvin Wharton. *Rowing.* Erin, Ontario: Boston Mills Press, 1994.

Lee, J. J., and Marion R. Casey, eds. *Making the Irish American: History and Heritage of the Irish in the United States.* New York and London: New York University Press, 2006.

Lehmann, R. C., with F. S. Kelly, R. B. Etherington-Smith, and W. H. Eyre. *The Complete Oarsman.* London: Methuen & Co., 1908.

Leish, Kenneth W., ed. *The American Heritage Pictorial History of the Presidents of the United States.* New York: Simon and Schuster, 1968.

Lemmon, Jim. *The Log of Rowing at the University of California Berkeley 1870–1987.* Berkeley, CA: Western Heritage Press, 1989.

Leslie, Frank, ed. *Frank Leslie's Illustrated Historical Register of the Centennial Exposition 1876.* New York: Paddington Press, Two Continents Publishing Group, 1974 facsimile edition.

Literary Digest. vol. LXXXI (May 17, 1924), 38–44. "'Silent Charlie,' the Mayor Maker."

Look, Margaret K. *Courtney: Master Oarsman—Champion Coach.* Interlaken, NY: Empire State Books, 1989.

Lovett, James D'Wolf. *Old Boston Boys and the Games They Played.* Boston: Privately printed at the Riverside Press, 1906.

Low, A. Maurice. "Tammany Hall: Its Boss, Its Methods, and Its Meaning." In Norman and Roberts, *World's Work and Play*, 380.

Lucas, John A., and Ronald A. Smith. *A Saga of American Sport*. Philadelphia: Lea and Feibiger, 1978.

Macia, Xavier. "The Continuing Legacy of East Germany's Rowing Machine." *Rowing News*, October 2005.

Mallory, Peter. *An Out-of-Boat Experience . . . or God Is a Rower, and He Rows Like Me!* San Diego: Writer's Monthly Press, 2002.

———. *The Sport of Rowing*. Henley: River and Rowing Museum, 2011.

Manual of the Corporation of the City of New York. New York: Harper, 1869.

Mason, Tony. *Sport in Britain: A Social History*. Cambridge: Cambridge University Press, 1989.

Mather, Frank Jewett Jr. "Thomas Eakins's Art in Retrospect." *International Studio*, January 1930, 44–49 and 90ff. Schreiber Brothers painting leads the article, pictures courtesy Babcock Galleries.

McCarthy, Eugene J. *Dictionary of American Politics*. Harmondsworth, England: Penguin Books, Inc., 1962.

McElroy, W. H., and Alex McBride. *Life Sketches of Government Officers and Members of the Legislature of the State of New York for 1874*. Albany, NY: Weed, Parsons and Company, 1874.

McFeely, William S. *Portrait: The Life of Thomas Eakins*. New York and London: W.W. Norton & Company, 2007.

Melville, Tom. *The Tented Field: A History of Cricket in America*. Bowling Green, OH: Bowling Green State University Press, 1998.

Mendenhall, Thomas C. *The Harvard-Yale Boat Race 1852–1924 and the Coming of Sport to the American College*. Mystic, CT: Mystic Seaport Museum, 1993.

———. "The Rowing Art of Thomas Eakins." *Rowing USA*, April/May 1983, 12–14.

———. *A Short History of American Rowing*. Boston: Charles River Books, 1980.

Miller, Bill. "The Great International Boat Race." Friends of Rowing History website, rowinghistory.net.

———. "Strange But True." Friends of Rowing History website, rowinghistory.net.

———. "Fred Plaisted—Professional Sculler," Friends of Rowing History website, rowinghistory.net, September 2002.

———. "The Wild & Crazy Professionals." Friends of Rowing History website, rowinghistory.net, 2003.

Mohr, James C. *The Radical Republicans and Reform in New York During Reconstruction*. Ithaca, NY: Cornell University Press, 1973.

Mooney, Katherine C. *Race Horse Men: How Slavery and Freedom Were Made at the Racetrack*. Cambridge. MA, and London: Harvard University Press, 2014.

Morris, Edmund. *The Rise of Theodore Roosevelt*. New York: Coward, McCann & Geoghegan, Inc., 1979.

Morris, Peter, William J. Ryczek, Jan Finkel, Leonard Levin, and Richard Malatzky, eds. *Base Ball Founders: The Clubs, Players and Cities of the Northeast That Established the Game*. Jefferson, NC and London: McFarland & Company, Inc., 2013.

Morrow, Don, and Mary Keyes, with Wayne Simpson, Frank Cosentino, and Ron Lappage. *A Concise History of Sport in Canada*. Toronto: Oxford University Press, 1989.

Moynihan, Daniel Patrick. "The Irish (1963, 1970)," chapter 21 in Lee and Casey, *Irish American*, 475–525.

Mrozek, Donald J. *Sport and American Mentality, 1880–1910*. Knoxville: University of Tennessee Press, 1983.

Myers, Gustavus. *The History of Tammany Hall*. New York: Boni & Liveright, Inc., 1917; Carlisle, MA: Applewood Books, 2012 reprint.

Nauright, John, and Charles Parrish, eds. *Sports Around the World: History, Culture, and Practice*. Santa Barbara, CA: ABC-CLIO, LLC, 2012.

Nemec, David. *The Beer & Whisky League: The Illustrated History of the American Association—Baseball's Renegade Major League*. Guilford, CT: The Lyons Press, 2004.

New York Clipper. New York: Frank Queen Publishing Co. Cited: July 29, 1865; June 1 and 7, 1872; October 12, 1878.

New York Clipper Annual 1893. New York: Frank Queen Publishing Co., 1893.

The New York Public Library Desk Reference. New York: Stonesong Press, Inc., 1989.

New York Times Obituaries Index 1858–1968. New York: New York Times, 1970.

Norman, Henry, and Henry Chalmers Roberts, eds. *World's Work and Play*. London: William Heinemann, 1903.

Norsen, Irene Ward. *Ward Brothers, Champions of the World*. New York: Vantage Press, 1958.

Odlum, Catherine. *The Life and Adventures of Prof. Robert Emmet Odlum, Containing an Account of His Splendid Natatorium at the National Capital*. Washington, DC: Gray & Clarkson, Printers, 1885.

Optic, Oliver. *The Boat Club or The Bunkers of Rippleton*. New York: Mershon Company, 1896 reprint.

Pagen, Mary Jane, and Thomas E. Weil Jr. *Reflections on a Tradition: English and American Rowing Art*. Catalogue for an Exhibition by Georgetown University and the 1990 US Rowing Convention. Georgetown University Fine Arts Gallery, 28 November to 15 December 1990.

Palchikoff, Jan. "The Development of Women's Rowing in the United States." (Paper at the University of Massachusetts, Amherst, cited in Dodd, *World Rowing*.)

Palmer, Harry Clay. *Athletic Sports in America, England and Australia*. Philadelphia: Hubbard Brothers, Publishers, 1889.

Personal Name Index to the New York Times *Index 1851–1974*. Succasunna, NJ: Roxbury Data Interface, 1977.

Peverelly, Charles A. *The Book of American Pastimes: Containing a History of the Principal Base-Ball, Cricket, Rowing, and Yachting Clubs of the United States*. New York: New York Printing Company for the author, 1866.

The Philadelphia Record Almanac 1890. Philadelphia: Philadelphia Record, 1890.

Pickelhaupt, Bill. *Club Rowing on San Francisco Bay, 1869–1939 Featuring the South End Rowing Club*. Published by the author, 2014, second edition.

———. "Professional Rowing in the United States and Canada." *Maritime Life and Tradition*, no. 17 (Winter 2002), 60–69.

———. *The Rowing Clubs of California*. New Braunfels, TX: The Ellen Weber Regatta Club, a division of Flyblister Press, 2016.

Porter, Fairfield. *Thomas Eakins*. New York: George Braziller, Inc., 1959.

Potter, Merle. "The Red Wing—Stillwater Boat Race." In *101 Best Stories of Minnesota*. Minneapolis: Schmitt Publications, Inc., 1956.

Powers, John. *The Head of the Charles Regatta: First 50*. Cambridge: Head of the Charles Regatta, 2015.

Price, E. D., and A. I. McLeod, eds. *Oarsman's Pocket Guide*. Detroit: Daily Post Book and Job Printing Establishment, 1876. Full title: *Rowing in 1876, or, the Oarsman's Pocket Guide, containing A Graphic History of the Great Regattas at Toledo, Detroit, Saratoga and Philadelphia, Together with Facts and Figures of Practical Value to Every Oarsman*, by E. D. Price (Boating Editor "Detroit Post") and A. I. McLeod (Captain Zephyr Boat Club).

Prince, Carl E., and Mollie Keller. *The U.S. Customs Service: A Bicentennial History*. Washington: Department of the Treasury, 1989.

Pringle, Henry Fowles. *Theodore Roosevelt: A Biography*. New York: Blue Ribbon Books, 1931.

Proceedings of the Board of Aldermen of the City of New York, vols. 150 and 151. New York: Martin G. Brown, 1878.

Proceedings of the Board of Councilmen of the City of New York, vol. 107. Delhi: Pranava Books, 2020. (Reprint of the 1868 publication.)

Proctor, John Clagett. "Courtney in Recollections of John Hadley Doyle," *Washington Sunday Star*, April 6, 1930.

Prominent Families of New York. New York: Historical Company, 1897.

Putman, J. D. R. *The Rower's Manual and Boat Club Register*. New York: Herald Book and Job Office, 1858.

Rader, Benjamin G. *American Sports: From the Age of Folk Games to the Age of Televised Sports*. Englewood Cliffs, NJ: Prentice-Hall, 1983 and Upper Saddle River, NJ: Prentice-Hall, 2004.

Rasmussen, C. A. *A History of the City of Red Wing Minnesota*. Red Wing, MN: Published by the author, copyright 1934 by C. A. Rasmussen.

Redmond, Patrick R. *The Irish and the Making of American Sport, 1835–1920*. Jefferson, NC: McFarland & Company, Inc., 2014.

Reeves, Thomas C. *Gentleman Boss: The Life of Chester Alan Arthur*. New York: Alfred A. Knopf, 1975.

Rickards, Maurice, and Michael Twyman, eds. *The Encyclopedia of Ephemera*. New York: Routledge, 2000. Rowing entry by Diana Cook.

Rinehart, Rick. *Men of Kent: Ten Boys, a Fast Boat, and the Coach Who Made Them Champions*. Guilford, CT: The Lyons Press, 2010.

Riess, Stephen A. *The American Sporting Experience: A Historical Anthology of Sport in America*. New York: Leisure Press, 1984.

———. *City Games: The Evolution of American Urban Society and the Rise of Sports*. Urbana: University of Illinois Press, 1989.

——. *Sport in Industrial America 1850–1920*. Wheeling, IL: Harlan Davidson, Inc., 1995.

Rischin, Moses. *The Promised City: New York's Jews 1870–1914*. New York: Harper & Row, 1962.

Rode, Charles R. *The New York City Directory for 1853–1854*. New York: Charles R. Rode, 1853.

Rosenwaike, Ira. *Population History of New York City*. Syracuse, NY: Syracuse University Press, 1972.

"Rowing." In *The Universal Cyclopaedia*. New York: Appleton and Company, 1900, 199–201.

The Rower's Almanac. Bethesda, MD: Rower's Almanac, Inc., 2005 and 2012.

The Rowing Almanack and Oarsman's Companion 1877. London: Virtue & Co. and New York: Virtue & Yorston, 1877.

Royle, Marlene, and Carmen Marquez, eds. *The Rower's Almanac 2004-2005*. Bethesda, MD: Rower's Almanac, Inc., 2004.

Rule, Henry B. "Walt Whitman and Thomas Eakins: Variations on Some Common Themes." *Texas Quarterly* 17 (Winter 1974).

Safire, William. *Safire's New Political Dictionary*. New York: Random House, 1998.

Sante, Luc. *Low Life*. New York: Macmillan, 1991.

Sargent, Rachel L. "The Use of Slaves by the Athenians in Warfare." *Classical Philology*, vol. 22, no. 3 (July 1927), 264–79.

Schaelchlin, Patricia A. *The Little Clubhouse on Steamship Wharf: San Diego Rowing Club 1888–1983*. Leucadia, CA: Rand Editions, 1984.

Schendler, Sylvan. *Eakins*. Boston: Little, Brown and Company, 1967.

Schlup, Leonard, and James G. Ryan, eds. *Historical Dictionary of the Gilded Age*. Armonk, NY, and London: M.E. Sharpe, Inc., 2003.

Schnapper, M. B. *American Labor, A Pictorial Social History*. Washington, DC: Public Affairs Press, 1972.

Schnell, Dieter, Karl-Hans Arndt, and Herbert Lollgen. "Development of Sports Medicine in East Germany from 1945 to 1990." *Deutsche Zeitschrift fur Sportmedizin*, Jahrgang 63, no. 12 (2012).

Seeger, Pete, and Bob Reiser, *Carry It On! A History in Song and Picture of the Working Men and Women of America*. New York: Simon and Schuster, 1985.

Senate Committee on Investigation and Retrenchment. *Testimony in Relation to Alleged Frauds in the New York Custom-House*, 3 vols. Washington, DC: US Government Printing Office, 1872.

Sewell, Darrel, ed. *Thomas Eakins*. Philadelphia: Philadelphia Museum of Art, 2001. Catalogue for the 2001 "Thomas Eakins: American Realist" exhibition at the Philadelphia Museum of Art, Musee d'Orsay, and Metropolitan Museum of Art.

——. *Thomas Eakins: Artist of Philadelphia*. Philadelphia: Philadelphia Museum of Art, 1982. Catalogue for the fall 1982 exhibit of Eakins work at the Philadelphia Museum of Art and the Boston Museum of Fine Arts.

Seymour, Joey. "The History of the Resilient San Diego Rowing Club." *Journal of San Diego History*, vol. 57, nos. 1 & 2 (Winter/Spring 2011).

Sheldon, Henry D. *Student Life and Customs*. New York: Appleton, 1901.

Siegl, Theodor. *Philadelphia: Three Centuries of American Art*. Philadelphia: Philadelphia Museum of Art, 1976.

———. *The Thomas Eakins Collection: Philadelphia Museum of Art*. Nashville: Falcon Press, 1978.

Simpson, Marc. "The 1870s," in Sewell, *Thomas Eakins*, 2001, 27–40.

Smith, Ronald A. *Sports and Freedom: The Rise of Big-Time College Athletics*. New York and Oxford: Oxford University Press, 1988.

Stebbins, Theodore E. Jr., Carol Troyen, and Trevor F. Fairbrother. *A New World: Masterpieces of American Painting 1760–1910*. Boston: Museum of Fine Arts, 1983.

Stewart, Robert. *Rowing: The Experience*. Philadelphia: Boathouse Row Sports, Ltd., 1988.

Phelps Stokes, I. N. *The Iconography of Manhattan Island 1498–1909*. New York: Robert H. Dodd, 1928.

Stokes, Stewart. "It Was a Fearful Stroke, But They Made Their Old Boat Hum. A Social and Technical History of Rowing in England and the United States." Amherst: University of Massachusetts, 2000.

Stowe, William A. *All Together: The Formidable Journey to the Gold with the 1964 Olympic Crew*. New York: iUniverse, Inc., 2005.

Strahan, Edward. "The Pennsylvania Academy Exhibition," *Art Amateur* 4, no. 6 (May 1881), 114–115.

Strauss, Barry. *Rowing Against the Current: On Learning to Scull at Forty*. New York: Scribner, 1999.

Sullivan, John Lawrence, and Dudley Allen Sargent. *Life and Reminiscences of a 19th Century Gladiator*. Boston: J. A. Hearn & Co., 1892.

Summers, Mark Wahlgren. *Rum, Romanism, and Rebellion: The Making of a President, 1884*. Chapel Hill: University of North Carolina Press, 2000.

Talamini, John T., and Charles H. Page, eds. *Sport and Society: An Anthology*. Boston: Little, Brown, 1973.

Taylor, Bradley F. *Wisconsin Where They Row: A History of Varsity Rowing at the University of Wisconsin*. Madison: University of Wisconsin Press, 2005.

Thorn, John. Our Game website, http://ourgame.mlblogs.com.

———. "Introduction to 'Peverelly's National Game'" thornpricks.blogspot.com, April 28, 2005.

———. "New York Base Ball Club (a.k.a. Washington BBC, Gotham BBC)" in Morris et al., *Base Ball Founders*, 46–62.

Tilden, S. J. *The New York City "Ring:" The Origin, Maturity and Fall, Discussed in a Reply to the New York Times*. New York: Press of John Polhemus, 1873.

Tomlinson, Alan. *The Atlas of Sports: Who Plays What, Where, and Why*. Berkeley: University of California Press, 2011.

Tunstall, Brian. *Introductory Notes on the Art of Rowing*. Revised Michaelmas, 1956. Greenwich, England: Alfred Peacock, Ltd., 1956.

Twain, Mark, and Charles Dudley. *The Gilded Age: A Tale of To-Day*. New York: Penguin Books, 2001.

Twombly, Wells. *200 Years of Sport in America*. New York: Random House, 1976.

The Universal Cyclopaedia. New York: Appleton and Company, 1900, 199–201.

Updike, John. "The Ache in Eakins," a review of *Thomas Eakins: The Rowing Pictures* exhibit and catalogue, *New York Review of Books*, August 8, 1996, 10.

Volkwein-Caplan, Karin A. E. *Culture, Sport, and Physical Activity*. Aachen, Germany: Meyer & Meyer Verlag, 200.

von Drehle, David. *Triangle: The Fire That Changed America*. New York: Atlantic Monthly Press, 2003.

Walker, Donald. *British Manly Exercises*. Philadelphia: T. Wardle, 1837.

Watson, James, ed. *Rowing and Athletic Annual for 1874*. New York: Published by the editor, 1875.

Weber, Lutz. *Rekonstruktionsversuch der Agyptischen Rudertechnik in der 18. Dynastie, Unveroffentilchte Diplomarbeit an der Deutschen Sportochschule*. Cologne, Germany: 1978. Cited in Hans Georg Brecklinghaus, *The Human Beings Are Awoken, You Have Set Them Upright: Body Structure and Conception of Man in Ancient Egyptian Art and the Present Day*. Fereiburg: Lebenshaus Verlag, 2002.

Weil, Thomas E. Jr. *Beauty and the Boats: Art & Artistry in Early British Rowing*. Henley, UK: River and Rowing Museum, 2005.

———. "An Introduction to Rowing Prints." *Rowing USA*, April/May 1983, 6–10.

———. "A Preliminary Survey of Boat Clubs and Associations Formed and Recorded Rowing Races and Regattas Held in the United States and Canada (except Quidi Vidi) Through 1860." Draft, June 22, 2008.

———. "A Time Line of Rowing History." Friends of Rowing History website, rowinghistory.net.

———. "Why Rowing Is Unique Among Team Sports." Friends of Rowing History website, rowinghistory.net.

Weiss, Nancy Joan. *Charles Francis Murphy, 1858–1924: Respectability and Responsibility in Tammany Politics*. Northampton, MA: Smith College, 1968.

Welch, Richard F. *King of the Bowery: Big Tim Sullivan, Tammany Hall, and New York City from the Gilded Age to the Progressive Era*. Albany: State University of New York Press, Excelsior Editions, 2008.

Werbel, Amy. *Thomas Eakins: Art, Medicine, and Sexuality in Nineteenth-Century Philadelphia*. New Haven & London: Yale University Press, 2007.

Whitehead, Ian. *James Renforth of Gateshead: Champion Sculler of the World*. Newcastle: Tyne Bridge Publishing, 2004.

Whitney, Caspar, "The Guiding Hand of Faculty in College Sports," *The Outing Magazine* XL (July 1902), 497.

Whiton, James M. "The First Harvard-Yale Regatta (1852)." *The Outlook*, vol. 67 (June 1901), 286.

Wilcox, Ralph. "Irish Americans in Sports: The Nineteenth Century," in Lee and Casey, *Making the Irish American: History and Heritage of the Irish in the United States*, 451.

———. "The Shamrock and the Eagle: Irish-Americans and Sport in the Nineteenth Century." In Eisen and Wiggins, *Ethnicity and Sport*, 55–74.

Witness. "Sports in America" Special Issue, vol. 6, no. 2, 1992.

Wulf, Steve. "Title Waves," in *ESPN The Magazine*, June 14, 2012.

Wood, W. *Manual of Physical Exercises*. New York: Harper & Brothers, 1870.

Woodgate, W. B. *Boating*. London: Longmans, Green, and Co., 1891. Badminton Library of Sports and Pastimes.

Woodham-Smith, Cecil. *The Great Hunger: Ireland 1845–1849*. New York: Harper and Row, 1962.

Yanega, Lt. M. J., et al., *Centennial Issue, Fire Department 1865–1965*, a commemorative booklet by the Fire Department of the City of New York, New York, FDNY, 1965.

Young, Charles Van Patten. *Courtney and Cornell Rowing*. Ithaca, NY: Cornell Publications Printing Co., 1923.

Index